By All Accounts

Race and Culture in the American West
Quintard Taylor, Series Editor

By All Accounts

General Stores and Community Life in Texas and Indian Territory

Linda English

University of Oklahoma Press : Norman

Library of Congress Cataloging-in-Publication Data

English, Linda, 1969–
 By all accounts : general stores and community life in Texas and Indian Territory / Linda English.
  pages cm. — (Race and culture in the American West ; volume 6)
 Includes bibliographical references and index.
 ISBN 978-0-8061-4352-1 (hardcover)
 ISBN 978-0-8061-6883-8 (paper)
  1. General stores—Texas—History—19th century. 2. General stores—Oklahoma—History—19th century. 3. Community life—Texas—History—19th century. 4. Community life—Oklahoma—History—19th century. 5. Texas—Social conditions—19th century. 6. Oklahoma—Social conditions—19th century. 7. Oklahoma—Social conditions—19th century. I. Title.
 HF5429.4.T4E64 2013
 381'.14—dc23
                                                              2012039451

By All Accounts: General Stores and Community Life in Texas and Indian Territory is Volume 6 in the Race and Culture in the American West series.

The paper in this book meets the guidelines for permanence and durability of the Committee on Production Guidelines for Book Longevity of the Council on Library Resources, Inc. ∞

Copyright © 2013 by the University of Oklahoma Press, Norman, Publishing Division of the University. Paperback published 2021. Manufactured in the U.S.A.

All rights reserved. No part of this publication may be reproduced, stored in a retrieval system, or transmitted, in any form or by any means, electronic, mechanical, photocopying, recording, or otherwise—except as permitted under Section 107 or 108 of the United States Copyright Act—without the prior written permission of the University of Oklahoma Press. To request permission to reproduce selections from this book, write to Permissions, University of Oklahoma Press, 2800 Venture Drive, Norman OK 73069, or email rights.oupress@ou.edu.

Contents

Illustrations	VII
Acknowledgments	IX
Introduction	3
1. Who's Minding the Store?	23
2. Regional Particularities: Cotton, Cattle, and Coal	52
3. In the Presence of Ladies	78
4. Recording Race	105
5. The German Imprint	147
6. Commodities from Local, Regional, and National Perspectives	173
Conclusion	194
Notes	201
Bibliography	241
Index	259

Illustrations

Figures

1.	Lyne T. Barret	134
2.	Blackstone Hardeman, Jr.	135
3.	Nacogdoches, Texas, c. 1882	136
4.	Captain George Benjamin Hester	137
5.	James Jackson McAlester	138
6.	Mrs. Rebecca McAlester	139
7.	McAlester home	140
8.	F. B. Severs's Cash Store, Okmulgee	141
9.	Mrs. Anna Martin and her sons	142
10.	Anna Martin's store and home	143
11.	Page from McAlester's ledger	144
12.	Page from McAlester's ledger	145
13.	Newspaper ad for Mrs. A. J. Hyde's boardinghouse	146

Maps

1.	Texas stores, 1870–1890	4
2.	Indian Territory stores, 1870–1890	5

Acknowledgments

THIS PROJECT STARTED WITH fifty-five feet of ledger records that I discovered at the Western History Collections while working on a graduate school paper at the University of Oklahoma. It quickly became obvious that the ledgers, from J. J. McAlester's store in Indian Territory, were rich in detail and provided a unique snapshot of the region's history. From this collection, I expanded the scope of my study beyond Indian Territory into the neighboring state of Texas. As a consequence, I found myself crisscrossing the nation's second-largest state looking for other store ledgers, most of them covered in dust and yellowing with age.

From a dissertation, the project evolved into this book (after much revision, of course). The completion of my degree would not have been possible without the assistantships and fellowships offered to me by the Department of History at the University of Oklahoma. I would like to thank Professor Morgan for supporting graduate research through the generous Anne Hodges Morgan and H. Wayne Morgan Dissertation Fellowship. I also received research and conference support from the Graduate College and the Graduate Senate at OU, the Clements Center at Southern Methodist University, and the Bea Mantooth Estep Travel Fellowship offered through the Department of History at OU. After completing my degree, I also received travel monies for research while working for the Department of History at the University of Northern Colorado.

During my travels, I received courteous and professional assistance from the staffs of the following archives: the DeGolyer Library, the Southwest Collection, the East Texas Research Center, the Sam Houston Regional Library & Research Center, the Austin History Center, the Center for American History, Baylor University, the Daughters of the Republic of Texas Library, and the Oklahoma Historical Society. I would like to extend a special thanks to the staff at the Western

History Collections, where I spent numerous afternoons poring over ledger books. I would like to single out particular archivists who helped with finding new materials and photographs. Special thanks to Becky Laughner and Kristin Aguilera at the Museum of American Finance and Kyle Ainsworth at the East Texas Research Center for all of their assistance. I also want to thank the professionals at the University of Oklahoma Press who lent their tremendous talents to this project, specifically Jay Dew, Steven Baker, and Pippa Letsky.

In academia, everyone is short on time. Thus, I would like to thank those who served on my dissertation committee for giving me some of their precious time as well as their suggestions and comments—thank you, David Levy, Catherine Kelly, Linda Reese, Robert Rundstrom, and Albert Hurtado. I am neither the first nor the last to single out the contributions of Professor David Levy for his humor, wisdom, and kindness over the years. My advisor, Professor Albert Hurtado, has been an invaluable source of knowledge and guidance (and a much-needed rock when my confidence wavered). I am also grateful to my former colleagues at the University of Northern Colorado for providing helpful suggestions for the chapter "In the Presence of Ladies." As part of the Coalition for Western Women's History (CWWH) Writers Group, I also received valuable feedback on this chapter from Sue Armitage. Thanks to all. Along these lines, I would like to thank Elizabeth Jameson both for serving as a professional mentor (through the CWWH Mentoring Program) and also for suggesting the book's title. Finally, I would like to thank my present colleagues at the University of Texas–Pan American for their kindness and continual encouragement. Over the years, I have presented my ideas at various conferences, especially the Western History Association Annual Conference; consequently, I have received valuable insights and suggestions from audience members, fellow panelists, and comment/chairs.

Where would we be without our friends? For their personal and professional support, I would like to thank "the Sisterhood"—Sarah Eppler Janda, Robyn McMillin, Jana Vogt, Heather Clemmer, and Holly Berkley Fletcher. In addition, I would also like to thank Kristin Shamas and Lance Janda. Finally, I would also like to acknowledge the love and support of the significant men in my life: Joseph English,

Alexander Gall, and Chris Davis. My father, Joseph English, not only encouraged my scholarship from a young age but also proved steadfast and unconditional in his support. Throughout the writing process my son, Alexander Gall, provided both joy and patience. Finally, I could not imagine successfully completing this book without the love and generosity of my partner, Chris Davis.

By All Accounts

Introduction

ON NOVEMBER 27, 1871, MARGARET JACOBS entered the Hardeman & Barret General Merchandise store in Melrose, Texas, and purchased the following items:

three (hoop) skirts	$5.25
two pairs of women's shoes	$5.00
a sack of salt	$2.50
a bucket	37¢
twenty yards of print fabric	$3.00
two spools of thread	20¢
two packs of needles	20¢[1]

On the surface, the transaction seems neither surprising nor significant. One can imagine that women obtained similar items from their local general stores in communities across the United States, undoubtedly on this very same day. The purchases were subsequently recorded in the merchants' ledgers—the balance to be paid by Jacobs at a later date. This, as the saying goes, is where the story gets interesting. In the unraveling of seemingly inconsequential sales data from ledger records, a larger narrative emerges—one that reveals a complex web of relationships among merchants and customers involving commodities and prevailing cultural assumptions, local and regional economies, and communities and their inhabitants.

On this visit to the store, Jacobs acquired several sewing items. Unlike Hardeman & Barret's male clientele, who could select ready-made clothing off the store shelves, female customers could acquire from the retailers only the "raw" materials for their future dresses—fabrics, needles, and thread.[2] After that, it was up to them. By the 1890s, factory

Map 1. Map of Texas Stores, 1870–1890. Cartography by Erin Greb.

labor and mass production would eventually mean that women's ready-to-wear clothing could appear on department store shelves in northern cities. However, this was Melrose, Texas, in the early 1870s—thousands of miles and several decades away from such innovations.[3] What is not clear from this entry is whether Jacobs expected to use the materials to sew something for her household or for someone else's. Census records indicate that Jacobs worked outside her home as a "housekeeper," an occupation typical among many women in the late nineteenth century.[4] The census taker used precise language in

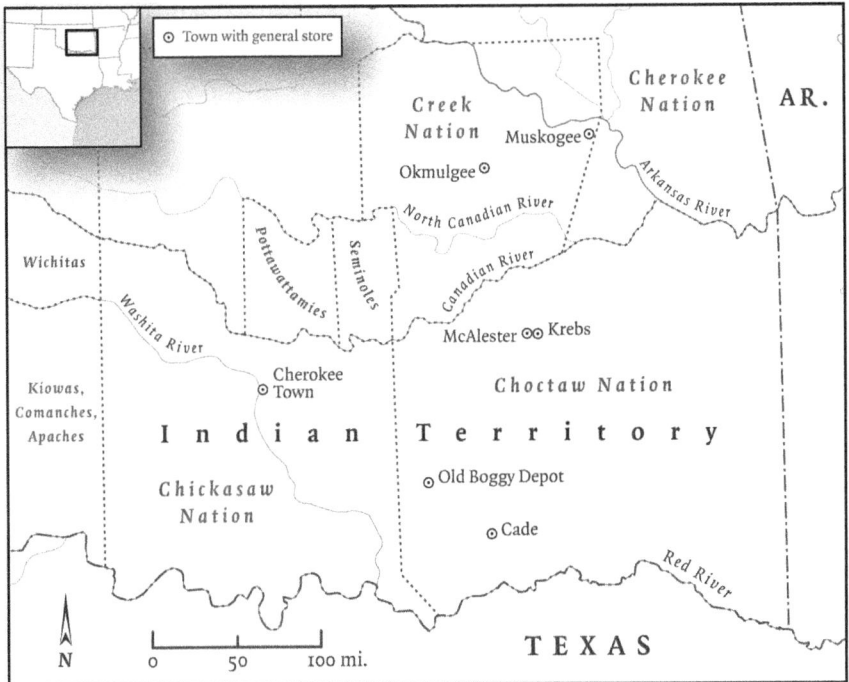

Map 2. Map of Indian Territory Stores, 1870–1890. Cartography by Erin Greb.

classifying the occupation of the smaller group of women in the community who worked as housekeepers—not to be confused with the majority of married women who "kept house." In 1870, Margaret Jacobs lived with her two teenage daughters, May and Hannah; thus, she functioned as her family's "head-of-household," the principle provider and decision maker for their home. With three females residing in the Jacobs household, the purchase of two pairs of women's shoes and hoop skirts, in addition to the sewing items, makes perfect sense. In her dual role as consumer and laborer, Margaret Jacobs provided a vital contribution to the economic lifeblood of the Melrose community.

One would think that the action of recording this sales transaction in the business logs for the day would be a relatively mundane task. Returning to the ledger entry itself, the retailers failed to include the distinction of Mrs. or Miss before Margaret Jacobs's name—a peculiar omission given that so many other women listed in the ledgers merited the distinction. For example, the ledger includes the purchases of Mrs. A. Blakely, Mrs. Amanda Johnson, Miss Mary S. Haynes, Mrs. E. K. Lavender, Miss P. Parks, Miss Sally E. Davis, and Mrs. Harriet Hall—many of whom made purchases quite similar to those of Margaret Jacobs.[5] So despite the fact that the store owners commonly included the distinction of "Miss" or "Mrs." in their customer accounts, they failed to do so for Margaret Jacobs.

The clue to this exclusion lies in the initials that appear after her name in the ledger: "F.W.C.," meaning "free woman of color."[6] In other words, Jacobs was African American. Both a courtesy and a gesture of respect, the distinction of "Miss" or "Mrs." appeared on the accounts of white women customers; for the store owners, their female African American clientele evidently did not warrant the distinction (although certainly these customers were indeed either married or single). The omission is a telling indicator of the inferior position of African American women in East Texas during the Reconstruction era. The insertion of Jacob's status (free) and race (of color) is also worthy of note; "free white" customers most certainly did not need to be singled out in the store's ledgers.

So who were these retailers and why might they make such race-based distinctions in their sales books? In the 1870s, the Hardeman & Barret General Merchandise firm was owned by Blackstone Hardeman, Jr., and Lyne T. Barret. Despite the partnership, the day-to-day operation fell on the shoulders of the latter partner. Indeed, L. T. Barret maintained a frequent and prominent presence in the store, charging household items almost daily to his personal account.[7] Both store owners possessed a fine pedigree in terms of Texas circles; their family backgrounds in the state dated back to the early years of the Republic. Blackstone Hardeman, Sr., was a prominent physician who grew up and received his medical training in Tennessee before moving his family to Texas in 1838.[8] His son, Blackstone Hardeman, Jr., operated several successful retail ventures before entering his partnership with Lyne T. Barret in the early 1860s. Originally from Virginia, the Barret family also migrated to Texas in the years of the Republic. The Barrets prospered in their new home, establishing a plantation in East Texas and emerging as one of Melrose's wealthiest slave-owning families.[9] Land and wealth distinguished these two store owners—in a rather stark contrast from the experiences of Margaret Jacobs, the "free woman of color" who frequented the Hardeman & Barret store in November 1871.

Stepping away from the specifics of the ledger entry, it is important to consider the Jacobs sales transaction in the context of the period. Located in Nacogdoches County, a cotton-rich region in East Texas encircled the small community of Melrose, a community much closer in character to Shreveport, Louisiana, than to the larger commercial centers of Central and South Texas such as Houston, Galveston, or San Antonio. Census records confirm that the bulk of Hardeman & Barret's clientele, whether blacks or whites, engaged in cotton farming. For African Americans in post–Civil War Texas, poverty and discrimination limited their opportunities to purchase land, so many of them became sharecroppers. A mixed blessing at best, sharecropping afforded African Americans access to land for cotton production, but the new system replacing slavery often led to constricting debt cycles, with landlords and merchants who charged exorbitant interest rates to their borrowers. Merely six years after General Granger's "Juneteenth" announcement that freed Texas slaves from bondage, African Americans in 1871 struggled to overcome abject poverty and often endured severe discrimination and intimation from whites during this period, which came to be known as Radical Reconstruction. Although lesser known than the Ku Klux Klan (largely defunct in Texas by 1870), white vigilante groups such as the Knights of the White Camellia and the Knights of the Rising Sun used tactics like night riding, whippings, and lynchings to terrorize blacks in the state, an effort intended in part to affirm and maintain the pre–Civil War racial status quo.[10] As an African American in Reconstruction Texas, Margaret Jacobs faced inordinate challenges in her day-to-day life. From sewing items, to class and race assumptions, to Reconstruction, much can be drawn from a single sales transaction made at the Hardeman & Barret store in Melrose, Texas.

This book explores similar transactions carried out at general stores across Texas and Indian Territory and places these exchanges in the context of late-nineteenth-century America. Examining persons on both ends of sales transactions—merchants and consumers—provides valuable insight into the complex relationships and power dynamics that developed in local communities. Communities are critical to this analysis. Few sources rival general store sales ledgers and daybooks in granting access to the lived experiences of those residing in small, predominantly rural, communities in the region. Everyone needed something from the store. General stores served as a forum for bringing together people with very different backgrounds and experiences—people like Margaret Jacobs and L.T. Barret. The focus on transactions carried out at general stores, by both individuals and representative groups, means that consumerism and consumption themes necessarily constitute a significant portion of this study. Store records provide critical information on commercial relationships beyond purchases, however, including inscribed distinctions of race, gender, and class made by store owners as they recorded sales and account information in their ledgers. Indeed, such records demonstrate that race, gender, class, and ethnic distinctions were determined and reinforced during commercial exchanges carried out at general stores.

On that day in late November 1871, Margaret Jacobs probably entered the Hardeman & Barret store through a wide front door, which welcomed patrons and invited them to enter, peruse the store's wares, and leave with purchases in hand. The store itself probably featured a large designate sign, highlighting offerings such as "Dry Goods and Groceries," affixed, perhaps, to an oversized square front—an extremely popular design among retailers of the day. In other instances, mercantile enterprises featured sloped roofs and large covered porches (see images of F. B. Sever's Cash Store and Anna Martin's store in Hedwig's Hill in the illustration section). With a smaller sign, many rural stores alerted passersby of another service offered by the retailer—the presence of a U.S. Post Office. Typically, the postal outlet, with its official oak partition or its homemade bars and numerous locked boxes, stood somewhere near the front door, obvious and readily available to customers entering the shaded confines of the stores. The services rendered by the U.S. Postal Service included stamps and delivery, connecting even the remotest of rural patrons to the outside world.

Along one side of the structure one might find feed or shed rooms, often serving as a storehouse for excessive or oversized goods. At the back of the shed room of the Charles Schreiner General Merchandise store located in present-day Kerrville, Texas, was a cellar that held barrels of coal oil, beer, whiskey, and molasses as well as other necessities for frontier life. Relying on the recollections of "old-timers who have traced the patterns of pioneer life" as well as interviews with family members, Charles Schreiner's biographer described the layout of the store: "Down the length of the building on the right, from the front, ran the rough board counter, across which, for more than a decade, was to be handed the homely commodities to meet the simple needs of the pioneers of the Texas Hills." The L-shaped counter featured a small space for an office and sheltered, at its base, barrels of sugar, coffee, rice, lard, and dried fruit. On the back wall of the store was an array of groceries, "while the long counter to the side cut off the dry goods that lay in assorted bolts of calico, jeans and hickory on rough shelves along the wall." On the opposite side, harnesses and saddles dangled on hooks near the front, while further down the wall hung wooden items such as buckets, kegs, and tubs.[11]

While the presence of a long counter and shelving on all the walls were standard features of general stores of the period, the size and sophistication of the apparatus used to exhibit store stock varied considerably. Some stores featured rows of heavy drawers with stout knobs and finger pulls, employed to hold a variety of small or loose merchandise. Brogan shoes—a popular line of mass-produced men's footwear—were often stored in drawers rather than on shelves. Heavy barreled items such as whiskey, molasses, lard, salt, coffee, rice, sugar, and vinegar were usually found at the back half of the store. Nicer establishments might also boast glass showcases to display the store's finer merchandise, such as buttons, needles, pens, hatpins, bows, hairpins, jewelry, perfume, slate pencils, watches, and scissors.[12] Given the elite background of the Hardeman & Barret store owners as well the store's location in a thriving Texas town, one can image that Margaret Jacobs might have selected the more intricate items of her purchase, the needles and thread, from an upscale glass showcase.

This study of general stores is both a social and a cultural history of a particular time and place, specifically Indian Territory and Texas during the 1870s and 1880s.[13] From a regional perspective, Indian Territory and Texas in the post–Civil War years experienced tremendous growth and change. "Burgeoning" seems a particularly appropriate term to describe these regions in the late nineteenth century. For while it is true that by the 1870s East Texas had enjoyed decades of demographic growth and prosperity because of the westward expansion of King Cotton, both West Texas and Indian Territory were relatively less settled and economically developed than their eastern counterparts. During the war years, Texas escaped the major devastation experienced by its southern counterparts, since most of the fighting stayed to its east. In fact, Texas agriculture remained productive throughout the war years with enough surpluses to feed both the Confederate army and the home front. In Indian Territory, the Civil War bitterly divided the nations of the Five Civilized Tribes, and the destruction of war and factionalism stymied growth in the territory both during and after the war.[14] Further still, the Indian nations paid a heavy price in "surplus" land relinquished to the federal government as retribution for their decision to side with the failed Confederacy. By the late 1880s and early 1890s, shifts in population significantly altered these regions, resulting in sweeping social, political, and economic transformations. These shifts were due, in no small part, to the great land runs that opened Indian Territory to a flood of predominantly white settlers and to incursions by both farmers and cattle ranchers into Central Texas as they competed for increasingly scarce agricultural lands. The hordes of new settlers not only realized the farming potential of their new region but created fresh economic opportunities in the newly formed towns established during the period.

As regions, Indian Territory and Texas offer remarkable perspectives on the changing nature of race relations in late-nineteenth-century America. With a large African American population, primarily the result of the legacy of slavery in the state, Texas grappled with redefining race relations in the post–Civil War environment—socially, politically, and economically. It was by no means a smooth transition. Race was similarly a complicated and evolving issue in Indian Territory. Unique to Indian Territory, members of the Five Tribes played a significant role in governance and, by extension, in shaping race relations and defining citizenship in their respective nations. This distinct region presents the opportunity to examine not only the interrelations of American Indians and whites but also relations among African Americans residing in the Territory. In the 1870s and 1880s, America as a whole was forced to reassess its racial divisions and forge new social arrangements in a period when racial tensions were in sharp relief and highly contentious.

In exploring people and processes, this analysis is rooted in social and cultural history, although no general store history could be told without incorporating some elements of business history. As a record of consumption, store ledgers shed light on the material possessions, dispositions, assumptions, values, and experiences—in essence, the culture—of the thousands of persons whose transactions are recorded on pages now yellowing with age. A useful definition of both consumption and consumption studies is that "consumption implies a process or means by which consumer goods and services move through the general economy. Thus, the study of consumption ranges widely to include the institutions that produce, market, and retail those goods and services."[15]

Both methodologically and epistemologically, my historical approach draws heavily on the New Social History as well as the New Western History. Of particular importance to this study, for example, is the everyday life of ordinary people living in the American West, including women, immigrants, and minorities. Power is a central organizing principle to this analysis. As one New Western historian observed, "the West has in fact been a scene of intense struggles over power and hierarchy, not only between the races but also between classes, genders, and other groups within the white majority."[16] Such a perception turns on its head Frederick Jackson Turner's depiction of the West as a classless region that ultimately served as a beacon of freedom and democracy for the rest of the nation.

Further, this study's discussion of the relationship between goods and people, such as African Americans and spelling books or Germans and Christmas ornaments, reflects sensitivity to material culture studies —a field defined somewhat broadly by archaeologist James Deetz as "that sector of our physical environment that we modify through culturally determined behavior."[17] Studies in material culture stress the way human-made things (such as spelling books) fit together or interact with people (African Americans, for example), shifting in focus from objects to people to social group to culture or the other way around.[18]

With the focus on individuals like Margaret Jacobs, an African American female laborer living in Reconstruction Texas, it also seems safe to consider this work as "history from below." No one would confuse Jacobs (or others like her) as having access to the corridors of power or as setting the political agenda in the state.

General store records provide a fresh perspective on both new and old historical questions. For instance, such data can be used to challenge or confirm preconceived notions of who shopped and what they bought. How significant were female consumers to store owners? Did the shopping habits of African Americans differ from those of whites? More simply, what kinds of things were people buying and why? Store accounts supply direct evidence of consumer behavior, particularly with regard to day-to-day needs. Similar studies of other regions and earlier periods provide useful models for examining both the role of merchants in the economic life of early America and the complex ties of rural communities to both regional economies and distant markets.[19] In one study of Kentucky frontier purchasing, for example, the author asserts that consumption of manufactured goods from eastern centers and the display of metropolitan styles by local inhabitants transformed the Kentucky backwoods into a consumer frontier: an economic border region situated between subsistence and capitalist modes of production and containing aspects of each. Tracing how general stores integrated consumers (including those in marginalized groups) into market society is a central feature to this study. By synthesizing the consuming experiences of diverse populations, such as merchants, women, African Americans, Mexicans, American Indians, and German immigrants, who frequented general stores in Indian Territory and Texas during the 1870s and 1880s, we find important clues on the experiences of those often left out of traditional histories.

It should be noted that the word "ledger" was often employed as an all-inclusive term. In some cases, the ledger was only a cash charge book or record of settlement with the store owner, while a journal carried the itemized and chronological accounts. Daybooks typically contained individual purchases and the day-to-day transactions between store owners and their clients. This information was later transferred to an account ledger, which tallied each customer's purchases. The terminology used to distinguish record books and the methods of account keeping tended to be highly personalized, subject to the preferences and proclivities of the individual storekeeper. Although richly filled with consumer information on account holders, ledger books in themselves provide no cohesive narrative on late-nineteenth-century society; as a consequence, the responsibility falls to the researcher to derive meaning from the historical evidence. As cultural historian Lynn Hunt asserts, the deciphering of meaning, rather than the inference of causal laws of explanation, has become the central task of cultural history.[20] Of course, the interpretative task of decoding meaning from the sources—comprised mostly of names, products, and prices—is necessarily shaped by the cultural dispositions and speculations not just of the past but of the present.

The majority of people whose names are listed in account ledgers are not familiar, and most of the items they purchased are neither surprising nor extraordinary; staple items like tobacco, flour, coffee, salt, potatoes, and domestic fabrics appear most frequently on customers' accounts. But it is the everyday, seemingly inconsequential purchases of the stores' clientele that prove so revealing to this study. It is doubtful that the merchants gave any thought to the historical significance of Margaret Jacobs's purchases as they recorded the data into their sales ledgers; they were merely doing business. Retailing in largely agricultural areas often entailed extending credit to would-be consumers; as a result, merchants kept meticulous records of their customers' accounts. To a great extent, the solvency of their businesses depended on careful record keeping. For farmers, book credit often tided them over until they were able to make good on their crops.[21] In this respect, largely cash-poor farmers necessarily relied on merchants for their economic well-being.

Despite their dependency on merchants for credit, many rural customers complained vehemently that merchants practiced shady bookkeeping; as such, ledger books took on a mysterious aura with customers. The popular perception of merchants, as one southern historian argues, was that they squeezed every drop of profit that could be had from every minor purchase: "Everyone knew that the men behind the counter appeared friendly and warm while the credit bill grew, but revealed another face when settling time arrived."[22] The relationship was not entirely one-sided, however; store owners also relied on the business of the local community. Thus, general store ledgers not only enhance our knowledge of consumption patterns in the past but also underscore important aspects of local economies and the complex relationship between merchants and their clientele.

In countless ways, general stores functioned as the economic heart of their communities. As mercantile establishments, they provided the opportunity for area residents to enter market relations—as producers, consumers, and in many cases, debtors. Who owned these stores? Who frequented them? What did they sell? Where were they located, when did they operate, and why should they be studied at all? The last point— why should general stores be studied at all?—requires explanation at the outset. Although they no doubt had their moments, general stores were probably not the most exciting establishments in western towns. While other, more salacious, institutions like saloons and brothels have garnered more than their fair share of attention from western historians, general stores have largely fallen under the radar of scholarly analysis.[23] And yet, general stores drew in people from all classes, races, and genders. In especially small communities, store owners often found themselves without any competition, which allowed them to be the sole purveyors of not just staple goods but also specialty items. As local gathering sites, stores provide unrivaled access into the social dynamics of the communities in which they operated. Few other local institutions can make such a claim.

Given the importance of general stores to local economies and rural community life, there has been surprisingly little written about them, especially in the last half century. One of the earliest historical contributions on the subject was Lewis Atherton's *The Pioneer Merchant in Mid-America*. Published in 1939, Atherton examined storekeepers in the upper Mississippi area from the period between 1820 and the Civil War.[24] Five years later, in 1944, Thomas D. Clark picked up the story of rural stores essentially where Atherton's study left off, although Clark concentrated exclusively on southern stores. Focused on the period from the post–Civil War to the 1920s, Clark's *Pills, Petticoats, and Plows: The Southern Country Store* remains the benchmark history of country stores. Eloquently written and meticulously researched, Clark's book scoured hundreds of account ledgers and daybooks for historical insights into the communities of the New South. The 1920s, according to Clark, coincided with the decline in the country store's importance to the southern economy. While the store remained central to his analysis, his study was also a social and economic history of both the southern farmer and southern life. In 1949, Atherton followed up his earlier publication with *The Southern Country Store, 1800–1860*, and, like Clark, examined the role of the storekeeper in the southern economy, highlighting especially the store owner's role as petty capitalist agent to the large non-slaveholding population.[25] The fact that these three important books were published in 1939, 1944, and 1949 respectively, suggests that a fresh contribution to the historiography of general stores is long overdue—if for no other reason than to add those people who are generally left out of these accounts of the larger history of Texas and Indian Territory during this period—specifically, women, African Americans, and American Indians.

In addition to histories of general stores, this book also needs to be placed in the context of studies dedicated to consumerism or consumption behavior. Beginning in the 1980s, a growing field of historical inquiry has focused on consumer culture, its origins in American history, and its social ramifications. An outgrowth of such studies has been a revived interest in material culture studies. From the outset, two divergent schools of thought emerged—one describing the movement toward a consumer society and the "consumer revolution" that took place during the late seventeenth and early eighteenth centuries and the other focusing on consumer society in the late nineteenth and early twentieth centuries. Those studying the earlier period attempt to identify what people had and what items were available to them, as well as the larger economic, social, and cultural developments that influenced consumption behavior. Historians analyzing the latter period tend to focus on the changing meanings of things as well as on factors influencing the experience of consumption, such as the role of department stores and advertising in shaping consuming desires.[26] Since most studies of the late nineteenth century examine consumerism from an urban perspective, there is ample need for further exploration of rural consumption and the role of country stores in the late nineteenth century.[27]

While neither rigidly defined as a study in material culture nor focused exclusively on general stores, cultural historian Ted Ownby's *American Dreams in Mississippi* incorporates evidence from account ledgers to examine consumption patterns in Mississippi from the antebellum period to the present. In his study Ownby uses a number of sources from ledgers to letters, journals, and diaries to discuss not only what people bought in the various periods he examines but the reasons consumers made the choices they did. In other words, he provides the cultural context behind their purchasing. His early chapters, which examine the last decades of the nineteenth century, provide useful comparisons with consuming practices in Texas and early Oklahoma, particularly his discussion of women and African Americans.[28]

As former slaveholding regions, Texas, Indian Territory, and Mississippi found themselves in the 1870s having to adjust to a very different world—life after slavery. All these regions shared in the turbulence of race relations that defined the period of Reconstruction. That said, this study will demonstrate that the demographic composition and political structure of Indian Territory created a unique racial environment, not always in accordance with social climate evidenced in other Confederate regions.

While the contributions of Atherton and Clark fall short in addressing contemporary historical questions, these antiquated studies present a theme of particular importance to the present study and, for that matter, to any discussion of general stores in rural settings in the nineteenth century: the centrality of the merchant to both the local economy and the community as a whole. Store owners not only sold to their clients goods ranging from patent medicine to spelling books, they also served their communities in their roles as the local banker, postman, and central connection to the outside world. Further, beyond functioning as a source for consumer goods, the country store often served as a marketing agent for crops and proved a critical source of credit for area residents. The general store operated as a conduit within the larger market economy, linking local farmers with the more transient clientele as well as with distant eastern and overseas markets. Market society breached the frontiers of Indian Territory and the remote farming communities of Central Texas, connecting local and regional economies to the national economy. In many ways, store owners fashioned themselves not only as the suppliers of consumer items from the eastern centers but also as purveyors of more cosmopolitan culture. Moreover, they conflated their own identities and worth through their connection to the outside world. Their role as creditors only served to fortify their privileged position in rural society.

In his study of country stores in rural America, material culture historian Thomas Schlereth relates the waning significance of the country store in the late 1880s and early 1890s to the influx of mail order catalogues.[29] It is not a coincidence that this study concludes at roughly the same point. The prevalence and importance of catalogues from retailers such as Montgomery Ward and Sears, Roebuck significantly altered rural shopping habits and ultimately undermined the role of the general store in rural life. This said, the scarcity of banks and the merchants' willingness to issue credit to their patrons extended their importance to community life. In addition to the proliferation of mail order catalogues, shopping options expanded in Texas and Indian Territory as populations in these regions increased. In Indian Territory, for example, the opening up of Indian lands to white settlers led not only to more stores but also to diversification in retailing choices. Instead of an all-encompassing general store, larger communities increasingly boasted retail outlets like pharmacies and specialized shoe and clothing stores. At the nexus of these studies is the intersection of material culture, consumption patterns, rural living, and, more broadly, culture and economics. Economic and social issues are not treated as separate thematic strains from cultural issues, rather such themes are perceived as integral facets of culture.[30] Similarly, this study of general stores employs ledgers and daybooks as a means to understand the culture of late-nineteenth-century America, integrating both a local and a national perspective into the analysis.[31]

In terms of cultural identity and regional boundaries, Indian Territory and Texas spread over a number of "contested" regions within the United States, specifically the West, the South, and the Great Plains. Disagreement among scholars as to the parameters of the West further complicates the issue of regional identity. Does the West start at the hundredth meridian, the beginning of the Great Plains? The ninety-eighth meridian? The Rocky Mountains?[32] Many historians of Texas have tended to stress the state's connection with the West, particularly the great cattle drives and the rugged individualism associated with cowboy culture. The state's cultural links to the South and cotton production, on the other hand, have often been downplayed. As one Texas historian observes, "Cattle gave the state cowboys and western glamour; cotton made it southern, hence Confederate, defeated, poor, and prosaic."[33] The present study affirms the connection of Texas and Indian Territory with both the West and the South, recognizing the cultural influences of both regions. From a socioeconomic perspective, Texas and Indian Territory had much in common. There was some diversity in the economies of the two regions, but the cattle and cotton industries (followed by lumber, coal, corn, and grains) dominated the social and economic development of both Texas and the future state of Oklahoma.

While most of the general stores studied here were located in very small agricultural communities, there are some notable exceptions. Ledgers from stores located in the mid-sized Texas towns of Jacksonville, Athens, and Nacogdoches provide useful comparatives, as do records from Charles Wolf's store in the city of Austin. In the 1870s, Austin was a fairly small but budding state capital with 4,428 residents in 1870 and 11,013 in 1880.[34] In 1870, Texas had only nine towns or cities that met the definition of an urban center: a town or city with a population over 2,500. Much would change in the period under analysis. The population of the state of Texas exploded in the late nineteenth century—in 1870 the total population was 818,579 (95 percent rural) and it grew to 2,235,521 in 1890 (90.5 percent rural).[35]

Indian Territory experienced similar growth, albeit on a smaller scale. In the early 1870s, the mining town of McAlester was little more than a rural outpost, with a general store and not much else. Although it would eventually become the capital of the Creek Nation, Okmulgee was also a modest community in the 1870s. The same can be said for most of the other communities discussed here, including Hedwig's Hill, Industry, Fischer's Store, Cherino, Oakland, Fort Hubbard, Matagorda, Kerrville, Webberville, Refugio, Comanche, Hidetown, Melrose, Manor, Cade, and Old Boggy Depot. An aspect shared by all these communities was their strong connection—economically and culturally—with the rural hinterland. Stretching from the northeast corner of the present-day state of Oklahoma to the South Texas community of Refugio and then moving laterally across the state from near the Louisiana border to the West Texas plains, this book covers a lot of terrain—literally and figuratively.

Precious few of the ledger collections examined here record decades of a store's history; examples that do include McAlester's store in the Choctaw Nation and the McKinney & Brown store in Jacksonville, Texas. These collections document thousands of customer transactions over several decades and provide extraordinary access into local developments, giving us the ability to track "change over time." In other instances, there is only a single extant ledger book, which provides only a brief glimpse into the day-to-day consumption and credit activities of a particular community. From 1870 to 1890 much changed in these regions of the country, but country stores still reigned supreme, sustaining and shaping the course of rural economies. With growth, competition, and specialization (and the introduction of the mail order catalogue), the general store gradually lost its position of prominence.

While the focus on general stores located in small communities scattered throughout Texas and Indian Territory suggests a micro-approach to the study of history, the topics addressed in this work extend far beyond the local into much broader national issues. Of particular interest is the intersection of national historical developments and attitudes with those at the local level. Stores and their retailers served as conduits, connecting local communities to the outside world. Through the commercial relations between store owners, customers, and an examination of the commodities themselves, this study explores a host of social and cultural questions, especially those pertaining to class, gender, race, and ethnicity in postbellum America. In fact, one of the motivating factors behind this work is the desire to integrate the West, specifically Texas and early Oklahoma, into the larger national narrative. Survey texts for the late nineteenth century contain chapters on Reconstruction, industrialism, immigration, urbanization, the more general notion of Gilded Age acquisitiveness, and possibly some discussion of Victorianism or, more likely, the ascendancy of middle-class values. Then, in its own separate chapter, there is the West, a region somehow divorced from the major historical processes and cultural attitudes prevailing in the rest of the nation. But no boundary separated the West from the developments that textbooks ascribe to either the East or the South. Further, the migrants who ultimately settled the sparsely populated regions of Indian Territory and Central Texas brought with them their eastern, southern, and European perspectives and, by extension, all the challenges associated with those perspectives. Ledger entries are an effective source for tracing the impact of national concerns such as Reconstruction, racism, the pursuit of "progress," domesticity, immigration, and temperance campaigns in the smaller centers of the country.

The term "Reconstruction" requires some explanation at the outset. While contemporary historians generally agree on the events and time period associated with the term, in recent years the scope of Reconstruction has expanded from strictly a southern phenomenon to one encompassing both the North and the West. In his article, "Reconstructing Race," Elliott West implored his readers to consider Reconstruction as part of a larger social process that included developments before the Civil War and applied to race relations not only in the South but also in the West: "During what might be called the Greater Reconstruction, 1846–1877, territorial acquisitions as well as southern slavery forced a new racial dialogue between West and South, unsettled race relations and presumptions, and finally led to a new social order encompassing western as well as southern people of color."[36] This work adopts Elliott West's expanded vision of Reconstruction, applying it not just to events taking place in the former slave state of Texas but also to the equally important issues of race that surfaced in Indian Territory. Much as in the East, there was little uniformity in the reactions to larger social issues by those residing in the regions; rather, responses tended to be nuanced, multifaceted, and relative to the perspective involved.

The role of merchants in late-nineteenth-century rural society is assessed in Chapter 1. Focusing exclusively on store owners, in this chapter we consider their social status, their roles in their respective communities, and their cultural influences, along with concepts such as Victorianism and Gilded Age acquisitiveness and their impact on the region. A once accepted, if vaguely defined term, inspiring literally hundreds of studies, "Victorianism" has increasingly fallen out of favor with scholars of the nineteenth century. The exception is perhaps in histories of the American West where the term has proved remarkably resilient in describing the "civilized" elements in burgeoning communities. The term is generally used to describe the values, dispositions, possessions, and social actions shared by the middle classes in Great Britain and America during the last half of the nineteenth century.[37] Those who challenge the term argue that "Victorian" implies a political and cultural homogeneity that never existed on either side of the Atlantic. The relevance of Victorianism as a trope and its applicability to the merchant class in Texas and Indian Territory is also addressed in Chapter 1.[38] In Chapter 2 culture is related to regional identity, focusing on both the socioeconomics of the region and the critical role that store owners played in the economic lives of those residing in their respective communities. Since the relationship of credit practices and power are of primary concern to this chapter, class and social hierarchies continue to be relevant themes in the developing narrative.

In the next three chapters the focus shifts to store customers—in particular, women, African Americans, American Indians, and German immigrants. These consumer-centered chapters explore the class, gender, race, and ethnicity dynamics revealed in ledger records. Women's roles as consumers of general store goods are traced out in Chapter 3, and comparisons are drawn with women's experiences in other regions of the country. Included in this discussion is the relevance of the "cult of domesticity" and the doctrine of separate spheres in this part of the country. Increasingly, historians have argued that separate sphere ideology represented an ideal, realized by few.[39] This ideal, for example, did not reflect the lived experiences of most minority or working-class women in the nineteenth century. Ledger records from stores in early Texas and pre-statehood Oklahoma indicate that women in these regions maintained diverse roles in their respective communities, particularly with regard to work. Many of the women who frequented general stores did not experience the domestic ideal that confined women's roles to the home. As a consequence, this examination of general store ledgers mounts yet another challenge to separate sphere ideology, suggesting that the social construction of true womanhood or female domesticity found only a marginal base in the realities of rural life in Texas and Indian Territory.

Chapter 4 examines how the racial divisions endemic to the Reconstruction era shaped commercial relations in the region. As an African American woman, Margaret Jacobs, described in the opening paragraphs, straddled the themes presented in these separate chapters; she essentially wore two hats in that she faced both the gender and the racial challenges prevalent during the period. In Chapter 5 the focus is primarily on the German immigrants of the Texas Hill Country and their roles as both retailers and consumers, tracing the remarkable stability of the German communities and their cultural imprint on the larger expanse of Central Texas. Finally, in Chapter 6, the story moves away from representative groups to examine the connection between particular consumer items sold at general stores and the region's rural identity.

General stores connected residents of rural Texas and Indian Territory with the values and experiences of those living in other parts of the United States. The desire for genteel culture and refinement, for example, crossed the Mississippi with the waves of settlers who traveled from the East to the West in the nineteenth century along with their class assumptions. The same can be said for the problems of race associated with Reconstruction and other defining aspects of the national experience. Westerners often wrestled with many of the same questions as their eastern counterparts. Thus, store records from Texas and early Oklahoma open an important window on late-nineteenth-century American society, revealing that a multitude of social and cultural issues transcended regional boundaries. From an intracommunity perspective, extant general store daybooks and ledgers also provide valuable access to the social dynamics present at the local level, including the desire to reinforce nineteenth-century perceptions of class, race, gender, and ethnicity. If we extend the discourse outward from individual sales transactions to the larger social questions of the day, much can be learned from a brief visit to the general store.

Chapter 1

Who's Minding the Store?

SEPTEMBER 20, 1876, MUST HAVE BEEN a pretty big day for sixteen-year-old Lon Dixon. His stepfather, William A. (W. A.) Brown, purchased two suits for Lon (Alonzo Dixon, as he was formally known), recording the purchases under the account he held at his dry goods store, McKinney & Brown, in Jacksonville, Texas. One suit was clearly nicer than the other: the first cost $11.50 and the second only $5.25.[1] Still, such purchases were of no small consequence to the new store owner, particularly in rural Texas and particularly in the 1870s, when the country was still climbing out of the depression sparked by the Panic of 1873. W. A. Brown was likely suiting his stepson in clothing appropriate for an apprentice store clerk, a position that Lon would hold in his stepfather's firm until he assumed a partnership in 1886, at which point the company's name changed from McKinney & Brown to Brown, Dixon & Company.[2]

The experiences of this general store owner in East Texas exemplify both the fascinating class dynamics evidenced in small rural communities and the diversity present within those dynamics. Merchants often served as the economic nuclei of their respective communities. More often than not, their fortunes were integrally tied to the fortunes of their clientele. Because of differences in their backgrounds, value systems, career aspirations, and achievements, it is virtually impossible to pinpoint one merchant as typical of all the store owners in Texas or, for that matter, in any region of the country. From a class perspective, a handful of store owners examined in this study smoothly transitioned from the plantation elite to the post–Civil War, post-slavery merchant elite, a group still able to exert considerable influence over the economic fortunes of individuals—black and white—residing in their communities. A far more significant number of store owners were self-made men (and, in one instance, a self-made woman), with more humble backgrounds, who had responded to favorable markets and increasing demand for agricultural products in the North by establishing successful retail and credit outlets in their rural districts. Despite boom and bust cycles, demand for cotton and cattle—chief exports of both Texas and Indian Territory—grew in the decades after the war. By 1890, Texas had emerged as the largest cotton-producing state in the nation.[3]

Some merchants used retailing as a springboard into bigger and better financial opportunities, exhibiting all the cutthroat business tactics associated the Gilded Age, while others seemed satisfied with more modest retail ventures. Aggressive tactics could reap pecuniary rewards, but competitiveness, speculating, and general wheeling and dealing might also draw sharp criticism, or worse still, enemies. Some store owners developed their careers through extensive training and apprenticeship (notably W. A. Brown and his stepson Lon Dixon), others happened into retailing by chance. A common thread that can be found among retailers in Texas and early Oklahoma, regardless of where they started or where they ended up in terms of wealth and status, is that all were committed to "boosting" their small towns, both economically and socially. They obviously had a vested interest in doing so. Nonetheless, many seemed genuinely interested in the moral development of their communities, especially through the establishment of churches and schools. This was certainly true for W. A. Brown. Ultimately, all merchants responded to and were influenced by local conditions and circumstances as well as by the value systems and attitudes that prevailed throughout the United States in the late nineteenth century.

By all accounts, store owner W. A. Brown was the industrious sort, professional and sober in his approach to both business and life. In describing Brown's business achievements, Dr. W. H. Campbell, a longtime family friend, stated in 1916, on the occasion of the Browns' fiftieth wedding anniversary, "It is easy to account for his success, for he has always been honest, energetic, truthful and accommodating, the four traits that make success."[4]

Like his stepson, Brown had himself apprenticed at the retail firm of Clapp & Brown before it was purchased by William McKinney in

1874. After McKinney took over, he appointed Brown as a managerial partner for the store and changed the name of the firm to McKinney and Brown. In 1874, Jacksonville was a small but promising community. The town was initially located at a different site, but it moved in 1872 for a position on the rail line of the International & Great Northern Railroad, which completed its track that year. The businesses of "Old Jacksonville" reestablished themselves on the new site, and shortly thereafter, the new town of Jacksonville incorporated in May 1873.[5] Under Brown's skillful management, the mercantile firm diversified and expanded. Such fiscal success allowed the merchant to buy out his partner, and the firm came under the sole possession of the Brown family. As he diligently and dutifully reinvested his profits back into his firm for future rewards, W. A. Brown demonstrated keen business acumen. His cautious approach to retailing enabled his business to withstand the bank failures and panics endemic to the last decades of the nineteenth century. And while Brown invested in a mercantile firm in a neighboring community and became a partner in a local furniture store, his principal pursuit remained his Jacksonville store.[6] He poured his efforts into improving his store so that one day he could pass it on to his sons.

Besides growing his business, Brown served as a principal director for the Jacksonville Education Association, the group responsible for erecting a new public school for Jacksonville in 1891, after a storm demolished the town's only school.[7] The Browns, according to Dr. Campbell, "had always been kind to the broken-hearted, charitable to the poor, and a help to the community in which they lived."[8] Time and again, W. A. Brown demonstrated both the restraint and the "striving mentality" associated with the last decades of the nineteenth century.[9] By counseling his sons to reinvest in the business, by stressing that "times were hard" and "money was scarce" and that they "would have to be very careful of the funds," W. A. Brown promulgated the middle-class virtues of conscientiousness and fiscal restraint. In addition to Lon Dixon joining his stepfather's firm in the mid-1880s, Brown's second son, J. L. Brown (or Lem), would shortly enter his father's firm after returning from college. Later, describing his father's influence, Lem Brown stated, "But father toted fair, as for seeming boyish sacrifices we were given an ever-widening vision of successful business management."[10] Heeding their father's advice, Brown's sons exercised similar pecuniary cautiousness in their future business dealings.

While he sought success in business, W. A. Brown endeavored to meet his moral, social, and civil responsibilities. Besides his involvement in the development of educational institutions in the Jacksonville community, he and his wife were active members of the Presbyterian Church.[11] The couple were both charitable and influential town citizens. Brown's purchases reflected his desire to project a tasteful and sophisticated public image, while concurrently exercising the fiscal reserve needed to see his business prosper. Typical ledger entries from his general store included practical items like food and fabrics. For example, on August 2, 1876, he picked up bleaching, lining, cotton and lawn fabrics, in addition to eggs, salt, and medicine. However, specialty purchases such as dishes, place settings, goblets, cashmere fabric, table linen, and perfume enabled the Browns to be tastefully attired and well equipped for entertaining, as was fitting for one of Jacksonville's leading merchant families.[12] Skipping ahead several decades, W. A. Brown and his stepson Lem brought to the community of Jacksonville a clear indicator of early twentieth-century material comfort—a Hudson automobile. The acquisition and the arrival of the car to the community merited an announcement in the local newspaper.[13]

Unlike W. A. Brown's slow but steady rise to prominence, the owners of the Clark & Hyde mercantile store in Nacogdoches, Texas, had attained their elevated status well before they ventured into the retail trade. Indeed, these merchants must have considered themselves the social superiors of their often struggling cotton-farming clientele. Both store owners were lawyers with distinguished careers before they purchased the store in 1872 from another attorney, G. F. Ingraham.[14] Nacogdoches had a storied history as a center for trade—and smuggling—dating back to the early eighteenth century. Spanish explorers ventured into the region, initially an Indian settlement, in the early 1700s and established the Mission of Our Lady of Guadalupe of Nacogdoches in 1716. Shortly afterward they were forced out of the region by the French, in the first of many challenges for the small community. In the late eighteenth century, Spanish officials briefly pulled back the military and missionary presence in the Nacogdoches area only to see stubborn East Texas residents return to the abandoned region a few short years later. The town persisted. Despite frontier threats, Nacogdoches weathered the troubled years, and by 1870 the town boasted a permanent population of over three thousand residents.[15]

Store owners William Clark III and William F. Hyde were not only among the elite, in the Nacogdoches sense, but were prominent persons in the ranks of Texas society as a whole. Born into a prominent Texas family, Clark's father, William Clark, Jr., was a signer of the Texas Declaration of Independence and served in the Second Congress of the Republic. William Clark III practiced law in San Augustine for a number of years before moving to Nacogdoches, where he continued to practice law, pursuing promising business ventures on the side. He was a delegate from the Nacogdoches region to the state secession convention and was one of the "Seven, serious, sober, sensible" men who voted "No" on the proposition to secede. Once the Civil War broke out, Clark raised a company of men and joined the Confederate Army, being commissioned captain of Company G. After the war, he returned to Nacogdoches to practice law, investing with William Hyde in the mercantile business as a silent partner. Indeed, Clark had little time for running a dry goods store since he provided legal services for the Houston East & West Railroad Company and served a number of terms in the Texas Legislature.[16]

By the time he acquired a share in the mercantile firm Clark & Hyde, William Clark III had positioned himself in the highest ranks of Texas society. His account records reveal not only that he purchased staple items from the store but also that he acquired many small indulgences and specialty items for himself and his family—consumption patterns that closely corresponded with many of his upper-middle-class contemporaries in regions across the United States. On November 2, 1872, for example, he purchased one box of milk, oysters, and chocolate, a tasty collection of delicacies for his Saturday visit to the store. On November 27, Mrs. William Clark charged to her husband's account:

two yards of cashmere fabric	$2.86
sixteen yards of calico	$1.92
twelve yards of binding	36¢
buttons (including brass buttons)	48¢
total	$5.58[17]

At a cost of $1.43 a yard, cashmere would probably not appear on the shopping list of those with a modest budget. In addition to fabric and thread, on January 31, 1873, Mrs. Clark bought a roll of wall paper from the store; perhaps she sought to adorn her walls in a manner appropriate for an upper-class household.[18] Two sets of shoes were purchased from the store on March 29, 1873, and this purchase was picked up for Clark by a "Negro Woman," which suggests the family had some domestic help on hand, in a situation not so different from the middle- and upper-class families on both sides of the Atlantic.[19]

According to census records, Lyne T. Barret, of the retail firm Hardeman & Barret located in Melrose, Texas, had a domestic servant named Edward Archibald residing in his household. Barret was a shining example of "old money" in the post–Civil War Texas sense, meaning that his family's wealth was acquired before the war, primarily through the plantation economy. Listed as a white male domestic servant from Ireland, Archibald lived in the Barrets' home along with Mrs. Angelina Barret and her five boys: William, Ralph, James, Robert, and Charles.[20] One of the occasional responsibilities charged to Archibald was to fetch items from the store and deliver them to the family home. On September 5, 1870, large quantities of flour and sugar were charged to L. T. Barret's account per "Ed." With Mr. Barret minding the store and the five young boys occupying Mrs. Barret's attention, Edward was likely the only adult available to run errands for the household. Sometimes twelve-year-old Willie or ten-year-old Ralph were similarly called upon to fetch grocery items from the store to home.[21] It is not surprising that Barret secured domestic help for his family, given both his and his wife's backgrounds—both of them came from wealthy slave-owning families. Angelina had grown up in the home of Tom Johnson, a relative, and according to later accounts, the Johnsons and the Barrets owned most of Melrose and a great deal of the surrounding country.

Because of his family's wealth, Barret initially received an exemption from military service during the war so that he could oversee his mother's plantation. However, he eventually served the Confederacy as captain in the Third Brigade, Texas State Troops, Nacogdoches District.[22] Evidently, Barret's affluent background enabled him to be "high-minded and aristocratic in his ways and tastes."[23] Undoubtedly, such qualities were suitable to gentlemen of the period not just in the South, but nationwide. Like many southerners, the Barrets emerged from the war with less money than they had at the outset. Nevertheless, in terms of landownership and business interests, they were doing better than most in the district. In the post–Civil War period, Barret transitioned from the slave-owning elite to the merchant elite—a trend consistent with a growing number of wealthy Texans during the period. In antebellum Texas, the majority of the wealthiest Texans were from the farmer/planter class; in 1870, they were merchants and bankers.[24]

Both owners of the Hardeman & Barret Merchandise store listed their occupations in the 1870 census as retail merchants, suggesting that both focused their professional endeavors on retailing. They established their retail partnership in the early 1860s and maintained their business relationship through the Civil War. In the immediate postwar period, however, Barret actively engaged in developing an oil company, which would capitalize on the region's rich oil reserves. In December 1865, Barret and a handful of investors established the Melrose Petroleum Oil Company, and the company began drilling for oil in the area in the summer of 1866. In late 1866 and early 1867, Barret traveled to New York and Pennsylvania seeking advice and financial interest on how best to develop the region's potential. Unfortunately, low oil prices and concerns by northern investors about the stability of Reconstruction Texas left Barret without sufficient investment capital to proceed; in fact, he suffered extensive financial loss through his involvement in the project. As a result, he abandoned his oil company ventures and returned to the business of retailing.[25]

Like his partner, Blackstone Hardeman, Jr., maintained a large family, which in 1870 included his wife and ten children, although ultimately he and his wife, Rebecca, would have a total of sixteen children. Blackstone Hardeman, Jr., boasted a fine pedigree in terms of Texas social circles: his father was a prominent physician who grew up and received his medical training in Tennessee before moving to Texas in 1838. Dr. Blackstone Hardeman, Sr., bought land just west of Chireno, Texas, and apparently the local precinct now known as Chireno initially bore the name Hardemans in honor of the distinguished founding family.[26] Indicative of the political prominence of the Hardeman family, Dr. Blackstone Hardeman's younger brother, Bailey Hardeman, had been a signer of the Texas Declaration of Independence and secretary of the Treasury under President Burnet. His older brother was active in the Second Congress of the Republic of Texas, while their father had sat in the Constitutional Conventions of both North Carolina and Tennessee.[27]

Although Blackstone appears less frequently in the store's ledgers, partner L. T. Barret made purchases from the firm almost daily, recording them under his personal account. Not surprisingly, these quotidian purchases were typically food and household basics. There are some interesting exceptions, however. The storekeeper ensured that his sons were both well clad and well equipped for pursuing their studies. In October 1870, Barret procured two pairs of shoes for his boys, one for Robert and the other for Charley. Ralph Barret was the lucky recipient of an arithmetic book in May 1870, a speller and a penholder in November, and a new pair of brogans on December 17, 1870.[28] It appears that L. T. Barret not only used his mercantile business to provide for his family's present needs but, in supplying his sons with educational resources, he demonstrated a commitment to "improving" them and their career opportunities. Education increased in importance for Texans across the socioeconomic spectrum in the early 1870s. Thanks to initiatives put forth by the Republican Reconstruction governments of the early 1870s, a new public school system was put in place for the state, which offered education to both black and white students, though the schools were segregated by race.[29] According to Victorian historians, upper-middle-class Americans during the period manifested an extreme form of "future-orientation" in their ambition, their interest in education, and their willingness to reinvest profits, all demonstrating their preoccupation with planning ahead and using their time wisely. Barret's purchases on June 25, 1870, of a top, a harmonica, and a set of marbles indicate, however, that it was not always study time for the boys in the Barret household—they were able to indulge, at least a little, in the pleasures of play.[30]

Whether for themselves or for their families, it seems store owners on the Texas frontier attained the commodities that befitted their status as the local elite. The rural middle class shared with their urban counterparts the desire for the latest in available goods. While rural inhabitants' interest in "scarce commodities" was not merely a product of the late nineteenth century, the increased proliferation of ready-made, mass-produced commodities expanded that interest exponentially. Persons living in rural locales, however remote, reinforced their elite status through the acquisition of fine goods produced in far-off urban centers. The fervent desire to possess certain items by people living in both rural and urban locations, particularly items that would demonstrate their gentility and respectability, implies that many in the period defined themselves by what they owned.[31] Items that Alfred B. Lewis purchased from his own dry goods store in Manor, Texas, for example, indicate that the merchant had reached a relatively high degree of success. On May 10, 1883, Lewis purchased a suit of clothes for $12.00; he acquired another suit for $12.42 in September 1883; and he followed up these purchases the next year by buying a coat and vest for $13.79. Factoring in the hat he bought for $3.40 in July 1884, the pants he purchased for $6.32, the suspenders, coat, shirts, and hose he purchased in the same period, Lewis emerges as one particularly well-dressed retailer. On December 31, 1884, Lewis charged to his account an especially costly purchase: a buggy for $145.00 and an accompanying harness for $16.50.[32] At such a high cost, Lewis's buggy was well beyond the reach of most of his farming clientele. Store merchants' purchases of luxury items affirmed their elite status, especially when compared to the more modest purchases made by their largely rural clientele. In this regard, consumer goods helped to establish and enhance social differentiation, particularly in regions perceived as being on the "frontiers" of civility. It is worth noting that by the time of these purchases Alfred Lewis was in his early sixties and, having enjoyed some measure of success, was preparing for his son to take over his business. At the time of the 1880 census, Ashby W. Lewis was clerking at his father's store; he and his brother-in law Henry C. Fristoe took over the business in the 1890s and operated an affiliate in Taylor, Texas, as well.[33]

The privileged position of the merchant in local communities was not limited to Texas and Indian Territory. Store owners sat at the top of the social hierarchy in Kansas cattle towns; merchants and stockmen represented the "civilized element" in the burgeoning frontier communities. In his classic work on southern country stores, Thomas Clark described merchants as the local elite, observing that storekeepers became the local "rich men." They lived in the best houses, generously contributed to local churches and schools, and essentially ran local politics and social affairs. Although such prestige followed only after they reached a certain level of success, the owners of general stores in Texas and early Oklahoma achieved the elevated status of their counterparts in Kansas and the southern states. Local prestige came not only from business success and community activism but also because merchants cast themselves as purveyors of eastern cosmopolitan values and goods. Another southern study of country stores and consumerism posits that owners saw themselves as part of and agents for cosmopolitan culture; they tied their own identity to the goods themselves and to their part in knowing what were the latest trends coming out of the East. In effect, merchants fashioned their roles as the gatekeepers of all things modern and sophisticated for those living on the peripheries of metropolitan society.[34]

Elite status was manifest not only in the consumption practices of the merchants on the Texas frontier but also in their community activism. A bulwark of middle-class culture was the emphasis placed on both education and the Christian religion. The school and the church were institutions that both promoted such ideals as duty, discipline, virtue, and morality. Community success was measured not simply by prospering businesses, although these were critical, but also through flourishing schools and churches. It is in this philanthropic capacity that W. A. Brown served as a director for the Jacksonville Education Association, raising funds to rebuild the school in Jacksonville, Texas. In their commitment to their community's moral development, the Browns established a reputation for being charitable to the less fortunate in their community.[35] In reviewing the accomplishments of the burgeoning community of Jacksonville, the *Texas Intelligencer*, a local newspaper, considered the establishment of schools and churches as a key factor in the town's success, along with its thriving industries. The editorial cited a population increase of 25 percent in 1875 as proof of the town's growth and future success. The *Intelligencer* observed that "A religious, moral, and social influence has grown and extended, and today we can safely say with excusable pride, that Jacksonville's future is assured and firm; that commercially, socially, and morally, she has no superior, of equal (and in many instances, of greater) size, among all the towns in this grand State."[36]

Philanthropist, rancher, and store owner Judge John C. Lynch of Shackelford County, West Texas, was a local "big wig" in all senses of the word. In this predominantly cattle ranching county, J. C. Lynch operated one of the largest cattle ranches in the area, owned roughly fifteen thousand head of cattle, and served as the principle employer for scores of laborers—including foremen, cooks, washerwomen, cowhands, teachers, and preachers.[37] Records from J. C. Lynch's store in the 1880s trace the employment transactions that were funneled through his store. Lynch issued credits to various account holders for "seven days with herd," "driving steer to Fort Worth," "by 2 days washing," "Miss Netty and Mary Manning for teaching John," and "cash paid Preacher Tremble."[38] Local histories credit J. C. Lynch with establishing a school in his county, in his effort to develop his community's potential: "In those days there was no such thing as a public school in Western Texas, but in 1868, or thereabout, Judge Lynch, a big cattleman living on the Hubbard, some fourteen or fifteen miles east of the Ledbetter Salt Works, employed a private teacher, and all the people throughout the surrounding country were at liberty to send their children to this school, a cherished opportunity of which they heartily took advantage."[39] Ledger records indicate that Lynch drew money from his own store account to pay for the school upgrades. In addition to his benevolent activities, the store owner distinguished himself as local elite through his consumption practices—Lynch regularly purchased big ticket items from his store and charged them to his private account, including luxury fabrics, fancy linens, expensive clothing ($25.00 suit and $7.00 hat), and a $27.00 sewing machine.[40]

The exploits of merchant and cattleman Charles Schreiner epitomizes the onward-and-upward narrative of the rugged frontiersman to wealthy community philanthropist. As a teenager Schreiner traveled to Central Texas with his family in the early 1850s. Originally from the Alsace-Lorraine border region of Germany and France, the family members spoke both languages fluently, a skill that proved vital to the future success of the store merchant in the heavily German regions of the Texas Hill country. Schreiner's father died shortly after the family arrived in the Hill country, and Charles's mother died in 1857, a few years after her husband, which forced each family member to seek their own strategy for survival. For Charles Schreiner, that survival strategy included joining the Texas Rangers at the ripe age of sixteen. Unlike L. T. Barret, Schreiner was clearly not a product of "old money." In the late 1850s, he entered both the store and the ranching business with his brother-in-law in Kerr County, Texas, where he purchased a modest ranch on Turtle Creek with a small herd of cattle and sold beef to the troops stationed at Camp Verde. During the Civil War, Schreiner fought on the side of the Confederacy. This was rather atypical for German immigrants living in Central Texas during the outbreak of hostilities; in fact, Charles was the only one of four Schreiner brothers to fight on the side of the South.

Like many of their Texas counterparts, the Schreiner family struggled financially in the immediate years after the war. The family relocated from Turtle Creek to the small hamlet of Kerrville. With the financial backing of a fellow German countryman, August Faltin (who served as a silent partner for the mercantile firm for the next decade), Charles Schreiner opened a general store in Kerrville, Texas, on Christmas Eve, 1869. On the first day of business, the store owner recorded only three entries in his account ledger—including a small cash advance to himself.[41]

From this modest beginning, Schreiner's business grew and diversified. He engaged in land speculation and banking and returned to his earlier fascination with cattle ranching. At their peak, his landholdings amounted to over five hundred thousand acres in Central Texas. At the turn of the century, the Charles Schreiner Company was one of the largest employers in the community of Kerrville, including its holdings the Schreiner Cattle Company and the Charles Schreiner Bank. Schreiner also ventured into wool and became a leading proponent of mohair; over time, Kerrville would become known as the "Mohair Center of the World." The management of the company would eventually pass from Charles Schreiner to his sons, and his vast estate would similarly be divided among the next generation.[42]

This fiscal success allowed Schreiner to move into the realm of philanthropy. The store owner offered scholarships to Kerrville's local high school; gave land for a community church; provided a ten-thousand-dollar endowment to the high school of a neighboring community, Junction, Texas (which prompted them initially to name the school for him); and most significantly, provided extensive funds for the Schreiner Institute, a small Presbyterian college located in Kerrville that opened in 1923 and is still in operation today (now Schreiner University). On Schreiner's commitment to his community, his biographer waxed sentimental: "The poor and shiftless found as ready, as kindly, and as friendly an ear in him as did the rest. . . . His love of the land and its people and his innate modesty and sense of good taste linger now, long after he is gone, as a civilizing influence in a world of business that badly needs it."[43]

Schreiner was not alone in his commitment to education and community development. Described as "the first citizen of Muskogee in benevolence," Mrs. Elizabeth Fulton Hester, wife of store owner G. B. Hester, moved to Indian Territory in 1856 to work as a teacher and a missionary among the Chickasaws.[44] She married retailer Captain George Benjamin Hester two years after she arrived. In 1861, as the War Between the States drew nearer, the Hesters decided to put their missionary work on hold, and they relocated to Old Boggy Depot, a small community in the Choctaw Nation. In their new location, Mr. Hester resumed his mercantile business, and Mrs. Hester became a teacher in a National School provided by the Indian Legislature. Thus, Mrs. Hester was able to render both spiritual and educational direction even to those in the presumably "civilized" tribes. According to his contemporaries,

Hester served a critical role in the development of this community: "He supplied the surrounding community of farms and stockmen with farming implements, food, clothing, guns and ammunition for the upbuilding of his community. He also helped Reverend J. S. Burrow in organizing schools, churches, and the Masonic Lodge at the location that is now Boggy Depot, Atoka County."[45] Clearly, Hester served his community in a variety of capacities.

In her later years, Mrs. Hester moved to Muskogee and continued providing her philanthropic services—she held Sunday afternoon services at the city jail and played a key role in the founding of the Muskogee Day Nursery. Captain Hester was superintendent of the Methodist Sunday School for twenty-two years. Besides their retailing and missionary work, the Hesters were also the proud parents of Daisy Hester, who married Robert L. Owen, Indian agent and first U.S. senator from the state of Oklahoma.[46]

Other merchant families similarly displayed a firm commitment to developing the moral or religious character of their communities. So important were church services to the Gauntt brothers of Athens, Texas, that they made their contributions to the local preacher through the coffers of their general store. Ownership of the Gauntt Bros. mercantile firm was initially split between two brothers, William M. [Bill] Gauntt and Robert Lee [General] Gauntt, and a third brother, J. R. [Bob] Gauntt, bought into the business in the 1890s.[47] According to their account ledgers, both brothers paid the preacher for his services, recording the transactions in their daybooks. For example, listed under General Gauntt's account for May 3, 1888, is the ledger entry "paid Preacher $1.00." In the fall of 1888, Bill Gauntt's account includes the entries, on September 7, "cash to Preacher 50¢," and on October 1, "paid Preacher $1.00." Bob Gauntt was an active member of the Baptist church in Athens and served as both a member of the city council for eight years and a member of the school board for an impressive twenty years.[48] Western towns have often been depicted as being devoid of social hierarchies, a characterization dating back to Frederick Jackson Turner's writings on the frontier, where "Both native settler and European immigrant saw in this free and competitive movement of the frontier the chance to break the bondage of social rank, and to rise to a higher plane of existence." Nevertheless, class distinctions did exist in western communities. Popular images of the West include scenes of lawlessness, gunfights, and wild living in saloons and brothels. In an analysis of cattle towns in early Kansas, one historian contests the depiction of a "wild and wooly" West in stark contrast with the genteel, class-conscious East: "However pleasant and entertaining it may be to create a 'mythic West' separate from the East, Kansas—even Kansas of the western cattle towns—was a part of the nation and did not exist in some Brigadoon time warp."[49]

These cattle towns played host to countless cowboys who drove longhorns from South and Central Texas during the boom years of the 1870s and 1880s. After the Civil War, there was a huge demand in the North for Texas beef. Kansas cattle towns opened railroad links to markets north, specifically the future meat-packing center of Chicago. In welcoming the Texas cowboys, Kansas cattle towns experienced not only the economic perks but also the downside associated with boom times, having scores of rootless young men looking for amusements to kill time and spend money. Of course, not all men linked to the cattle industry bore such reputations for frontier shenanigans. For decades, the home of store owner and cattle rancher Mayer Halff was the center of social and cultural affairs in San Antonio, Texas, in part because Halff reportedly "possessed the unique ability to shed the trappings appropriate to a cow camp and assume the role of a highly refined gentleman."[50]

Progress, laissez-faire economics and Social Darwinism, all served as central tenets of the late-nineteenth-century mind-set. If historians have largely failed to recognize the role of class dynamics and gentility in the American West, the opposite can be said of the westerners' stress on principles such as progress, competitiveness, and town boosterism. Competition seemingly ruled the West—unapologetic, no-holds-barred competition—much like the cutthroat competition and ruthlessness associated with the robber barons of the East: "[phrases such as] 'survival of the fittest,' 'struggle for survival' and 'march to perfection' seeped into the public mind and everyday conversation. Western editors glibly used the terminology with the same ease as they would any other popular cliché."[51] The masthead of the *Oklahoma Star*, a newspaper established in the Choctaw Nation in the 1870s, read "Progress and a Higher

Civilization." According to one Oklahoman historian, the *Star* was essentially a "Boomer" sheet that not only promoted white settlement in Indian Territory but also frequently criticized the tribal administration and frankly asserted that "the white race was destined to own every foot of land on the American continent."[52]

As an advocate of progress, the *Star* endorsed all those who sought to "elevate and refine" the undeveloped territory. According to this newspaper, the retail merchant, cattleman, and mine owner James Jackson McAlester was a fine example. On its editorial page, the newspaper proclaimed, "Jim McAlester, the Osage Mining Company and everyone else in this country, who are trying to do anything tending to unveil and utilize its hidden wealth, will always find the *Star* defending them."[53] For some, the heroes of the West were those who battled the untamed, unforgiving, godforsaken land, seized the lands of the Indians through various means, and emerged triumphant; such triumphs culminated in the accumulation of personal wealth.

Similar to corporate innovators in the East, entrepreneurs such as J. J. McAlester capitalized on the new economic opportunities developing in the West and spearheaded the drive to accumulate wealth.[54] From a modest Arkansas upbringing, McAlester emerged as a prominent leader in business and political circles in both pre- and post-statehood Oklahoma. He operated a prosperous mercantile business, owned a large cattle ranch, invested in and administered a successful mining company, served as a U.S. Marshall for Indian Territory and was elected to both the Corporation Commission and the office of Oklahoma lieutenant-governor.[55] Truly a western success story, McAlester proceeded from meager circumstances after the war to establish himself among the highest ranks of the Oklahoma elite. However, his means of achieving this success have drawn criticism from some contemporary critics, who use terms like "interloper" and "exploiter" to describe him.[56] While there is no doubt that McAlester ultimately embraced the aura of middle-class gentility, neither his background nor his means of achieving wealth in the Choctaw Nation conformed to rigid notions of Victorian civility, particularly regarding issues of race and class.[57]

In a 1957 article celebrating McAlester's career titled "An Oklahoma Indian Trader as a Frontiersman of Commerce," the author contended that McAlester "was a stable businessman who was part of the frontier process, advancing the spread of civilization by establishing a connecting link between frontier and metropolitan areas."[58] According to this early perception, McAlester was a "civilizer," a community builder, and as the title suggests, a frontiersman of commerce. McAlester moved to the Choctaw Nation after obtaining a map from a geologist's survey that indicated rich coal beds were located in the area. In an interview conducted long after the fact, McAlester relayed the story of how he came into possession of the map. After serving the Confederacy during the war, young McAlester returned to his home in rural Arkansas only to find "a land possessed and controlled by those who had been his enemies." Hoping to improve his lot in life, he pursued an education. While attending school, he lived with a man named Weldon who had been a member of an engineering corps that surveyed the Choctaw Nation in Indian Territory. Weldon had witnessed the rich coalfields in Indian Territory firsthand. According to McAlester, his roommate was unable to take advantage of his knowledge himself, but he produced a map "with accuracy and great care," which he gave to McAlester, urging him to secure possession of the area as soon as possible. "School didn't interest me much after that," the future store owner declared.[59]

Seizing the opportunity to gain access to the region's untapped wealth, McAlester ultimately parlayed his insider information into a position of wealth and power. Arriving in Indian Territory, he accepted a position with the trading firm Reynolds & Hannaford, with the stipulation that he would open a trading post in the area known as "the Crossroads," a location conveniently near the coal outcrops. In 1870 he purchased Reynolds's share of the business and the firm's name changed to McAlester & Hannaford.[60] Eventually, McAlester bought out his remaining partner and became the sole owner of the dry goods store, expanding his business interests until his death in the early 1920s.

McAlester's shrewd opportunism drew the ire of some within the Choctaw Nation, particularly those in leadership roles. Grounds for this criticism lay not merely in McAlester's acquisition of Weldon's map but, rather, the fact that he continually forged relationships that allowed him to exploit the Choctaw Nation's wealth. For example, on August 22, 1872, he married Rebecca Burney, a Chickasaw woman, and one critic wrote,

"While it is unfair to suggest that he married only to gain access to the coal reserves, the fact remains that only through this union could he have access to them." The Choctaw and Chickasaw tribes had a dual citizenship agreement, so through his marriage to Miss Burney, McAlester gained citizenship to both tribes and thus access to tribal lands.[61]

The store owner also developed relationships with important tribal members that paid off for him in times of crisis. For example, he established business ties with the Pusleys, a prominent Choctaw family, through their mutual interest in the Osage Coal and Mining Company. This investment proved highly contentious. The Osage Coal and Mining Company lease paid no royalty to the tribe, just to individual investors (like McAlester). This arrangement garnered condemnation from many Choctaw leaders and from U.S. government officials, who saw it as a breach of U.S. law governing contracts between whites and Indians. Consequently, the issue led to a prolonged court battle and eventual settlement in McAlester's favor.[62]

His close relationship with Judge James Thompson proved advantageous for McAlester in various legal battles the store owner waged with the Choctaw leadership. Legal confrontations developed, in part, because there were some in the Nation who resented McAlester's ability to sidestep tribal law continually while concurrently amassing huge profits from his land and coal interests.[63] At times, the struggles between McAlester and the traditional Choctaw leadership went further than the court room. A dispute over mining contracts and railroad development prompted Chief Coleman Cole, principal chief of the Choctaws from 1874 to 1878, to send the Choctaw Light Horse Company to arrest McAlester and three others for treason. According to McAlester, however, the captain told him that he and his cohorts were to be shot: "Choctaw fashion, he left their prisoners on their own recognizance, while he and his force sought Tandy Walker [one of the perpetrators] . . . 'but we didn't wait for the Light Horse to return. I didn't want to be shot.'"[64]

Despite these disputes, the McAlesters represented the social and economic elite not just in the community of McAlester but in the Choctaw Nation as a whole. There is ample evidence that points to McAlester's financial success. For example, his account records indicate that he was moving large amounts of cash out of the Choctaw Nation and into his personal bank accounts—he cleared $215,343 through his checking account with the Commercial Bank of St. Louis in 1887–1888.[65] From store, cattle, and coal revenues, McAlester invested in a number of real estate and business ventures, including a gristmill and a sawmill. He later served as president of the Bank of McAlester, established in 1905.[66]

His elite status is also evidenced by his material surroundings, his prominent social network, and his widespread reputation. The McAlesters resided in a lavish home, complete with a cupola and porch all around, situated on a ten-acre lot surrounded by an ornamental fence.[67] Purchases such as peaches, currants, oysters, two and a half yards of table linen, ribbon, chambray, preserve dishes, and a $13.50 China tea set suggest that the McAlesters could afford to surround themselves with the niceties of their day. According to one observer (a Mrs. Cook, who spent much time in the household as a child), Mrs. Rebecca McAlester always wore diamonds, even when she was doing housework. Another indication of McAlester's prestige is the impressive list of supporters who promoted his appointment to the position of U.S. Marshall in 1893, including the principal chiefs of the Choctaw and Cherokee Nations, the president of the Choctaw Senate, the state treasurer of Arkansas, and prominent businessmen in Texas, Missouri, and Indian Territory.[68]

The fact that McAlester was white and Rebecca McAlester was American Indian points to the unusual social dynamics of Indian Territory. Strong relationships with tribal leaders were essential to those seeking social and economic success, and ties to Indian agents and the federal government also helped. Like most periods in American history, the issue of race in the late nineteenth century was tumultuous, fraught with tensions and contradictions. Generally, racial minorities found themselves at the bottom rungs of society. As one western historian wryly observes, classes in the West "were not rigid and arbitrary—providing, as prairie wisdom had it, 'you were free, white, and twenty-one,' a description that was intended to cover everyone except, of course, those in racial categories not yet assimilated into the American culture."[69] However, this generalization cannot easily be applied to Indian Territory. Access to land and resources in Indian Territory required some level of tribal consent. The McAlesters, a mixed-race couple, maintained a position of wealth and prestige both in the Choctaw Nation and later in the new state of Oklahoma. Indian Territory and early Oklahoma were exceptional places in this regard, general assumptions of race and class needed to be adapted to fit the unique circumstances of this region during this period.

Frederick Benjamin Severs, who operated a dry goods store in Okmulgee, the capital of the Creek Nation, met with challenges similar to those faced by McAlester in the Choctaw Nation. Like McAlester, Severs transitioned his success in retailing into other profitable business ventures and similarly converted his tribal citizenship into a large personal fortune. By the time of his death in 1912, Severs was considered one of the leading financiers in the region and one of the few millionaires in the early state. Severs acquired his wealth from retailing, land speculation, banking, and most especially, cattle ranching. He capitalized on cheap barbed wire prices and enclosed enough land to raise and sell between fifteen and twenty thousand cattle every year. In fact, Severs and fellow Creek rancher George Perryman were two of just sixty-one Creek citizens who between them controlled 1,072,215 acres in 1896—a figure that represented almost one-third of their nation's entire land surface.[70]

Born in Washington County, Arkansas, Severs moved to Indian Territory at the age of eighteen, initially clerking in a store at Fort Gibson and later teaching school in the Creek Nation at Concharty Town and Asbury Mission. With the outbreak of the Civil War, he enlisted on the Confederate side and served as first lieutenant in the First Creek Regiment, Captain Samuel Checote's Company of full-blooded Creeks. Apparently in honor of his service under Checote during the war, Severs was formerly adopted as a Creek citizen, a privilege afforded to no other white men afterward.[71] Severs later served as private secretary to Checote in his capacity as principal chief of the tribe. Severs did not rise to his position of wealth in Indian Territory without some adversity.

His tribal citizenship preceded his marriage to Miss Annie Anderson, the daughter of Chief George Anderson of Concharty Town. Born into a prominent Creek family, Annie's purchases months before her marriage to F. B. Severs indicate that she already maintained a comfortable standard of living before marrying the future millionaire. On July 7, 1869, Miss Anderson purchased from Severs's store:

one hoop skirt	$2.00
a pair of shoes	$3.00
two yards of ribbon	50¢
pepper	50¢
starch	50¢
hair oil	50¢
six yards of bleached domestic	$1.50

By October 1869, Miss Anderson appears in the store ledgers as Annie Severs, reflecting her change in marital status.[72]

In exploiting his tribal connections and amassing great personal wealth, J. J. McAlester attracted criticism from within the Choctaw Nation as well as from some present-day scholars. Likewise, Frederick B. Severs's relationship with the Creeks and his subsequent rise to prominence within the Creek Nation have garnered mixed reviews. Some tribal members resented the practice of fencing in large pastures for cattle, which hindered freedom and travel in the Creek lands. Critics viewed successful cattleman like Severs and a handful of other ranchers as exploiting the resources of the nation at the public expense. Similar criticisms surfaced against Severs and other speculators within the tribe for their acquisition of huge lots in the newly planned town of Eufaula.[73] Indeed, Severs seems to have played some role in virtually all the money-making opportunities available to tribal members. Early historical assessments of Severs, on the other hand, celebrate his "civilizing" influence on the Creeks, depicting him as a worthwhile cattleman who led in the "higher purposes" of frontier life and enabled the Indians to improve their own territory.[74] In early historical interpretations, economic success was construed as a positive good—the implication being that Severs's success contributed to Creek improvement and economic development, even if it came at the expense of others in the tribe.

There can be no doubt that Severs assumed a leadership role in the Creek Nation, due in large part to his considerable wealth. Besides his retailing business, he owned a large modern cattle ranch, built and owned a cotton gin at Muskogee, led in organizing the Muskogee Roller Milling Company there as well as the First National Bank. He was builder and owner of a number of large business buildings, including the five-hundred-thousand-dollar Severs Hotel.[75]

Like McAlester, Severs seems to have met all the criteria to be considered a Gilded Age success story. He was influential socially, politically, and economically in the burgeoning towns of the Creek Nation, specifically Okmulgee and Muskogee. According to his niece Sarah Trent, Severs "was very liberal to charity. Whenever the Indians had any of their ceremonial dances or the payment, he donated several beeves and hogs for them to barbecue during their stay. He loved the Indian and was very generous towards them." Furthermore, Trent continued, "He contributed to the Harrell Institute [a Methodist missionary school in Muskogee] and liberally to all churches and he always gave beeves and hogs to every public gathering."[76] From his personal life to his professional associations, Severs clearly had a close relationship with American Indians. It is difficult to know if Frederick and Annie Severs, as a mixed-race couple, would have been welcomed in genteel circles in other parts of America; however, they certainly represented the very best of the social elite in their region of the West.

Offering a challenge to the social mores of the period that was quite different from that of Severs, Anna Martin's rise to prominence as a store owner and banker in Mason County, Texas, during the 1880s has all of the qualities of a Horatio Alger novel. The story of the life of Mrs. Anna Martin is one of unusual interest because, as one biographer eulogized, "the reader can be impressed with the splendid spirit of this woman, of gentle birth, who came to the Texas frontier, and with true pioneer spirit entered upon that life of service and struggle that was to be crowned with success far above the average, but abundantly deserved."[77] In this rags-to-riches tale, Martin surmounted the obstacles placed before her, overcame abject poverty, and ultimately labored her way to a large fortune for herself and her two boys. The fact that Martin was a woman makes her triumph even more impressive. Indeed, such experiences challenged the current cultural ideals regarding women's proper roles, specifically notions of nineteenth-century domesticity, which limited a women's sphere of influence to the home. Of course, this was an ideal, and exceptions surfaced in America long before Anna Martin, not the least of which were visible in the growing moral reform and suffrage movements of the late nineteenth century.

In a letter to an interested New York banker, Martin relayed the circumstances that led to her assuming ownership of a dry goods store in Hedwig's Hill, Texas. Charles Martin, Anna's husband, was in the retailing business, but his health failed when he contracted inflammatory rheumatism, and the business suffered as a result. For fifteen years, Anna nursed her sick husband and cared for her two boys, Charles and Max. She kept the family afloat—barely—by servicing the El Paso–San Antonio mail line, boarding transients, selling a few grocery items to travelers, making butter for the post, sewing, and so on, "enough to keep us out of debt."[78] Charles Martin died in November 1879, and Anna borrowed $150 from a friend to reopen the store. The death of her husband motivated Anna to act: "I had made up my mind that I either be somebody in life or break down." She sank all her efforts into expanding the business, and her store began to flourish. Apparently, she bought cattle, wool, and produce, which she sold on commission. Her store also operated as the postal station, and she served as the postmaster.[79]

By 1881, Anna had accumulated "a nice supply of merchandise on hand all paid for." She reinvested her profits from the store into ranching land and cattle and then "drifted into the bank business." She relied on her sons to assist her in her various business ventures, as she explained, "My oldest son taking care of the ranches of which are today about 50,000 acres, all stocked with good cattle and horses. The younger is a cashier of the bank of which I have the honor to be president." Martin was the first female bank president in Texas and one of four founders of the Commercial Bank, located in Mason, Texas. Opening for business on July 1, 1901, the Commercial Bank is the oldest continuously operated bank in the United States that was founded by a woman.[80]

Existing ledgers from the Hedwig's Hill store deal only with the period from the mid- to late 1880s, the period after Anna and her sons had acquired many of their vast holdings. Unfortunately, there are no ledger records either from the period of the Martins' early struggles or from the years of transition in the early 1880s. By the mid-1880s, Anna's purchases resembled those of her fellow merchants in Texas and early Oklahoma who had reached a similar level of status and wealth. In early January 1886, she charged to her store account almost $10.00 worth of goods, including candy, kid gloves, flannel, and thirty-nine yards of dress goods. Later that month, she debited her account the rather large sum of $44.90 "for a trip to La Grange." She bought two cans of apricots and two of salmon on March 20, 1886—delicacies of sorts, reflecting the proliferation of canned food items in rural locations.[81] Overall, her purchases indicate a comfortable lifestyle. No longer did she have to piece together "just enough" to provide for her family. By the 1880s, the boys were grown men, successful in their own right. Compelling evidence of Anna's change in status is the entry from her 1884–1891 account book, which includes the credit of $1,754.05 for "profit on March." Further confirmation of Anna's rising fortunes was her ability to make one of several trips back to Europe in July 1889, a luxury few struggling immigrants could enjoy in the late nineteenth century. Demonstrating her commitment to the Hedwig's Hill community, she provided the funding for the construction of a new school, supervising the project herself. Indeed, this store owner had arrived.[82]

Whether it was Martin's store in Hedwig's Hill or any one of her retailing contemporaries, the key to a successful mercantile business was in knowing the clients and responding to their needs accordingly. It was in a store owner's best interest to develop a good rapport with his or her customers, so as to keep abreast of changes in their economic fortunes. Store owners' well-being was intrinsically linked to the well-being of their customers, even if they saw themselves to be the social superiors of those customers. Ultimately, as one historian observed, "Good crops were as important for merchants as they were for farmers, and the long stoveside farming sessions were always valuable sources of information about the condition of soil, crops planned, and the next year's credit prospects."[83] There was certainly more to the symbiotic relationship than mere economics; communal ties and friendships also linked the parties together. Store owners and their clients worshiped together, their children attended the same school, and in times of crisis they came to each other's assistance out of both concern and necessity. Still, economics formed the underlying connection between merchants and their customers.

Besides fostering relationships with their clientele, merchants also had a vested interest in expanding their communities and promoting their towns or outposts with the intent of increasing their customer base. According to the *Oklahoma Star*, McAlester was clearly interested in the development of his community: "J. J. McAlester, the master spirit of the embryo city, is doing an extensive mercantile business, and at the same time is sparing no trouble or expense to improve the town and increase its importance. He has now, nearly completed, a hotel building which will be one of the best in the Territory."[84]

Few histories of western communities have escaped the issue of town promotion or "boosterism." Local merchants and other community leaders played a central role in promoting the town's future. Town boosterism fostered social cohesion, uniting the interests of ambitious community leaders to the collective interests of the burgeoning towns they promoted.[85] Only by attracting new residents and exciting commercial opportunities could the future of the town be assured. Of course, the commitment and skill levels of the businessmen involved were an important factor in any successful booster campaign. As one historian has observed, a well-orchestrated booster campaign was essential for a city to achieve and maintain a competitive edge, whereas an apathetic and unfocused campaign signaled to all concerned that a community was in trouble.[86] Everyone wanted their town to be the next St. Louis, San Francisco, or Denver. Unfortunately, few towns ever achieved such success.

One way that store owners demonstrated their commitment to expanding their towns, or future towns, was to speculate in the real estate market. They counted on an increased demand for town lots, which would drive up the value of their land investments. As noted, F. B. Severs speculated in land in Eufaula as well as in Muskogee, and apparently his town lots "engrossed substantial areas." In Muskogee, Severs built and owned a number of large businesses besides his dry goods store (he relocated in 1884 because of "the school advantages for his children"), including the Severs Hotel, which clearly suggests that the merchant had a substantial stake in the town's future prosperity.[87]

Anticipating growth in the town that would bear his name, J. J. McAlester claimed or purchased the land that surrounded his tiny outpost as early as February 1873. McAlester's bill of sale showed the right of occupancy for the entire town of McAlester. However, this acquisition was not without its share of controversy. Initially, McAlester was challenged from within the Choctaw membership: Judge James Cheadle contested McAlester's ownership of the land around the trading post, countering with his own claim to the property. Next, a dispute over the property developed between McAlester and the Choctaw, Oklahoma & Gulf Railroad. After learning of the railroad's intent to come through town, McAlester encouraged his fellow speculators to raise the price of their land collectively. In what was becoming the norm in western towns, the railroad demanded money, some $10,000, to run the line through the town. When McAlester refused to meet the railroad's demand, it located its line a mile and a half south of McAlester, prompting the town of South McAlester to spring up. Undeterred, McAlester immediately began purchasing sites in the path of the new rail line—in the end, the store owner spent more than $10,000 acquiring and defending his land acquisitions. As McAlester himself recalled: "It cost me more than ten thousand dollars to get a hold of South McAlester; and when the cases went through the courts they learned that their titles were not good. I bought up the judgments and in that way became a large property holder in their townsite."[88]

In 1878, William Henry "Pete" Snyder established a store along Deep Creek—the first permanent building in the future community of Hidetown, which later became the city of Snyder, Texas (in honor of its first merchant). In 1881, Snyder moved away from Deep Creek to Colorado City, beginning a second store at his new location. Closely paralleling McAlester's experience, Snyder became involved in a contentious battle over the land surrounding his early store, land that was planned for the future town site. Upon hearing that Hidetown might be designated the county seat, Snyder quickly began staking out a town site, some 640 acres of prime Texas range land. Another early settler, T. N. (Tommy) Nunn had been using the same land for cattle and claimed ownership of the same 640 acres. Apparently, Nunn wanted to divide the land equally, but as the local story goes, Snyder told him, "You know the land is mine and I will have it all or nothing!" A court battle ensued. Because Snyder had moved away from Deep Creek, the Texas Supreme

Court ruled that Snyder no longer had legal claim to the land, awarding the land to Snyder's rival, Tommy Nunn.[89] So, unlike McAlester, Snyder was unable to reap the benefits of being the first to settle the Deep Creek area. Evidently, being the first one in itself did not always pay dividends.

Speculating on a town's potential conformed closely to the competitive, progress-oriented mentality of the Gilded Age. The memorable Beriah Sellars character from Mark Twain and Charles Dudley Warner's *The Gilded Age* also engaged in town speculation. The belief in and desire for progress permeated all aspects of American culture; indeed, economic progress fostered growth and change in virtually all spheres of life and labor. Such progress was often accomplished with what later generations would call dubious means, for sure, but "progress" was accomplished nonetheless.[90] While fitting and colorful in its own right, Twain and Warner's *Gilded Age* description fails to capture the full essence of the last decades of the nineteenth century. It wasn't all reckless no-holds-barred competition and ruthlessness. Competing value systems, particularly those focused on gentility and moral probity, also surfaced in communities across America.

According to a number of scholars, the culture of Victorianism and its precepts best explains the dominant class structure of the period. In his history of the American West, for example, Richard White attributes efforts toward community building and moral reform in small communities to Victorian culture: "Community for these Victorian merchants meant women and families, and women and families demanded standards of respectability to thrive."[91] According to White, middle-class values and Victorianism were synonymous concepts. As many examples have shown, merchants resolved to improve their communities by supporting the development of churches and schools in their early settlements. However, the term "Victorianism" fails to capture the nuances of the elite merchant class in rural Texas and Indian Territory. The term itself is imprecise and overly vague. As a class, merchants were a multifaceted group. In the community of Jacksonville, for example, W. A. Brown might easily be placed in the petit bourgeoisie. He accrued modest wealth and exercised cautious business ambition, choosing instead to focus his efforts on growing his retail business for future generations.

He stressed to his sons the stalwart values of thrift, discipline, and hard work, yet despite his measured approach to business, he clearly took some risks. William Clark III, Blackstone Hardeman, Jr., and Lyne T. Barret came from privileged backgrounds; indeed, the latter came from a prominent slaveholding family, which allowed him to move smoothly from the slaveholding elite to the merchant elite. Barret also speculated in the oil business at its very earliest stages in Texas. James Jackson McAlester was very much a self-made man. He exhibited the intense drive often associated with Gilded Age success stories and amassed tremendous wealth and some enemies along the way. For his contemporaries in Indian Territory, McAlester was very much a part of the genteel elite, no different from fellow store owners Blackstone Hardeman or L. T. Barret in East Texas. Although Anna Martin happened into retailing only because of her husband's sickness and early death, she also successfully ventured into other industries and reaped the financial rewards of such risk taking.

Despite different starting and finishing points, there was also common ground among the merchants, who represented an elite class in their respective communities, though the level of their wealth varied immensely. In part, their elevated status derived from their critical role as creditors to a large percentage of their clientele. Further, through their trade connection with urban centers, store owners saw themselves as agents of cosmopolitan culture, linking their own status with their ability to purvey the latest trends of the East to their rustic environments. According to his ledger records, J. J. McAlester purchased almost all of his goods in the 1870s from wholesalers in St. Louis and, to a lesser degree, Kansas City. By the 1890s, however, his trade connections included wholesale houses in Dallas, Chicago, New Orleans, New York, as well as a slew of smaller cities. The ledgers of both William Clark's store in Nacogdoches and Anna Martin's store in Hedwig's Hill include debits for buying trips that were subsequently applied to the store owners' accounts. Thus, merchants served as significant cultural links between their local communities and the outside world, which only helped to heighten their already elevated social status.[92]

Store owners drew upon all the prevailing cultural influences of the late nineteenth century, including the middle-class emphasis on community responsibility and moral probity as well as the Gilded Age preoccupation with progress and money-making schemes. It was hardly an either/or issue, since most merchants exhibited some degree of both value systems. Some morphed from frontier opportunists, like J. J. McAlester and F. B. Severs, to genteel community leaders in the span of a few short years. As the local elite, store owners provided their respective communities with social and moral leadership; they served in political capacities and promoted their towns' potential. At the same time, they engaged in all sorts of wheeling and dealing typical of the period. In effect, they were very much products of their time as well as products of their place, in both the larger sense (the nation as a whole) and the smaller sense (the regional particularities of Texas and Indian Territory).

Chapter 2

Regional Particularities

Cotton, Cattle, and Coal

INCLUDED AMID THE EXTANT BUSINESS RECORDS for Hermann Fischer's store in Comal County is a "cotton book" for the years 1885–1886. In this specific ledger, Fischer registered the allotted weights and prices assigned to his customers' cotton crops. In an entry from October 29, 1885, for example, the store owner listed the weight of John Frebely's cotton crop at 550 pounds. Fischer assessed Frebely's crop at eight cents a pound, a respectable price only slightly lower than the nine-cent market average for the year.[1] After calculating the total, the merchant applied the credit to Frebely's account.[2] The ledger is hardly an unusual find, given the period, the popularity of the crop, and the critical role of store merchants as both creditors and marketers for farmers in the South. Certainly, similar records of such transactions can be found in ledgers across the cotton South.[3]

There is something striking about Fischer's cotton book, however—the location of the transaction itself. Situated in Central Texas, Comal County is a long way from East Texas, the region historically associated with cotton growing, slavery, and southern society in general. Comal County lies on the eastern edges of the Texas Hill Country and encompasses the northern outskirts of the large metropolitan area of present-day San Antonio. The county seat of New Braunfels reflects the influence of early German migration to Central Texas. Ledger entries from Fischer's store capture this region in a period of significant economic transition. In the 1870s and 1880s, King Cotton marched to both the western and northern counties of the state. Assisting in this march was the arrival of thousands of miles of railroad track connecting Texas to points east, west, and north. Commercial agriculture followed the tracks as they crisscrossed the state. To the frustration of many stock raisers, farmers increasingly encroached upon territory previously dedicated to cattle ranching. Fischer's business records also include ledgers that trace credits for hides and skins channeled through the store between 1888 and 1891—most of the hides were beef, although some were deer and goat hides.[4] While cotton was a significant and expanding crop in Comal County, cattle still maintained an important role in the local economy. In the state of Texas generally, the shift from predominantly cattle to predominantly cotton was not an even or an easy transition.

Fischer's ledgers not only highlight the westward expansion of cotton production but also demonstrate the ties of store owners to the local economy and, by extension, the economic fortunes of their clientele. Through their role as creditors, merchants maintained an elevated position of prestige in their respective communities. For many, however, their own success was predicated on the success of their store patrons. Merchants needed people to settle their accounts. Indeed, this was the case for a number of industries, not just cotton farming. The relationship of stores and merchants to the economic livelihoods of their customers is a fascinating story. General stores not only provided the forum for entrance into the market but also mediated market relations between merchants and consumers, creditors and debtors, and local industries and the national economy. Ledger records provide evidence of the interdependence of retailers, consumers, and their purchases.

Although cotton production—and specifically sharecropping—increasingly emerged as the principal economic activity in Texas during the late nineteenth century, this reality has not always been a source of state pride. When they think historically, many Texans prefer to stress their ranching heritage rather than their significant sharecropping history, and thus their connection to the West, rather than the South. Unfortunately, this emphasis distorts the historic record of the economic and cultural development of the state. Texas historian Robert Calvert argues that cattle ranching linked Texas to images of cowboys and western glamour while cotton tied Texas to the defeated Confederacy and southern poverty.[5] The disconnection of Texas with its southern roots prompted another Texas historian to write, "Texans escaped from the defeated, isolated, impoverished, brutally bigoted South by remaking memory, but that escape bore a price. The divorce of memory and reality, the erasing of the record of long and close association between Texas and the South, means as William Humphrey pointed out, that knowledge about Texas's past often sinks to the level of comic books."[6] The influence of the South on Texas was not merely a post–Civil War phenomenon; in fact the southern imprint began during the earliest period of extensive American migration, the 1820s.

Whether Texans wore it as a badge of honor or not, sharecropping, cotton, as well as strong cultural and regional ties to the South, all reflected the reality for the majority of Texans in the late nineteenth century. By 1890, the state of Texas produced 20 percent of the nation's cotton, leading all other states in cotton production.[7] While it is true that ranching and the much-heralded cattle drives constituted an important part of the Texas past, in the period under study, cotton increasingly reigned as king in the state. In the decades after the Civil War, most African Americans and many poor whites in Texas found themselves "farming on the halves," which essentially meant turning half of their crops over to someone else. As in other parts of the South, a farming hierarchy developed in the state; unfortunately, the chances of poor farmers to move up the agricultural ladder did not improve over time, especially for African Americans. Landowners not only owned the land but usually employed others to farm their land for them. Tenant farmers owned their farming equipment and work animals and rented land from landowners. These farmers were lucky enough to keep the majority of their harvest as profits (usually three-quarters of their cotton and two-thirds of their corn). Of course, the lowest ranking of the three in terms of social and economic standing were the sharecroppers. They were essentially farm laborers who lacked tools, work animals, and most important, land of their own.[8] Landowners hired them to produce cotton on their land and then paid them one-half of the proceeds of their harvest, minus any debts the sharecroppers owed for supplies. With their half of the cotton proceeds, sharecroppers proceeded to pay their debts at the local store. In the end, most sharecroppers were left with little or no profit, often carrying a balance with the store owner into the next season.

Rather than growing subsistence crops and eking out enough to feed and house their families first before taking their product to market (the customary strategy during the antebellum years), the trend after the war was to move toward cotton specialization. It is worth noting that many agricultural reformers during the period warned against specialization, instead arguing for diversification—and, in particular, for subsistence farming, which would be less susceptible to economic or environmental catastrophes. Still, cotton farmers in Texas pressed on. They did so because, despite slumping prices, cotton almost always returned more per acre than other suitable alternatives. The proliferation of railroad lines enhanced specialization, since farmers could acquire cheap food items from elsewhere and focus their attention on the more lucrative cotton crop. Because Texas farmers lacked capital, they needed to engage in crop-lien systems and sharecropping with local merchants and landowners. With the crop-lien system, merchants secured the credit they offered to cash-poor farmers by placing a lien on the future crop. If their crop returned as much profit as anticipated, then the farmer successfully paid off his debt with the merchant. However, if the crop brought in less than what was expected, and this happened with increased frequency in the late nineteenth century, then the farmer risked falling into a downward spiral of debt with the merchant. For farmers, cotton promised the best return on investment for both borrowers and lenders, so store owners encouraged the expansion of cotton farming with their accessible credit policies. Unfortunately, few farmers realized either economic independence or substantial wealth through cotton production.[9]

The influence of cotton on Texas's social and economic development was not uniform but, rather, varied in scope and region. In his study of cotton in Central Texas, Neil Foley examines the evolution of cotton culture and its impact on race relations in Texas from the postbellum period to the New Deal. He argues that a distinguishing feature of sharecropping in Central Texas, specifically the highly fertile Blackland Prairie region, was the high percentage of white tenant farmers and sharecroppers. Indeed, the predominance of white cotton farmers contrasts sharply with the economic demographics of other regions in both the cotton South and the counties of East Texas, where blacks comprised the majority of the workforce before the Civil War and then moved into sharecropping roles after emancipation.[10] Because of its unique racial dynamics, Central Texas emerged as a distinct economic and cultural region; however, the same cannot be said of its eastern counterpart. The culture of East Texas was more closely aligned with that of other southern cotton-producing states. As Foley observes, East Texas "fits comfortably within the cultural and historiographical boundaries of the South, with its slavery, cotton, and postemancipation society."[11]

Ledger records from general stores in these regions not only affirm the regional and racial distinctions posited in Foley's study and also demonstrate the centrality of the merchant-client relationship in these largely agricultural regions, a relationship that affected both white and black farmers. Located in the heart of East Texas, the Hardeman & Barret general merchandise store in Melrose featured a large African American clientele reflecting the racial demographics of the region. Store owner L. T. Barret distinguished race in his ledgers, generally by identifying his customers as either freedmen or freedwomen beside their names in his account books. Moreover, census records for the Melrose precinct confirm a high number of black farmers in the region in comparison to the demographics of Central Texas.[12]

The account of Charles Byrd, Jr., provides a useful example of how ledger records reflect economic activity in the region. Specifically, this entry reveals the ways in which customers settled their debts at the local store with their cotton crops. Identified in Hardeman & Barret's ledgers as a freedman, Charles Byrd, Jr., received a $100 credit on his account for his cotton crop in 1870, which conveniently (and exactly) settled his $100 debt with the store owners. His debt derived from an amalgam of store purchases including fabrics, food items, shoes, clothing, and tobacco.[13] Census records indicate that Charles Bird was a fifty-six-year-old black farmer at the time of the 1870 census. Born in Georgia, he lived with his wife, Amy, and their seven children, who ranged in age from two to twenty-two. As noted, Bird's occupation was recorded by the census-taker as "farmer."[14] In fact, virtually all of the store's African American customers were listed in the census as farmers; examples include Jesse Powers, Dick and Darthula Taylor, Starling

Kyle, and Berry Rusk.¹⁵ No distinction is made between sharecroppers and tenant farmers, or for that matter, landowning farmers.

The imprecise use of the term "farmer" in the census merits some discussion. On the one hand, it suggests that both store owners and former slaves in the region saw themselves as farmers, not field hands. After all, they worked a plot of land without supervision, and through their agreements with landowners, they established a "share" in the proceeds of their labor, a situation very different from slavery. On the other hand, the use of the generic term "farmer" to describe virtually all agricultural occupations in the region in 1870—sharecroppers, tenants, and landowners—may simply have been the least complicated means of collecting and categorizing data, no doubt an important consideration for an overburdened census taker.

Concerning landownership, relevant data available from the census is provided under the column "Value of Real Estate Owned" which is then divided into "Value of Real Estate" and "Value of Personal Estate." None of the sharecroppers listed above owned any real estate (briefly defined as land and the structures permanently attached to it). In the latter category, Charles Byrd, Jr. (or Bird, as he is in the census), valued his personal property at $145; Jesse Powers at $150; Dick and Darthula Taylor at $250; Starling Kyle at $275; Berry Rusk at $415. An analysis of census data for the community of Melrose provides a telling snapshot of African American landownership in East Texas. The population for District 3 in Nacogdoches County, Melrose and its surrounding area, in 1870 was 1,734: 1,171 whites and 563 blacks (so roughly two-thirds white and one-third black). According to the census, only one black farmer, John Simpson, owned land in the district—real estate valued at $350, with an additional $350 in personal property.¹⁶ While it is true that not all whites in the community owned land, the difference in rates of landownership between whites and blacks was dramatic. With the one exception of John Simpson, it is safe to say that in the Melrose district in 1870, landowners were white.

In this former slaveholding region, as in other parts of the South, landownership was a luxury that few freedmen could afford. Lack of African American landownership was not simply a question of means (although this was an important factor); most whites were not inclined to sell land to blacks even if the latter could afford it. In 1870, Reconstruction was in full swing in the South, and the terror campaigns of groups such as the KKK, the Knights of the White Camellia, and the White Caps were a powerful social force. Resentment on the part of white southerners toward both Radical Republican policies and their former slaves resulted in deliberate efforts to restrict African American landownership. Sharecropping, it may be supposed, was the only available reality for most African American customers of the Hardeman & Barret store.

At the McKinney & Brown store in Jacksonville, located in adjacent Cherokee County, store owner W. A. Brown similarly extended credit to his largely cotton-farming clientele, many of whom were African American. Account holders such as Perry Bolden, Sandy Chandler, and March Kessentiner, all frequent and long-term customers of the store, received credits from the store owner for their cotton crops. For example, on December 12, 1881, Bolden received a $44.80 credit on his account "By net proceeds 1b/c [bale of cotton]." Sandy Chandler received a $66.00 credit on his store account on November 12, 1881, "By cash on cotton." And finally, March Kessentiner received a $50.70 credit from the store owner "By net proceeds 1 b/c" on November 21, 1881.[17] Bolden, Chandler, and Kessentiner not only acquired necessities for their households from McKinney & Brown but also purchased work-related items such as bagging and ties for their cotton bales.

Ledger entries from this same period also reveal an interesting accounting practice employed by W. A. Brown for these particular customers' accounts. He applied a 10 percent interest charge to purchases made by both Bolden and Chandler in the spring of 1881; unusual in part because the store owner did not apply the practice across the board to other account holders, but just in certain instances. For example, on April 30, 1881, Brown applied a 10 percent charge of 40¢ to Bolden's purchases, which totaled $4.00; his purchases included fabrics, hose, oil, snuff, buttons, and candy. Another 10 percent was added to Sandy Chandler's account on May 23, 1881, after he purchased such items as gloves, ribbon, ties, handkerchiefs, and a parasol. Chandler's bill totaled $5.75 and the added 10 percent charge was 57¢.[18] In both cases, these were large orders somewhat atypical of the number and kinds of items purchased by other African American customers. Tellingly, during the same spring, the white doctor and frequent store customer J. T. Simpson charged to his account a large purchase order, which included a lace scarf, buttons, hose, a variety of fabrics, and two boy's suits—with no additional interest charge applied to the account by the store owner.[19] Indeed, large purchases made at other times by Bolden and Chandler did not merit the additional interest charge. The seemingly random application of the interest penalty is particularly odd. Of course, no rationale is given by the store owner for the unusual charge; however, since it applied only to black store customers, the ledger evidence suggests there was clearly a racial component to the practice.

Another interesting ledger entry that highlights McKinney & Brown's credit policies is witnessed on the account for Dick Coleman, listed in the ledgers as a "Mulatto." In this instance, the merchants indicated in their ledgers a credit limit of $150, assumedly per annum. What prompted the limit by the store owners is unknown. Credit limits were a fairly common occurrence in the New South, especially because of the preponderance of the crop-lien system.[20] In the case of the McKinney & Brown store in Jacksonville, the consequences of prolonged debt with the firm was that creditors were subjected to extra interest charges, as in the examples listed above, or in more extreme cases, customers had to sign notes or give mortgages on property to cover their unpaid balances.[21]

Bookkeeping practices and debt policies varied considerably and depended on the proclivities of the merchant involved. Despite such variation, there was widespread consensus among store clients that they were being taken advantage of by the merchants.[22] While there is little evidence in ledgers from stores in Texas and Indian Territory, in the way of signatures or initials, of public access to account records, merchants no doubt "opened their books" when pressed by their clients. After all, despite their exploitative reputation, merchants depended on their customers just as their customers depended on them. In many cases, a general crop failure not only threatened a store owner's livelihood but could place his business in utter ruin. The perception of merchants as callous swindlers, fleecing poor farmers out of land and the fruits of their labor, is flawed for it fails to address the complexity of the credit relationships in the postwar South. As creditors, merchants assumed an enormous amount of risk, a general crop failure promised ruin for the store and inevitable bankruptcy for the borrower. As Thomas Clark points out, "A hundred credit customers who religiously settled their accounts at the end of each crop season were often forced to pay the accounts of another hundred who did not."[23]

Part of the risk absorbed by merchants as credit issuers is that they themselves were subject to interest rates. Country store owners primarily obtained their merchandise on credit, granted to them by supply houses located in distant urban centers. In this sense, they were in a similar boat as their credit-dependent clientele. Relying heavily on the credit records of R. G. Dun & Company, a New York–based credit report agency, Scott Marler examined the volatility and risks associated with retailing in both pre- and postwar Central Louisiana. Citing evidence of low business survival rates in the postbellum environment (a consequence of volatile markets, a debt-beleaguered clientele, and merchants' own unremitting credit obligations), Marler challenges the idea that retailers always profited on the backs of patrons. Indeed, southern historian C. Vann Woodward warned against casting merchants as the villains in this story: "The prices and interest rate were exorbitant, but so were the risks the merchant took," as they "paid outrageous rates of interest to factors." In part, store owners charged their customers interest rates in an effort to offset the risk and, more specifically, the interest they accrued with their creditors.[24]

Even if they had total access to a merchant's books, not all store customers could make sense of what they were seeing. Some merchants used shorthand and symbols in their ledgers, which only they and their clerks understood. As well, not all store clients could read. High illiteracy rates distinguished African Americans in the postbellum period, although many former slaves sought to rectify this problem by attending the newly established freedmen schools. Illiteracy rates were also higher for poor whites in the South compared to the national average. For example, in 1880 when the national average for white illiteracy was about 9 percent, between one-quarter and one-third of whites in southern states could not read.[25]

Perhaps in an effort to contain their own risk, owners of a mercantile firm in Chireno, Texas (described in their 1887 ledger book as the vague "Chireno Alliance"), enforced credit limits on their customers through a trading card system.[26] Located in East Texas, the small community of Chireno is located eighteen miles east of Nacogdoches and roughly ten miles from Melrose, Texas. Account data from this general store indicate that the clientele engaged primarily in agricultural pursuits, especially cotton, and often settled their accounts with bales of cotton. Census records confirm that most of this community's residents in the 1880s were farmers.[27] Evidently, store owners issued trading cards to their customers that specified the credit available at the store. For example, the amount of Levi Morton's trading card was $30.00; he received a $20.00 credit for his crop. During the same period, J. H. Fuller's trading card was also $30.00, T. W. Layton's trading card was $35.00, and M. Sargent's trading card was $50.00.[28] As in other instances, the rationale concerning what qualified the customer for a higher trading card remained in the control of store owners. The trading card system employed by the Chireno Alliance denoted a unique twist on an old system—a system that set limits on the credit available to the customers and thus reduced the store owners' own risk in the trading relationship.

The process for debt collection varied depending on the store and the circumstances concerning the individual account. No doubt, some methods for collecting outstanding accounts met with greater success than others. General appeals for customers to meet their debt obligations with their local merchant were likely the least effective. In 1872, an ad appeared in a Jacksonville newspaper that read as follows: "Our merchants will start on to lay in their spring stocks in a few weeks. They would like for every Tom, Dick and Harry, and every other man and woman to come forward and settle up."[29] Store owners also sent out their clerks to collect outstanding debts. While working as a store clerk for the Dickson & Green mercantile firm in Comanche County, Texas, J. D. Sherrill recorded entries in his diary that recounted his collection experiences. On January 1, 1884, he wrote, "Worked all morning making out accounts. Collected all evening, had very good luck." In an entry dated January 22, 1884, he noted, "We rolled out this morning and went to Gaines and got him to mortgage his crop."[30] Besides working in the store, one of Sherrill's key responsibilities was evidently collecting overdue accounts. Since a number of entries mention such transactions, many overdue accounts were settled through the exchange of mortgages on both crops and property, which could then be transferred from farmers to the store owners to pay off debts.[31] Under the crop-lien system, landowners had the first right to a tenant's crop, which left little for other creditors such as merchants or bankers to cover their own losses. As a result, the chattel mortgage system arose, which provided additional security for merchants and bankers. If a tenant could not meet his credit obligations with a merchant or a banker with the proceeds from his crop, the lenders had a right to seize his property, as shown in Sherrill's diary. Sherrill also collected cash when available and applied it to the overdue balances. For example, he recorded the following entry in his diary on November 28, 1882: "Went down to T. M. Coudrons [sic] today and collected $40.00 from him for Dickson & Green."[32] While Sherrill's diary provides insights into the more extreme cases of the crop-lien system, most debtors settled with store owners when they could—this usually meant when their crops came in. In cotton regions, most merchants were also ginners and cotton buyers. When their customers brought in their freshly harvested cotton crops to be marketed, store owners were able to collect on their overdue store accounts.

Cotton regions were particularly susceptible to credit/debt systems in which local merchants assumed the role of principal creditors for the region. In a cash-poor economy, the dominant method of exchange tended to be book credit, and this was certainly the case in the agricultural regions of East Texas. As one Texas historian observed, the state suffered chronic shortages of investment monies, which at times became acute: "This situation was particularly desperate in the interior parts of the state, far from the larger cities, and especially so in the predominantly agricultural sections where small farmers needed loans to enable them to buy supplies until they could harvest their crops."[33]

While most store customers relied on credit, cash transactions also appeared in ledger records. Merchants both received and dispersed cash to their clients, as a number of examples from the McKinney & Brown store in Jacksonville will show. A debit was charged to Cal Arnwine's account in February 1881 for "cash handed you $1.00." In October 1883, Dick Coleman received a debit "to cash handed you" for

$13.00. And in November 1885, Sam Lacy's account was debited $2.00, again the rationale for the charge being "cash handed you."[34] Presumably, these three individuals needed cash for purchases or payments outside the store's credit system. In this capacity, the store owners assumed the role of local banker for their clients, in addition to the many hats they already wore within their respective communities.

A striking feature of census data for the communities of East Texas is the strong southern heritage evidenced by farmers listed in the records. In both the Jacksonville and Melrose communities most farmers who were born outside Texas had emigrated from other southern states. This was true for both blacks and whites. Of the aforementioned African American customers who frequented the Hardeman & Barret store in Melrose, all were born in Confederate states.[35] The same could be said of black customers at the McKinney & Brown store—for example, Perry Bolden and March Kessentiner were born in Alabama, while Sandy Chandler was born in Mississippi.[36] The white farmers who settled in East Texas had migrated from regions all over the South; in fact, store owners Blackstone Hardeman and L. T. Barret were both born in former slaveholding states.[37]

As the century progressed, the southern stronghold on the state increased. By 1887, southerners constituted nearly three-fifths of the population, although their numbers steadily declined after the turn of the century.[38] East Texas was linked to the South not just economically and demographically but culturally as well. The fact that East Texas was heavily influenced by the South meant that it shared the social ruptures and turmoil associated with the Reconstruction period, especially regarding race relations. In short, cotton was by no means the only connection between Texas and the South.

Situated on the southern boundary of Central Texas, between San Antonio and Houston, the Neer & James mercantile firm in Oakland, Colorado County, maintained a racially diverse clientele principally engaged in cotton production. Ledger records indicate that both black and white customers received credits on their accounts for some share of their cotton crops. For example, the store owners applied a $150.80 credit to the account of A. E. Easterling, "By 2 b/c 1040 lbs @ 14½," on September 5, 1871. Distinguished in the ledgers as a freedman,

Stephen McKinnon received a $64.96 credit on September 4, 1871, "By 1 b/c 448 lbs @ 14½." Another freedman, Irwin Dawes, received $74.34 credit from the store on September 11, 1871, "By 1 b/c 504 lbs @ 14¾." Indeed, numerous examples of such credits appear throughout the ledger, which highlights not only the region's commitment to cotton production but also the central role of merchants in extending credit to their farming clientele. Moreover, ledger records indicate that both blacks and whites engaged in growing cotton in Colorado County, and given the political and racial dynamics of the period, most of these customers were likely sharecroppers.[39]

As noted, in the late nineteenth century, cotton production increasingly spread from East Texas into the counties of Central Texas. The process eventually spread as far north as the southern banks of the Red River.[40] Thus, the impact of cotton expansion was felt in regions across Texas. The "cotton book" described earlier from Hermann Fischer's store in Comal County contained the names of farmers largely of German descent, which was appropriate given the large numbers of German immigrants in the Texas Hill Country. These names include George Stubbs, Otto Schlamens, Herm Linartz, C. Sachtleben, and Freidrich Frerichs. The Hill Country experienced a spectacular expansion in cotton production, beginning in 1870s and 1880s, especially among Germans, two-thirds of whom were raising cotton in the region by 1880.[41]

While Germans certainly dominated the Hill Country in the 1850s, this influence steadily decreased in the latter decades of the nineteenth century, as the counties of Central and South Texas attracted more ethnically diverse populations. By the 1880s, the urban centers of Dallas, Houston, Austin, Corpus Christi, and San Antonio all encompassed persons from a myriad of locations. To some degree, Spanish, French, German, African, Mexican, English, Polish, Czech, and other ethnic groups all left their cultural imprint on this remarkably heterogeneous region. As the nineteenth century drew to a close, rural and urban centers across Texas progressively developed into a complex hodgepodge of different ethnic and racial influences, prompting one geographer, Terry D. Jordan, to describe the region as a "shatter belt" of diversity. In the late nineteenth century, the central region was not only experiencing increased diversity, but was also coping with the effects of the westward expansion of cotton.[42]

Like the ledgers from Hermann Fischer's store in Comal County, ledger records from J. L. McInnis's store in Travis County provide a snapshot of the region in a period of economic transition, giving insights into the ethnic and racial composition of this centrally located county. Situated fifteen miles east of Austin, the community of Webberville was comprised of a variety of cultural influences, including Scots, northerners, southerners, and native-born Texans as well as a composite population of both blacks and whites. African Americans listed in the store records include blacksmith Sandy Haden and farmer Samuel Hancock.[43] The store not only provided goods but extended credit to farmers for a share of their cotton crop. Jasper Romine, a white farmer from Mississippi, received a $29.60 credit at the store "by cotton" on December 4, 1874. McInnis equipped his customers with the goods necessary to bring their product to market. For example, Michael O'Conner purchased bagging and ties on November 7, 1874. Suggesting that cattle ranching also remained prominent in the region, the account of John Meeks included credits for "beef hides," applied by the store owner to the account in May and August of 1874. In fact, both cotton and livestock constituted the principal commodities shipped from the area in the 1870s and 1880s.[44]

If the introduction of cotton was relatively new for the western and northern counties of Texas in the 1870s and 1880s, the same could not be said of the future state to the north. Cotton production in Indian Territory dated back to the 1830s, the earliest period of resettlement by the Five Tribes. Pushed out of southern states, many tribal members brought their knowledge of cotton production to their new lands. After arriving in their new territory, many wealthy Choctaws immediately began engaging in cotton farming and established plantations on the banks of the Red River with the labor of black slaves. As early as 1867, cotton emerged as the main export of the Choctaw Nation, closely followed by cattle.[45]

General stores located in the Nation in the 1870s and 1880s reflect the dual nature of the agricultural economy. Several entries from G. B. Hester's ledgers for his store in Old Boggy Depot demonstrate the importance of cotton in the local economy. Zach Gardner received credit "by five bales of cotton" on his account on January 30, 1874. A. Conner received a $14.00 credit to his account for 350 pounds of cotton on January 6, 1874. During the same period, bagging and ties were sold to A. D. Irwin, Joshua Irwin, and Giles Thompson. While cotton remained the principal agricultural pursuit of farmers in the region, Hester's ledger records indicate that there was some economic diversity as well—customers received credit at his store for both corn and deerskins.[46]

In other regions of the Choctaw Nation, cattle figured more prominently in store ledgers than cotton. It is not surprising that the ledgers of Choctaw principal chief W. N. Jones reflected many of the key aspects of the local economy, given that he established his mercantile firm in part to service the needs of those working on his cattle ranch. Indeed, his store ledgers record the sales of cows and calves among purchases charged to customers' accounts. At F. B. Severs's store in Okmulgee, the capital of the Creek Nation, a number of clients received credit for "beef hides." Examples include the $2.00 credit applied to Toney Burgess's account on August 26, 1869, Cono Fixoco's account on September 17, 1869, and Henry Duncan's account on November 20, 1869. In diversifying their business activities beyond retailing, both Jones and Severs created substantial fortunes out of their cattle-ranching interests in Choctaw and Creek Territories.[47]

Reflecting on the period he spent working in the Severs store in the late nineteenth century, William P. Morton described both the nature of Severs's business and his credit practices: "The Severs store handled everything from tobacco to coffins, and most of the trading was on credit. People paid their bills yearly, this being the center of the Creek Nation and a large cattle industry. The cattlemen received their money in lump sums, as did the Indians, and paid their bills accordingly." According to Morton, Severs had a simplified bookkeeping strategy: "Each item such as coffee, shoes, etc. was not charged on the books. Instead, if the credit extended an individual was $50.00, he was charged with this amount and a due bill issued to him. Four marks made a dollar, each representing a quarter, and as the holder traded, the due bill diminished." At one time, Morton served as the head of F. B. Severs's land department, and he looked after rentals and collections. He observed that Severs, at different times in his career, held as much as thirty thousand acres under his supervision, requiring much diligence on Morton's part to keep track of the numerous farms and tenants.⁴⁸

A. J. Kennedy worked for Severs in the early 1890s and also recalled what he described as the store owner's "all credit business." According to Kennedy, "If an Indian established credit, he would make arrangements with the store for a certain amount of credit and this amount would be charged to him in one lump sum. There would be no itemized accounts. If the customer wanted a $100.00 credit, as an example, he was charged $100.00 and due bills were given for him for the amount in bills of $5.00 and $10.00 denominations." Kennedy continued, "These due bills read for example as follows: Okmulgee, Indian Territory, September 1, 1892. Due in merchandise to bearer John Wildcat at my store $5.00 ı ı ı / ı ı ı ı / ı ı ı ı / ı ı ı ı / ı ı ı ı /F. B. Severs." Each short mark represented twenty-five cents and each long mark represented one dollar. When a twenty-five-cent purchase was made the clerk would take his scissors and clip off one of these short marks.⁴⁹

Robert Hamilton also worked as a clerk and a drummer (a traveling salesman) for Severs in the 1880s, and he remembered a similar credit practice utilized at the store, though he used slightly different terminology and described Severs's "due bills" as "certificates": "Captain F. B. Severs issued scrip to be used as money by the people trading with him. He never issued the brass tokens as issued by Parkinson-Trent [a rival store in Okmulgee]. One-fourth of this certificate was twenty-five cents and the Creek for it was con-sot-ca-hongon. These were the first Creek words I learned." According to Hamilton, he came to Indian Territory in 1885 and got a job clerking for Captain (F. B.) Severs; he initially worked in the Okmulgee store, but after a year, Severs transferred him to the Muskogee store. Hamilton remained in the Creek Nation for the next several decades of his life, witnessing the shift from Indian Territory to the state of Oklahoma.⁵⁰

While ranching was being pushed increasingly westward and northward (into Indian Territory, for example) during the 1880s, it still maintained an important presence in southern counties as well as in a number of communities in Central Texas, particularly in the sloping grasslands of the Hill Country. Early settlers to Central Texas, particularly those who arrived in the 1830s and 1840s, raised more cattle and corn than cotton. This transition began in the 1870s and 1880s, the period when the large cattle drives from South Texas to railway links in Kansas reinforced the image of Texas as predominantly western, rather than southern. Cattle drives were especially lucrative operations for landless cattlemen looking to make their start in the ranching business. Driving Texas cattle north for sale proved very profitable for a number of opportunistic drovers in the late 1860s and early 1870s. Consequently, the demand for cattle only grew. As the *New York Times* reported in 1876, "It is now ten years since Texas cattle, or 'the long-horns,' began to appear in large numbers on the Northern markets. Since 1867 over 3,000,000 head have been driven into Kansas, and shipped to Chicago and St. Louis. Large numbers have also been herded into Western Kansas, Colorado, Nebraska, and Wyoming."[51]

In 1870, more than five million longhorns roamed the Texas grasslands, many of them mavericks that could be claimed by anyone willing to affix a brand. It was precisely because of the preponderance of free and unbranded cattle in the Hill Country that many of the German immigrants listed in the ledgers at Anna Martin's store in Hedwig's Hill obtained herds and established ranches. Quality steers could be purchased in Texas for $4.00 and then sold in the North for up to $40.00, so there was more than enough incentive for persons willing to drive their cattle north, which was far less expensive than shipping cattle by train.[52] However, the days of the long cattle drives through Central Texas were essentially numbered. As Neil Foley notes, "The era of the Long Drive, with its powerful images of cowboys and roundups, was to endure for two decades following the Civil War. But during that twenty-year span the population of Texas was increasing rapidly, and new settlements pushed the cattle industry steadily westward beyond the central prairies and onto the rolling plains of west Texas." The process was already underway in the mid-1870s, as the *Times* reported in 1876, "The Western cattle trade has shown considerable change in the past two or three years. . . . Shipping points are also changing, the trails and stations, by legislation and otherwise, being gradually pushed further west."[53]

Straddling the boundaries of southern and Central Texas, Refugio County's residents focused their industry on the business of raising cattle.

In the postbellum period, Refugio was an inland county devoted mainly to stock raising.[54] Customer records from the W. E. McCampbell & Bros. store in the town of Refugio confirm the community's commitment to cattle ranching. Frequent store customers such as A. M. Dunman and R. S. West are listed in the store ledgers as "Cowhunters." Certain entries make specific mention of transactions involving cattle. For example, the store owners credited Davy O'Donald's account $20.00 for "Four head cattle" on December 27, 1876.[55] The sale of numerous six-shooters to store customers completes the imagined picture of rugged cowboys equipped with pistols, although their high cost priced them out of the range of most ranch hands.[56] Finally, the accoutrements of horseback riding such as leather stirrups, spurs, collars, and saddles also made frequent appearances on store accounts.[57]

As noted, the German immigrants who settled in the Hedwig's Hill community and frequented Anna Martin's store were heavily engaged in cattle ranching, as is evident in a number of ledger entries from Martin's store. In order to transport their bulk goods like cow hides and beef to market, cattle raisers needed to pay freight charges to haulers. Haulers, in turn, received credit on their accounts for transporting bulk quantities of freight. Store owners also needed to pay haulers for transporting store goods from larger centers outside of the region; likely the haulers would fill their wagons with store goods on their return trip to the community. Such transactions made their way into Martin's ledgers. For example, Theodor Weidemann's account is credited $18.00, "By 3600 lbs freight," on July 30, 1887. A few weeks later, William Tatsch received an $11.00 credit on his account for 2,200 pounds of freight on August 15, 1887. Perhaps, Weidemann and Tatsch hauled hides and beef to market, or possibly they received credit for transporting goods for Anna Martin's store—unfortunately, no further information is provided on their respective accounts.[58]

Involved in the cattle industry herself, Anna Martin brokered sales of cattle through her store, crediting her customers' accounts for specific cows or using the less precise term "by cattle." Store patrons paid bills with almost anything of value—crops, animals (including cattle, chickens, and turkeys), animal by-products (such as eggs, lard, bacon, and hides), freighting, and sometimes even cash. The problem was that there was a constant shortage of trustworthy exchange. To alleviate this problem, Martin began "commission buying." Her first commission was cattle, for which she received ten cents a head; later she expanded her commission options and bought items like pecans, cotton, and wool from local producers.[59] For cattle purchases, on July 8, 1886, John Bauer received a credit for $65.00, "By cattle delivered." The following day, Adolf Keller's account is credited $216.00, "By 27—year old steers @ 8.00." Both Max Reichenau and M. Bast received credits for $7.50 for one yearling each on September 15, 1886.[60] Martin credited Louis Eckert's account $86.00 on October 25, 1887, simply by noting, "By cattle." On May 8, 1888, Bill, Christian, John, and George Keyser all received separate credits on their account for steers, credits that ranged from $20.00 to $85.00.[61] All of these transactions highlight not only the economic activity of the region but also the ways in which the general store linked the socioeconomics of the Hedwig's Hill community together. Martin's store played a pivotal role not only in how cattle ranchers disposed of their income but also in how they acquired that income.

The cattle industry of the Hill Country underwent considerable change in the decades following the 1840s, when German immigrants first began ranching in the region. Cattle ranching itself in Central Texas (particularly in the San Antonio region) dated back to the mid-eighteenth-century mission period in Texas. A century later, Germans played a leading role in introducing innovations such as improved breeds (mainly Herefords) and in fencing the open range.[62] According to local history, Anna Martin was the first person to buy and sell barbed wire to ranchers in Mason County and in adjoining counties. The issue of barbed wire is a contentious one in the West. In many western regions, the introduction of barbed wire instigated feuds between farmers and ranchers, cattle ranchers and sheep ranchers, and large and small ranchers, all competing for that highly precious commodity, land. While barbed wire brought innovation to ranching by alleviating some of the problems of the open range, such as wandering strays, it also incited a new set of disputes between groups competing for available land.[63] Furthermore, by limiting access to free pastures and watering holes, Central Texas's appeal to cattle drovers and "free-grass" stockmen steadily declined; thus, barbed wire played a decisive role in transforming the region's main pursuit from cattle to cotton. From the early to mid-1880s, Texas ranchers embarked on the immense project of fencing their land. Marking the boundaries of their lands and dividing their land from that of their neighbors caused the lands in the public domain to shrink. Once large cattle companies obtained title to lands or permanent claims to a portion of the range, they immediately sought to fence in their land and herds to protect against poachers and the overstocking of pastures with strays.[64]

In counties just to the north of Mason County in Central Texas (specifically Clay and Brown Counties), barbed wire and the issue of fence cutting came to a head in the early 1880s. Once large ranchers began fencing major sections of their lands, it prompted small ranchers, who could not hope to pasture their animals on their relatively meager claims, and free-grass trail drovers, who needed access to trails and water holes, to cut the newly installed fences. A drought in 1883 escalated the need for access to water sources. The result was the Fence-Cutters' War of 1883–84, which led to a number of deaths in Clay County and near open warfare in Brown County. The violence forced the Texas legislature to act. Laws against both fence cutting and fencing in the public domain—as well as statutes in 1884 requiring stockmen to place a gate at every three miles of fence—ultimately put a stop to the fighting.[65]

Barbed wire appears in the purchases of many of Martin's ranching clientele in the 1880s, which shows that German ranchers in the Hill Country similarly engaged in the fencing trends of the mid-1880s. On July 2, 1886, Fritz Grote purchased 10 pounds of fleece twine, a pair of shoes, 198 pounds of barb wire, and 200 pounds of smooth wire. The total bill was $21.25. On July 17, 1886, Fritz Kothmann purchased 2,011 pounds of barb wire for $95.52 and 2,900 pounds of black wire. The total was $104.40. In September 1886, William Geistweidt acquired 5,300 pounds of wire for $185.50 and 144 pounds of barb wire for $5.13, while H. F. Keyser purchased eight spools of barb wire for $42.40 and 1,600 pounds of smooth wire for $64.00.[66] Clearly, not only was barbed wire a popular item among ranchers in the Hedwig's Hill community, but it required a fairly significant investment on the part of local consumers.

The large expenditures on various types of wire appear far less frequently in Martin's ledgers for the following summer and fall. In part, declining sales in barbed wire can likely be attributed to the fact that many of Martin's customers acquired such large amounts of wire in the summer of 1886. That said, the impact of the brutal winter of 1886–87 undoubtedly played a significant role in the declining sales of barbed wire in 1887. Taxed with a growing problem of overstocking, the plains suffered a series of environmental and economic calamities in the mid-1880s. Beginning with a blizzard in November, a fierce winter devastated the plains. Temperatures dropped, not only in the far stretches of the northern plains but as far south as Central Texas. Bitter cold gripped the nation. On the range, cattle died in alarming numbers. In the midst of the winter, one cattleman articulated the growing concern: "This winter found us with more cattle than grass, and it was generally conceded that nothing but a mild Winter could save us."[67] Unfortunately, the winter of 1886–87 was anything but mild. An economic depression followed the ecological disaster, as creditors called in their loans and ranchers scrambled to sell off their losses. Few ranchers successfully weathered the events of 1886–87; in fact, most had to cut expenditures and sell off at least a portion of their stock.[68]

Martin's store ledgers offer important insights into cattle raising and its influence on the Hedwig's Hill community, while similar records from Hermann Fischer's store in Comal County provide an interesting comparison and counterpoint. It seems these store owners took remarkably similar paths to Central Texas, and yet they chose opposite strategies for economic success on the Texas frontier. Like Anna Martin and many other German immigrants, Hermann Fischer had traveled from Germany shortly after the first waves of migration, arriving in northern Comal County in 1849.[69] Unlike Martin, who operated her late husband's store first before venturing into cattle ranching, Fischer initially engaged in stock raising on his 160 acres of land, but when the population of the area increased, he built a log store and developed a prosperous mercantile business. Fischer's store was located approximately twenty miles northwest of New Braunfels in the Hill Country of northern Comal County. Fischer, like Martin, provided postal services out of his store and served as postmaster in the 1870s. The community established around his store was aptly named Fischer's Store—becoming Fischer Store in 1894, and Fischer in 1950, both name changes came at the request of postal officials.[70]

In the 1870s and 1880s, it was cotton, not cattle, however, that increasingly came to dominate the agricultural activity in Comal County, hence the importance of the "cotton book" from Fischer's store records. According to one scholar, production of cotton by Germans in the New Braunfels area became quite widespread as early as 1859. Cotton's importance swelled during the postbellum period, and one observer described the fields around New Braunfels in the mid-1870s as being "snow-white with cotton."[71] Terry Jordan cites Comal County, in particular, as a county significantly affected by the expansion of cotton, noting that by 1885 the number of gins in the county had increased from one, in the mid-1850s when the first cotton gin was built, to twenty.[72] Apparently, by operating a gin behind his store, Fischer himself contributed to the growing number of cotton gins available to farmers in the county.[73] Thus, Hermann Fischer was not only a retailer to local farmers but also (for a fee) made his cotton gin available to them, which in turn drew them to his mercantile establishment. As retailer, postmaster, and gin operator, Fischer established himself as a prominent man of affairs, especially economic affairs, for his small community.

James Jackson McAlester occupied a similar position of importance in the burgeoning community that developed around the trading post he established in the "Crossroads" region of the Choctaw Nation in the early 1870s. From the outset, McAlester had his hand in virtually all the economic activities in the region, including retailing, cotton, ranching, and most important, mining. In large part because of the store owner's efforts, the community of McAlester developed and thrived from its proximity to the area's rich coal beds; of course, it was the potential of this geological bonanza that had drawn McAlester to the Crossroads in the first place. Ledgers from McAlester's store reflect the unique socioeconomics of the region, attesting to the importance of mining in the McAlester community and establishing, once again, the critical relationship of the store owner with the economic fortunes of his clientele.

An intricate web of contracts, networks, professional affiliations, and personal relationships linked McAlester to the interests of the Osage

Coal and Mining Company, a business that featured prominently in the store owner's ledgers in the 1870s and 1880s. McAlester and three business partners—Joshua Pusley, Tandy Walker, and Dr. Daniel M. Hailey—relinquished their individual coal leases (acquired in McAlester's case through marriage) for royalties in the Osage Coal and Mining Company, which was owned by the Missouri-Kansas-Texas Railway (MK&T). The collusion between the two companies was not publicly known—or at least not publicly admitted by the two parties. The railroad company claimed that the coal company was a separate operation, even though many of the mine's directors were also the MK&T's directors.[74] In the early 1870s, the mining company entered into an agreement with the Choctaw Nation that essentially permitted the company to do whatever was required to facilitate mining operations. The MK&T laid its track into the Nation's land with the specific intention of exploiting the region's rich coal beds. The railroad company learned of the territory's mineral wealth through McAlester. In 1871, he had hauled a wagonload of coal to Parsons, Kansas, for the railroad's officials to inspect. McAlester's strategy worked. The MK&T tracks reached the Crossroads area in 1872, and the tiny community was renamed McAlester in honor of the man who had first discovered the region's economic potential.[75]

The fortunes of the MK&T, its subsidiary the Osage Coal and Mining Company, and investor J. J. McAlester grew steadily over the course of the 1870s. By 1887 the eight mines were operating in the Choctaw Nation and had produced 685,911 tons of coal at a value of $1,286,692.[76] The critical role of coal in the MK&T's success during the period prompted two Oklahoma historians to observe that the shipping of coal over the MK&T rail lines was of more importance than all of the Texas cattle shipped over the same line.[77] Granted, this was during the era of the great cattle drives when it still proved cheaper to drive the cattle up from Texas than to ship it by rail. Still, the observation is a testament to the importance of coal to the region's economy during this period.

As one would expect, the occupations of miner and railroad agent figured prominently in McAlester's records. Both the MK&T and the Osage Coal and Mining Company maintained accounts at the store, and representatives from both companies also established their own individual accounts with the store owner. With no census available for the region in this period and with the transitory nature of both railroad work and mining, McAlester's inclusion of his customers' occupations is especially valuable for it reveals who worked in the region during the 1870s. A number of "railroad men" appear in ledgers from the mid-1870s, including William Dargetz, Larry Bowen, and David Woolf. In January 1874, McAlester also included in his records the account of J. T. Cowan, whose occupation is listed as "car trimmer." In their consumption patterns, these railroad employees tended to stick to the basics: their purchases included washing kettles, yeast, tea, sugar, beans, soap, potatoes, tobacco, and coffee.[78]

Although McAlester's general store was not an official company store, in many ways it operated as one. Area coal miners provided the largest customer base for the store. Furthermore, since McAlester was a principal investor in the Osage Coal and Mining Company (the primary employer of the majority of persons in the McAlester community), the miners listed in McAlester's ledgers were also indirectly his employees. There were few retail options available to consumers in the region, so miners had little choice but to give back to their quasi-employer a share of their wages. Commenting on the connection of McAlester to the coal company, one former miner later recalled, "A man by the name of J. J. McAlester was the head of the coal mining company mining the coal at this place at this time. I don't know but I think that this town was named after him. He was the biggest coal man there at that time."[79] According to store ledgers, the proprietor credited coal miner Charles Brown's account $38.30 "By cash collected of Coal Company from December 1874." Similarly, John Stoker's account was credited $11.17 "by cash of Coal Company for December." Another miner, J. McMullen, received a credit for payment from the Coal Company of $8.75 for December, $32.30 for January (which included some beef he sold to McAlester), and a $6.33 credit for February.[80] Indeed, there are ample examples of customer accounts paid by Osage Coal throughout the ledgers, affirming that coal mining constituted the principal economic activity in the McAlester district.

An entry involving one of McAlester's business partners, Dr. Daniel Morris Hailey, demonstrates the close connection of McAlester's store with the region's preeminent employer, the Osage Coal Company. As an investor, Hailey gained cash royalties from the coal company, and similar to the miners' employee checks, Hailey's royalties were funneled through McAlester's store. On May 10, 1875, for example, McAlester credited Hailey's account $248.60 "by cash of Coal Co. on royalty"; on June 1, Hailey received a $35.55 credit, and on July 1 his cash royalty was $28.12.[81] Evidently, investing in the upstart coal company proved lucrative for both Hailey and McAlester.

By and large, staples characterize the purchases made by the majority of McAlester's mining customers. Miner Mike Dunn's order from January 21, 1875, included flour, sugar, and soap; a few weeks later he bought more flour, cheese, lard, and a coffeepot. During the same period a fellow miner, U. A. Keith, purchased sugar, tea, tobacco, flour, salt, thread, and denim.[82] Knowing the needs of his clientele, McAlester stressed the "staple-nature" of his stock in his advertising. In an ad featured in the *Oklahoma Star*, McAlester emphasized that his mercantile establishment offered clothing, boots, shoes, hardware, queensware, tinware, hats, caps, blankets, fruit, and potatoes.[83] Since the needs of his predominantly male clientele were few, the store owner obviously saw no need to waste words in his advertisements; expensive specialty items were luxuries that these particular consumers could not afford.

As the community of McAlester matured in the last decades of the nineteenth century, its population rapidly grew and its economy diversified. Coal remained important but was no longer the sole focus of the local economy. With the influx of people attracted to the region initially because of the coal mining industry, opportunities in business and agriculture also developed. As in other parts of the Choctaw Nation, cotton emerged as the principle cash crop, yet the soil was also well adapted to fruits, vegetables, and corn. Attesting to the importance of cotton, there were three cotton gins within the McAlester city limits during this period as well as the Choctaw cotton compress (the largest compress located in either territory, Oklahoma or Indian), which processed forty thousand bales of cotton in 1900 alone. Much like Indian Territory's neighbor to the south, ranching and hay production also persisted in the region, although mining and cotton proved its most important industries.[84]

Whether the main business was cotton in East Texas, ranching in Central Texas, coal mining in Indian Territory, or some combination of all three, store records provide important insights into the social and economic dynamics of these different regions. Furthermore, by extending credit, marketing their customers' livestock and crops, and providing the goods necessary for industry and daily living, merchants themselves played an important role in the economics of their communities. It was during the 1870s and 1880s that Texas experienced a significant economic shift, as cotton farmers encroached upon the lands previously allocated to free-range cattle ranching. Ledgers from the period reflect this transition, evidencing both the western advance of cotton and the persistence of ranching in locations like Hedwig's Hill. Through their credit policies, store owners played a determining role in the move to cotton and the continued reliance on products such as cotton, cattle, and coal. As key players in the crop-lien system, so dominant in southern cotton-growing regions in the late nineteenth century, merchants significantly influenced their clients' economic fate. The era of the cowboy in Central Texas, still romanticized by some Texas historians, gradually gave way to the historically less-appealing reign of the sharecropper and tenant farmer. Still, cattle left a resilient imprint on the state, especially in regions in South and Central Texas and, increasingly, the western and northern counties. In Indian Territory, cotton, cattle, and mining competed to define the area's economic identity. Indeed, in both Texas and Indian Territory, each of these three industries shaped not only the regions' economic realities and demographics but also their cultural identities.

Chapter 3

In the Presence of Ladies

IMAGINE THE SCENE: IN A RURAL country store, a roomful of southern cotton farmers sit around laughing, playing checkers, and swapping stories, while the storekeeper looks on. In his 1944 classic, *Pills, Petticoats, and Plows: The Southern Country Store,* Thomas Clark invited his readers to envision these farmers with their heads bowed close together and voices toned down to practically an inaudible droning, while one salacious yarn after another was told and applauded. In stores where men did all the clerking, women were generally excluded. In fact, Clark supposed, "They stood near the front door with embarrassed grins on their faces showing clearly mixed feelings of eager curiosity and shocked modesty. They were caught in the unhappy situation of not knowing whether to stay until someone came to serve them or to leave the store."[1]

Contrast Clark's imagined scene of embarrassed women huddled at the front door of a general store with the experiences of Mrs. Anna J. Hyde of Nacogdoches, Texas. In November 1872, Mrs. Hyde purchased from the Clark & Hyde mercantile firm a large order of grocery items totaling $32.96. The order included basics such as bulk coffee, tea, bacon, butter, two dozen eggs, and a barrel of flour for $14.00. Typically, her purchases were recorded under the name Mrs. A. J. Hyde; some entries, however, particularly those for medicinal products, appeared under Mrs. Hyde's husband's name, Doctor Hyde. Doctor George S. Hyde purchased, for example, a razor and a vial of morphine from the store on December 30, 1872. A few days later, the purchase of some cottonade fabric and thread were recorded under Doctor Hyde's name "per [his] wife."[2] Further still, there were occasions when Dr. Hyde picked up some items for his wife, like flax and sugar, and the purchases were subsequently recorded under Mrs. A. J. Hyde's name "per [the] Doctor."[3]

In effect, there were two separate accounts for one household. Because store ledger entries were typically recorded under the name of the male head of household, the entries for Doctor and Mrs. Hyde are quite perplexing.

The clue to these unusual ledger entries lies in a small advertisement featured in the *Nacogdoches News* in 1877. The ad read as follows: "Mrs. A. J. Hyde, Private Boarding. Travelers Entertained. Transient persons will find it to their interest to stop at Mrs. Hyde's. Terms Moderate!"[4] According to the 1880 census for Nacogdoches County, Anna J. Hyde, the wife of sixty-nine-year-old physician George S. Hyde, lists her occupation in the census as hotel keeper. Hyde was born in New York State and was fifty-four years old at the time of the census. In 1880 the Hydes also had two black servants residing with them, eighteen-year-old Jeff McKnight and twenty-year-old Simma Young; in all likelihood, they assisted with the hotel-keeping duties and tasks around the home.[5] As a hotel keeper, Mrs. Hyde would need to keep her supplies well stocked with items from the local store. Because of the demands of her business, she frequented the store regularly and established a solid, mutually beneficial business relationship with the store owners. Bowing to practical considerations, the merchants deviated from the standard practice of listing purchases under the name of the male head of household, instead recording items under the name of the principal purchaser for the Hyde family, Mrs. Anna Hyde. It seems unlikely that Anna Hyde stood meekly at the door of the Clark & Hyde mercantile store wondering if she should enter and deliver to the retailers her large order of grocery items for the hotel. Mrs. Hyde's experiences challenge Clark's male-centered assumptions about country stores, their proprietors, and their clients. To be fair, Clark imagined his quaint scene in the 1940s; several decades before historians (both male and female) fully examined the role of women in shaping the American experience. This said, there are still many questions to be answered about women's experiences in influencing arenas previously thought to be exclusively dominated by males.

To be sure, not every woman in Texas operated a hotel, not every woman engaged in an enterprise separate from her husband's, and not every woman established a business relationship with local merchants.

Still, there are many examples of women in Texas and early Oklahoma who did not cower at the front door of their local general stores. They came through the door and bought items much like their male counterparts—whether they stuck around and swapped stories is another question entirely. What we do know is that women made purchases—and sometimes large purchases. Daybooks, account books, and sales ledgers are valuable resources for revealing women's consumption patterns in rural settings where shopping options were few. Store records indicate how often women visited general stores, the types of employment they engaged in, and the ways in which they contributed to the family income. This data is a useful springboard for examining women's overall participation in the day-to-day economic lifeblood of their communities. Further, such records confirm that, through their role as consumers, women wielded pecuniary power in their small towns.

Ledgers trace women's participation in the market in two separate, though related, ways. First, they provide evidence of women's physical presence in stores and thus their engagement in the public sphere, countering notions that they were confined to the inner sanctum of their homes. Second, the ledgers demonstrate not only that women participated in the market but that they proved significant economic players in their own right, and this provides a useful avenue to examining other economic and social contributions made by women to their communities. There was usually a strong correlation between women's occupations, their consumer behavior, and their relationship with store owners. However, ledger evidence suggests that not all women entered commercial relations on an equal footing. In some instances, storekeepers inscribed class distinctions for their women clientele into their books, often quickly followed by distinctions of race. As might be expected, account records confirm that economic divisions existed between men and women as well as between women in different socioeconomic classes.

While Thomas Clark was certainly one of the earliest historians to weigh in on the subject of women and country stores, recent studies have followed his lead by similarly marginalizing women's roles in the historical development of general stores, particularly during the nineteenth century. According to a more recent monograph on southern consumption, general stores were sites where white men talked about politics, told jokes, or shared gossip, often while playing checkers or whittling and spitting tobacco. Women acknowledged the fraternal atmosphere of stores by steering clear of where they were obviously not welcome. Apparently not content with just the interiors, men used space in and around store sites for recreational purposes. This study cites directly Clark's assertion that "men still offered to stand stallions for stud outside stores, and younger men and boys saw the area outside the stores as gathering places for wrestling, running races, and eventually playing baseball."[6]

One possible factor in women's reluctance to enter general stores was the preponderance of alcohol for sale. Merchants sold alcoholic beverages to principally their white male customers in the rear of their stores, beverages that apparently "offered strong taste and powerful after-effects that made trips to the store special occasions."[7] A good example in Texas of such activity can be found at the J. L. McInnis mercantile firm in Webberville, a rural community located in Travis County. Males comprised the majority of names listed in McInnis's 1874–75 sales ledger, with only a handful of women's names appearing. Further, both tobacco and whiskey appear in the purchases of many of the men who frequented the McInnis store. John Burleson, for example, on August 8, 1874, purchased sardines for fifty cents, whiskey and cigars for a dollar, and tobacco for twenty-five cents—hardly a grocery order.[8] Subscribing to rather rigid gender constructions, many in the middle class believed that women were far too delicate and moral for these male-dominated environments.

Another obstacle said by scholars to have limited women's visits to their local store was distance. According to this argument, women were less likely to travel long distances to acquire store items, preferring to send others in their stead. Rural women were often too busy with childbearing and child rearing to make such an excursion. In this scenario, women might choose to purchase goods from itinerant salesmen rather than from the local dry goods merchant.[9]

Given the time period, it is not surprising to find in store ledgers that the large majority of accounts in this male-dominated society were under the names of men. In his study of consumerism in Mississippi, historian Ted Ownby finds scarce evidence of female accounts, particularly in the antebellum period. Even as late as the 1890s, however, he notes that women were still very much in the minority, comprising only slightly more than 10 percent of accounts. While Ownby concedes that names in ledgers do not tell the whole story of how often women frequented general stores, he states, "It may seem likely women visited stores more often than those figures indicate and made purchases under the names of their husbands, but a few ledgers that recorded precisely who visited stores make clear that the stores were male institutions."[10] For Ownby, ledger entries that identified female customers— usually nameless—as the wives or daughters of the men who held store accounts only signified further that the men in charge considered women to be outsiders. However, gender historians who have broached the subject of women in account books have contended that such records need to be viewed with some degree of skepticism, especially in drawing conclusions regarding women's participation in the marketplace. These historians have argued that women's absence from account books does not in itself suggest that women were not significant economic players.[11] This is certainly the case for the women discussed below.

While account ledgers in Texas and Indian Territory tend to support findings that general store customers were predominantly male, they also reflect regional differences, which suggest that women visited stores more frequently in some locations than in others. In predominantly rural counties, whose populations exhibited a generally balanced sex ratio, women were more likely to visit their local store.[12] Alongside some rather significant female accounts, ledger books from the Clark & Hyde mercantile store indicate that women entered the store with regularity, charging purchases to the accounts of their husbands, fathers, and male employers. A sampling of account entries from the last two weeks in January 1873 include purchases for Mrs. A. J. Hyde, Letty Hyde per Julia, A. J. Simpson per daughter, L. E. Griffith per Martha, G. F. Ingraham per wife, L. E. Griffith per wife, and William Clark per wife.[13] Even though they appear in the ledgers under generic distinctions, women clearly patronized the Clark & Hyde firm. Women also appear quite frequently in ledgers from the McKinney & Brown general store in Jacksonville, Texas—either under their own accounts or under the male head of household's. In the last weeks of September 1874, the store owners recorded purchases under the following headings: Charles Gay per lady, A. J. Chessher (per lady), Samuel Gover (per daughter), Professor Patton (per lady), Tom Neely per sister, and John T Goodson per lady.[14]

A further point can be made regarding the issue of whether the above examples demonstrate that these women (and not a delegate with a grocery order in hand) frequented the stores. Standard practice at both the Clark & Hyde mercantile and the McKinney & Brown store was to note "orders" in their ledgers. For instance, on November 7, 1872, the purchases for G. F. Ingraham came into the Clark & Hyde store "per order."[15] Fabric, sewing items, and clothing purchases were made at the store on G. F. Ingraham account on November 4, 1872, "per mother." On most occasions, Mrs. Arkansas Sleet frequented the store herself; however, sometimes she sent in an order to the store owners "per Lem."[16] At the McKinney & Brown store, the purchase of some nails and a molasses pitcher by Mrs. S. A. Goodson were made "per order" on December 8, 1874.[17] Thus, ledger entries at the McKinney & Brown store that include "per lady," "per daughter," "per Negro," or "per washerwoman" denote the person who *physically* made the purchases, not the person who placed an order.[18] Thus, ledger records indicate that women were physically present in this presumed male enclave.

Such examples hardly suggest the need to revise earlier perceptions of women's roles in general stores; after all, even in these examples women were often in the minority of customer accounts. Though women were statistically less significant, ledgers indicate that the frequency of women's presence in the stores differed by location, and therefore, their importance to store owners as a customer base also varied. In Nacogdoches, for example, women maintained more than a marginal presence in store records, but there is little evidence in these scant examples that women challenged the male-dominated status quo. In fact, the listing of accounts under males' names only serves to reinforce the super ordinate roles of males in late-nineteenth-century society. In some cases, women appear quite frequently in ledgers (so they are not always in the minority), but when they do appear, they are often listed under their spouses' names, which suggests they occupied a subordinate role in both account ledgers and (likely) their households.

In many ways, the importance of women in store ledgers has less to do with their overall numbers and more to do with revisiting, or perhaps rethinking, their roles, however large or small, in commercial relations. In recasting earlier suppositions, women can be resuscitated from the perception of them as merely cowering at the front door of general stores. Instead, we can now recognize that some women were both vital and significant contributors not only to the economic viability of their local store but to the community as a whole.

Even in the farthest reaches of "civilized" society, middle-class culture and attitudes pervaded mid- to late-nineteenth-century American belief systems, affecting store owners in western/rural outposts as well as their clientele. For adherents to Victorian ideology, the home provided the most important locus for cultural transmission, and Victorians acknowledged this fact through their notions of domesticity.[19] However, the boundaries that limited women's responsibilities to the home proved far less rigid in America than is assumed in earlier nineteenth-century scholarly treatments. Idealized perceptions of domesticity were manifest in a myriad of different ways in western environments.[20] The perception of women as civilizing agents has proved to be a remarkably resilient trope in histories of the American West, partly because such sentiments were commonly expressed by western boosters and newspaper editors during the period.[21] That said, when nineteenth-century Anglo women left their homes in New England, the South, or the Midwest to live in the West they took with them some variant of domestic ideology. Many expected that their chief responsibilities in their new locales would be homemaking and child rearing. Further, many of them perceived themselves as the moral foundation of the family and society.[22] A logical extension of perceiving themselves as morally superior is to cast their sex as harbingers of civilization.

Understanding their prescribed roles in the domestic sphere often led to an outright rejection of their new frontier environment. Some women needed time to adjust to their new surroundings. Mrs. Mary Elizabeth Brown, the wife of store owner of W. A. Brown, expressed some concern upon seeing her new home in early Jacksonville, Texas. When W. A. Brown purchased the home in 1873, it was set back in the woods. There were no streets leading up to the new family residence, described by Mrs. Brown as a very small "uninviting house." According to local accounts, when Mrs. Brown came in a two-horse wagon to her new home, "she thought it a very lonesome place, and remarked that she didn't believe she would get out of the wagon, but for the fact that it was 'just home.' Considering the fact that she had been moving so much in the years just preceding, she was willing to locate at most any place, provided she call it 'home.'"[23] Many women believed that it was only a matter of time (and effort) before sod houses with musty air, splintery furniture, and dirt-covered floors could be turned into tastefully decorated family homes.

Whether arriving by train, on horseback, or in a covered wagon, women quickly commenced their homemaking responsibilities and provided their families as much comfort and refinement as their rustic circumstances would allow. Creating homes out of what was available in frontier Oklahoma and Texas was no small accomplishment. One Oklahoma historian noted, "Women expressed their individuality and pride in the comfort and decor of these first crude dwellings. They constructed shelves and furniture out of packing boxes . . . curtained off areas for privacy, planted flowers in pots, sewed bright window curtains, braided colorful rag rugs to cover the earthen floors or splintery wooden ones, and made decorative plaques from the dried gypsum that so tainted their water supplies."[24]

In their furnishings, women aspired to realize their dream of a comfortable house on the frontier. The purchases of Mrs. Susan Smith of Jacksonville from the McKinney & Brown mercantile provide a small but telling example. Smith lived with her brother Thomas Love, a resident farmer, and her twenty-year-old daughter, Nannie. The 1880 federal census listed Susan's status as housekeeper, the usual occupation for married women—and, evidently, sisters of farmers. Susan was in charge of shopping for the small family, and on November 13, 1876, from the McKinney & Brown store she purchased:

twelve yards of ticking	$3.60
one paper of needles	10¢
a lamp	35¢
a set of teaspoons	75¢
a cup and saucer	15¢[25]

While a thirty-five-cent lamp hardly qualifies as a symbol of gentility, Susan's purchases do reflect an interesting assortment of consumer items, some of which were intended to enhance the comforts of rural living. Indeed, fineries on the frontier came in all shapes and sizes.

In homes across America, the preferred showroom for material representations of Victorian gentility was a finely adorned parlor, and the prized possession of many Victorian parlors was a piano. More organs than pianos found their way into Victorians parlors because they were a less expensive alternative, but pianos maintained a position of prominence in the most genteel, well-to-do homes. Since the eighteenth century, pianos were featured in the homes of elite families who desired their children, particularly their young women, to be accomplished in the art of music.[26] Nellie Snyder—the wife of store owner Pete Snyder in Colorado City, Texas—apparently adored her piano and would sit for hours playing it. Snyder purchased the piano for his wife shortly after they were married and had it shipped from New York City to Colorado City, in Mitchell County, Texas, in the early 1880s. The Snyders were financially able, most of the time, to keep a housekeeper to help Nellie and afford her the time to play her beloved instrument. According to Charles G. Anderson's history of the store owner and his family, "beautiful music could be heard throughout the open prairie land."[27] While certainly not all Texas homes could acquire such luxuries, the Snyders did their best to bring the accoutrements of Victorian gentility to the West Texas plains. With her "beautiful music," Nellie Snyder brought a perceived sense of refinement and class to the rugged environment. The inclusion of the story of Nellie's piano in Anderson's nostalgic history reinforces the notion that is widely held in western histories of the civilizing influence of women in the American West, a problematic notion in contemporary historiography given its sexist and racist undertones.

Providing for her home and her hotel, Mrs. Anna J. Hyde's purchases tended to be fairly basic food items—not a surprise given the nature of her business. Perhaps the more provocative question with regard to the Hydes is why the wife of a mature physician, a woman of middle-class standing, engaged in any occupation at all? Misconceptions of class in the nineteenth century are rooted in the desire to generalize, simplify, and conflate experiences across lines of race, gender, and region.

Persons from all social classes, although most typically women, found themselves opening their homes to boarders in nineteenth-century America—this included perhaps a respectable widow or even middle- and working-class families.[28] Both middle- and working-class women continued to labor and contribute to their household economy throughout the nineteenth century, in both paid and unpaid labor capacities, even if that fact became increasingly hidden behind separate sphere ideology. Gender historians have argued that, in the early nineteenth century, the perception of women's work changed, and it became increasingly devalued, especially when compared to wage labor conducted outside the household. Respectable women no longer labored. One historian notes, "The language of the ideology of spheres was the language of gender, but its essential dualism was less precisely the opposition of 'female' and 'male' than it was the opposition of 'home' and 'work,' an opposition founded on the gendering of the concept of labor."[29]

In the small community of Nacogdoches, Texas, hotel owner Mrs. Hyde worked, and she did so in a social environment where such work may have been looked upon with disdain, especially among her middle-class contemporaries. A commonality of working women in the West (and South, East, and North) is that such women did so "in cultures that expected women to bear and care for children; to cook, keep house, and provide clothing for their families; and to provide sexual intimacy for men and emotional support for kin and community."[30] Mrs. Hyde's occupation closely aligned with women's traditional domestic roles, extending her housekeeping responsibilities to the upkeep of an entire hotel.

Sometimes boardinghouse keepers endured particular contempt of critics precisely because of the blurring of the lines between home and work: "For in boardinghouses the moral contagion of the market invaded relationships that ideally were to remain untainted by base economic concerns."[31] Mrs. Hyde might have worked out of economic necessity (her husband was sixty-nine years old). Perhaps she worked out of choice. Events outside the family economics, no doubt, factored into her decision to operate a hotel. Since she did not list her occupation as hotel keeper in the 1870s census, perhaps the fortunes of the Hyde family changed for the worse between 1870 and 1880, requiring that the Hydes become a dual-income family. Regardless of her reasons,

Mrs. Hyde's occupation expanded her responsibilities beyond her household and thus, however slightly, challenged the domestic model that confined women to the home and limited their responsibilities to the family.[32]

Operating a hotel in Nacogdoches at the same time as Mrs. Hyde, Mrs. Susan A. Durst also frequented the Clark & Hyde mercantile store. Like her contemporary, Mrs. Durst listed her occupation in the census as "hotel keeper," although the array of persons residing in her home suggests that Durst's hotel was little more than a boardinghouse.[33] In addition to her four children, a nineteen year-old store clerk called Robert Rainbolt, a thirty-eight-year-old man called Frederick Meier from Prussia and with no identified occupation, and a thirty-five-year-old domestic servant called Ed Mayfield all lived in the Durst household.[34]

In some locations, there was little distinction between hotels and boardinghouses. In her study of early Dallas, Elizabeth York Enstam argues that some boardinghouses were small, more or less exclusive hotels with complete staffs of maids, porters, and cooks, while others supplied only the most basic furniture, requiring their boarders to bring such comforts as featherbeds, blankets, pillows, and even linens.[35] It appears that Mrs. Durst's "hotel" fell into the latter, more modest, category. Rather than large purchase orders (such as Mrs. Hyde's $32.96 order, for example), Mrs. Durst rarely bought more than one or two items at a time. The extent of her purchases on November 27, 1872, from the Clark & Hyde store was a barrel of flour for $14.50.[36]

The 1870 census also indicates that Susan Durst was the "widow of Louis Orlando." With four children to support and no husband to help with the expenses, Mrs. Durst surely needed the income. In this capacity, she reflected a common regional pattern of the period that showed a strong economic link between boardinghouses and widows. For many widows, especially those with children, economic survival meant using all respectable means to support themselves. Running a boardinghouse was often the preferred choice among a limited number of occupations that were available to widows: washing, ironing, cleaning house, or prostitution.[37] Keeping boarders afforded women the opportunity to earn income while they remained in the home, expanding upon rather than interfering with their other housekeeping and child-rearing responsibilities. It is worth noting that, by the 1880 census, Mrs. Durst was no longer in the hotel-keeping business. In 1880, Susan Durst resided in the household of her son-in-law, Robert Irion, a real estate agent, and her daughter, Helena, and significantly, no occupation is listed for Durst in the later census.[38]

As boardinghouse keepers, women served the economic needs of their communities in a variety of often related capacities. They fueled the revenues of merchants by regularly frequenting the stores, acquiring the grocery items needed to prepare meals for both their families and their boarders. In their capacity as "hoteliers," women operated small businesses in their communities, however modest. In cash poor communities, they helped facilitate somewhat complex credit arrangements.

Store clerk Charles Schaffer worked at the Wolf General Merchandise firm in Austin in the early 1870s. Wolf credited Schaffer's salary to his store account at regular monthly intervals, and at the first of each month in 1873, Schaffer received a credit on his account: "By Salary $60.00" for the early months of the year, "By Salary $70.00" for August and September, which increased to $75.00 in October and the months beyond.[39] The account of Mrs. Martin, a frequent patron of the Wolf store, received credit by the owner for "2 months board $40.00" in February 1873; again credit for "2 months board $40.00" in April; and on May 9, credit "By cash per Charles S. $20.00." In his cash ledger, Wolf credited Mrs. Martin's account in August 1873 "for board C.S. $20.00."[40] Thus, Schaffer settled his rent with Mrs. Martin through her store account—either by a deduction from his salary or by paying cash on her account. Through credits and debits, the store ledgers linked the three interested parties—merchant Charles Wolf, clerk and boarder Charles Schaffer, and boardinghouse proprietor Mrs. Martin.

Evidently, a number of women worked as hoteliers in the burgeoning town of McAlester in Indian Territory. Ledger entries from J. J. McAlester's store reveal that both married and single women operated hotels or boardinghouses in the town, dating back to the earliest years of settlement. Two of the region's original settlers, Edward and Lena Sittel, operated a lodging establishment that evolved from a one-room boardinghouse into McAlester's first hotel, a fifteen-room dwelling named Elk House. Lena Sittel is said to have been the first white woman to arrive by train in McAlester, in 1872, along with their nine-year-old son, Fritz. Interviewed several decades after the fact, Fritz Sittel reflected on his mother's first impressions of McAlester: "When we first reached McAlester and my mother saw the little 6 x 10 ft. box depot and how wild and uninhabited the surroundings looked, she told the conductor to put her trunks back on the train—that she was going back to Maryland to a civilized country." According to a local historian, the Sittels' Elk House enjoyed a lucrative business in McAlester: "In the early days, the Elk House was the best place in McAlester to get a good meal and a clean bed. They had occasion to host many of the famous and infamous who passed by, including even Belle Starr and her companions." In the 1870s, McAlester recorded most of the Sittels' purchases under Edward's name; however, in the late 1890s, the store owner began listing the account under Lena's name, despite the fact that Edward was still very much involved in the business and would live for another two decades.[41] The shift in account headings indicates that Lena Sittel became the principal purchaser of goods for Elk House in the 1890s; possibly Mrs. Sittel was too busy cooking and cleaning for hotel guests in the early years to take on the additional responsibility of shopping.

According to ads in McAlester's earliest newspaper, the *Star-Vindicator*, another hotel—the McAlester Hotel—was operated by a Mrs. Sarah Fendall. In November 1877, the newspaper featured advertising that read, "McAlester Hotel—lately kept by Col. S. J. Brooks is now conducted by Mrs. Sarah Fendall." At the same time, McAlester listed Mrs. Fendall in his laborers' account book for 1877. On November 28, 1877, for example, McAlester included Mrs. Fendall among his "laborers," charging her fifty cents for a crumb brush and twenty cents for a half gallon of oil.[42] There is no census covering this period in the Choctaw Nation's history, so the marital status of Mrs. Fendall is difficult to confirm, but McAlester recorded the purchase of a "fancy" bottle of cologne for $2.00 under the account name "Mrs. Fendall for Dr. Fendall." It appears at least that this is another example of a doctor's wife—or at the very least, a doctor's female relative—operating a hotel. While hardly a pattern, both Mrs. Hyde and Mrs. Fendall demonstrate that working women in western settlements varied in marital status and class. In itself, marriage did not exempt women from the workforce.

Many married women engaged in business enterprises, contributing their share to the collective family income.

Female labor practices in Texas and Indian Territory were mirrored in communities to their immediate north. Women living in Kansas cattle towns engaged in occupations both inside and outside the household. In these archetypical western towns, many of the women who worked in their husband's businesses as clerks, bookkeepers, or boardinghouse operators often did much of the work themselves, and yet they were not recognized as being gainfully employed in census records. Most married women who worked did so out of economic necessity and not by preference; thus, they experienced few of the benefits of the cult of domesticity. Indeed, widowhood, an incapacitated husband, or a large family needing an additional breadwinner forced women to take on unusual roles.[43]

Choice would also be a factor. One could imagine that, besides helping the family's finances, work may have also been perceived by some women as an escape from the monotony of the private sphere, expanding their relationships to persons beyond their immediate household. Further still, there may have been some women who, despite the rigors of the task at hand, enjoyed the recognition and responsibility afforded by work outside of the home.

Other female hoteliers listed in McAlester's store ledgers include Mrs. Mike Holmes, Mrs. H. M. Mize, and Mrs. David Stark. The latter is distinguished in McAlester's records as a widow, again exemplifying the connection between widows and lodging establishments. As noted, boardinghouses and hotels on the frontier varied in both size and type of services—sometimes they provided, with some furnishing, only meals to clients, while others supplied both meals and lodging, and others offered a combination of services.[44] The large purchase orders associated with Mrs. Sittel's, Mrs. Holmes's and Mrs. Stark's accounts suggest that these women operated fairly substantial establishments, at least relative to those in comparable frontier settings.[45] These female entrepreneurs, either in partnership with their husbands or by themselves, provided much-needed food and lodging for McAlester's transient mining population.

Census data indicates that a large number of women in the farming regions of the West as well as other parts of the United States worked within the household under the distinction "housekeeper."[46] Seldom was housework recognized as an occupation, and it was rarer still that such work was considered a contributing factor to the household income. As one historian has argued, with the "pastoralization of housework" in the early nineteenth century, work inside the home increasingly became distinct from wage labor conducted outside the home.[47] Despite this changing perception, women continued to contribute to their households through both paid and unpaid labor. According to account records from the McKinney & Brown store in Jacksonville, a number of married women whose husbands kept accounts with the firm received credit by bringing in eggs, which were in turn sold by the store owners. For instance, Mrs. Joe Tilley received a $1.25 credit "by 10 dozen eggs" on June 17, 1876. Mrs. Tilley's husband, Joe, appears in store ledgers the following year when he purchased a knife for 50¢ and, two months later, two spelling books.[48] In another example, from November 1876, Mr. Lou Derit purchased tobacco and fabric from the store owners—three months after his wife, Mrs. Lou Derit, received a 65¢ credit "by six and a half dozen eggs" on August 4, 1876.[49] Mrs. Susan Smith contributed to her family's income by receiving a $1.60 credit for eight dozen eggs from the McKinney & Brown store on December 19, 1877.[50]

The sale of butter and eggs in the western environment provided a fairly steady source of income for women; in rural areas, one observer pointed out that women often supported their families through such funds while their husbands learned how to farm. Keeping chickens and selling their eggs, responsibilities conventionally assigned to women, linked them and their labor to the market economy; thus, women's economic contributions expanded beyond merely the household into the larger community. Moreover, a study of nineteenth-century rural Pennsylvania farm women demonstrates that this was a common economic strategy for families in other regions of the country and not just in Texas and Indian Territory.[51]

In early Dallas, much as in other parts of Texas, the majority of women continued to perform unpaid domestic work within the privacy of their homes, and this work had changed little since the early years of settlement. However, with specific types of labor such as operating boardinghouses or selling excess food products to store owners, women's work contributed to the market economy, at least in a visible sense. By tracing the myriad ways in which housework was intrinsically tied to the newly industrializing society of the early Republic, however, Jeanne Boydson demonstrates that unpaid labor was not divorced from market relations. She points out that many nineteenth-century households were in fact "mixed economies," economic systems that functioned on the basis of both paid and unpaid labor. The added responsibility of producing goods for the market did not absolve women from the demands of housework; such labor merely expanded upon an already burdensome workload. The "visibility" of labor seems to be the key here. As another historian states, "Shifting such work from the domestic use economy into the marketplace, the boardinghouses lifted labor usually done in private out of its invisibility within individual homes and into public view in the realm of trade and commerce." More than any other female occupation, keeping a boardinghouse indicated the fundamental economic importance of women's traditional work in the home.[52]

One story told by store records is that women engaged—and had for hundreds of years been engaging—in the "informal" exchange economy in which they traded goods produced in the household with their neighbors for reciprocal goods or services. Because women's involvement in the exchange economy neither garnered wages nor drew them out of their households, the contribution of such labor to family household has been largely ignored by historians. To be sure, Jeanne Boydston's discussion of "invisible work" and "unpaid labor" has done much to resuscitate women's roles in the mixed household economies of the nineteenth century. Through the exchange of goods and services, women were clearly participating in the public economy. Thus, women's work done within the confines of the family home was not necessarily limited to the private sphere. Furthermore, women often occupied critical roles in their husbands' business ventures, which again expanded women's responsibility beyond housework. With invisible labor, there was enormous flexibility, permeability, and overlap between women's and men's work.[53]

Living in rural hinterlands in no way guaranteed women any freedom from the rigors of their traditional domestic tasks. In many cases, the demand for domestic labor increased. Account records from McAlester's store demonstrate that regional socioeconomics influenced not only women's employment opportunities, specifically the types of work available to women, but also their consumption patterns. Spanning over forty years, McAlester's ledgers are an excellent historical source for revealing patterns in women's work in that area. Located in a coal-mining region in the Choctaw Nation, McAlester's store attracted mostly men as clientele, which is not surprising since they made up the majority of the settlement's early population. In fact, amid the hundreds of customer transactions listed in his 1874–75 sales ledger, the store owner recorded fewer than ten transactions between himself and female customers. Despite the small number of female transactions, the accounts of male customers make it possible to confirm women's presence, however, at least in early McAlester. James Donalson, for example, whose occupation was listed as miner, paid $3.50 for a pair of ladies' shoes on February 1, 1870. In another transaction, J. J. Cleary, a local butcher, paid the same price for ladies' shoes on January 9, 1875, and Mike Dunn, Enoch Cartlidge, and J. J. Wooten all made similar purchases in the early months of 1875.[54] As a general rule, coal mining camps maintained a disproportionate ratio of men to women. A characteristic feature of the mining frontier—whether mining for coal or precious minerals—was that most residents were young men, for few women or family groups came during the early boom times. In well-known boom towns such as Denver and San Francisco or in a remote mining center, men grappled with the issue of bringing their families west or marrying and settling down in more "mature" regions. After observing the characteristics of the mining frontier, many men concluded that such a setting was inappropriate for family life.[55]

The community of McAlester definitely fits into the small remote mining community model. In the few entries listed under women's names, account books indicate that the store owner paid a number of women to work in his employ as cooks and seamstresses. This is not surprising since it was often women's domestic skills that were most sought after in regions with high sex imbalances. Cooks, seamstresses, and washerwomen were in demand, particularly in the mining camps as well as in other areas where the population included a large number of single men.[56] Ledger entries indicate that Mrs. Annie Bowers began working for McAlester as a cook on Christmas Eve 1875. A week later, on December 31, she purchased from her employer's general store eighteen yards of fabric, thread, braid, lining, and a bottle of tonic for $8.90. This expansive purchase would take Annie roughly three weeks to make up in salary, since she earned only $3.00 a week as McAlester's cook. Her first lump payment came after seven and a half weeks of service, when she received $22.50, subsequently applied toward the debts she ran up at her employer's store.[57]

Three dollars hardly seems like an adequate salary to live on, and yet McAlester paid this wage to a number of female employees. In another example, Miss Mollie Sullivan commenced work as a cook for McAlester on March 30, 1876, at the rate of $12.00 per month—again, consistent with Bowers's wages.[58] McAlester immediately debited part of Mollie's salary, a total of $6.75, toward "cash paid for ticket from Chitopa." Apparently, Mollie needed to borrow from her employer in order to finance her trip to the town of McAlester. The store owner, in turn, desperately needed her labor. There was not only a shortage of women available to him, but it appears that the position itself turned out to be transitional. McAlester hired Mrs. Hattie Hood as a cook, only two days before hiring Miss Sullivan in March 1876, again, for $3.00 per week.[59]

As is clear from McAlester's records, women provided their cooking and sewing skills not only to the male mining town residents but also to their female counterparts, carving an economic niche for themselves in the frontier environment. Mrs. Fannie McElroy was the first woman to appear in McAlester's 1874–75 ledger. On November 25, 1874, she purchased coffee, sugar, tobacco, flannel, calico, denim, and a pair of shoes from the store for a total bill of $12.02. On January 14, 1876, McAlester cleared her account by applying a $12.02 credit, a credit earned "by dressmaking."[60] In another entry involving Mrs. McElroy, Annie Bowers's account is debited $3.00 because McAlester paid Mrs. McElroy that sum on Bowers's behalf—perhaps again for dressmaking services.[61] What is not known from these accounts is the level of training Mrs. McElroy brought to the craft of dressmaking.[62] Mrs. McElroy might have been a professionally trained dressmaker who migrated to Indian Territory to practice her trade, or perhaps she was an amateur dressmaker who took advantage of the frontier setting to fashion a lucrative new career for herself.

Women employed their domestic skills in a variety of capacities throughout Texas and Oklahoma. At the Gauntt Brothers dry goods store in Athens, Texas, for example, an account entry for Annie Richardson dated August 14, 1888, reveals a credit applied to Richardson's account "paid by washing." The debits accrued on her account came mostly from grocery items such as butter, sugar, flour, and candy.[63] Mrs. Regina Brinkman offered her specialized sewing talents to residents of Austin in the 1870s. Fortunately for Mrs. Brinkman, by the 1870s Austin was a bustling state capital with a number of mercantile firms, each seeking to expand their customer base. Mrs. Brinkman's account appears in ledgers for Charles Wolf's general merchandise store. In 1874 she purchased three pairs of scissors on April 6, a silk handkerchief on October 5, and a hat and shoes on December 15.[64] According to the *General Directory of the City of Austin, Texas for 1877–1878*, Mrs. Regina Brinkman was in the business of embroideries and worsted beadwork.[65] Given her occupation, the purchase of three pairs of scissors makes perfect sense. The directory indicates that Mrs. Regina Brinkman resided with Alexander Brinkman, a cabinet maker and a steady customer of Wolf's. This is another example where a household maintained separate accounts at the local store because individuals engaged in separate vocations.

Finally, account ledgers from the Clark & Hyde firm reveal that Mrs. Arkansas Sleet frequented the store with some regularity, typically buying fabric or other dressmaking goods. She purchased six yards of velvet ribbon on December 6, 1872, four yards of calico on December 18, 1872, one and a half yards of sash ribbon and three-quarters of a yard of belt sash ribbon on May 5, 1873.[66] According to the 1880 census, Mrs. Sleet was a dressmaker. The widow of Philip Sleet, she lived in Nacogdoches with her two daughters, Lilia and Estelle, and Lawrence, a twelve-year-old black servant.[67] Whether it was to complement the family's income or to serve the sole source of it, Annie Richardson, Regina Brinkman, and Arkansas Sleet fashioned careers in their respective communities that drew upon talents associated with the domestic sphere. The level of their training for their craft is unknown, though it is probably fair to say that extensive dressmaking training was neither required nor common in frontier settings. Austin was a larger center and probably a more competitive business environment, so perhaps Mrs. Brinkman needed to demonstrate professional training to her clients. Indeed, it is certainly possible that all of the women were trained craftswomen—the record is unclear.

Ledgers from William E. McCampell's general store in Refugio, Texas, affirm that employment opportunities for women on the South Texas frontier, like those in other parts of Texas and Oklahoma, were limited in scope and tended to be associated with traditional gender roles. For example, Elvira Peters, who later married and became Elvira Edwards, sustained herself in the Refugio community in part by working as a washerwoman for a prominent town resident. In April and May of 1877, McCampbell recorded various transactions under Elvira's account. On April 20, her purchases included a pound of candy, a dozen pearl buttons, seven and a half yards of Victorian lawn fabric, and three spools of thread; she received a credit on her account for $1.00, "by one day's labor." On April 21, she received a credit for $0.75, "by washing for Suicord," and a similar credit on May 12, 1877.[68] While it is unclear what other labor Elvira Peters performed, washing constituted one of the principal tasks she engaged in to support herself in the frontier community.

By 1877 Refugio was a modest settlement at best, located in a region largely dedicated to stock raising and equipped with only a handful of businesses, including a hotel, a courthouse, a saloon, a Masonic lodge, a chapel, and a couple of general stores. Captain William E. McCampbell established his store in the town in 1867 and operated it with his brother, Thomas P. McCampbell, until William's death in 1880. In 1934, Judge Rea, a town resident and contemporary of William McCampbell, described the McCampbell Bros. Store in 1868 as "a one-storey wooden building with a large wooden warehouse in the rear."[69] Within the walls of this wooden building, McCampbell's clientele came together to exchange stories, and to negotiate and conduct various business transactions, many of which involved women either directly or indirectly. To be sure, however, the majority of McCampbell's clientele were men.

Like McAlester's store, women maintained only a marginal presence in the account ledgers from the W. E. McCampbell and Bros. general merchandise store. The store ledgers reflect that customer accounts were generally listed under the names of the male heads of the household. Distinguished in McCampbell's ledgers as a "Cowhunter," R. L. Dunman's account clearly suggests the presence of a lady in his household. On July 2, 1877, McCampbell recorded the following charges under Dunman's account: one pair of boots for $5.00, one hat for John per Lady for $1.00, one card of buttons for $.25 and a parasol for $1.00.[70] It is doubtful that this rugged cowhunter himself donned a dainty Victorian parasol to ward off the sun's glaring rays.

While most accounts were listed under male names, the exceptions that do arise in McCampbell's records are revealing. A reoccurring figure in McCampbell's 1876–77 account ledger is Ann Shaw, who first appears under the date February 2, 1876.[71] Beside her name, in brackets, is the distinction "(col'd)," shorthand for "colored." This appears throughout the ledger beside many customers' names, both male and female. Along the same lines, the distinction of "(Mex)," short for "Mexican," also differentiates many names listed in the account book. McCampbell kept a separate ledger for employees (often racially distinguished as black or Mexican) than for employers and/or prominent town members.[72]

Returning to Ann Shaw's account, comparisons can be drawn between her consumption patterns and work experiences and those of Eliza Peters and the women who appear in McAlester's ledgers. She purchased on June 12, 1876, three spools of thread, one boy's hat, six yards of edging, one hair net, three sacks of salt, two boxes of lye, and three and three-quarter pounds of lard. Shaw's purchases reflect the preponderance of staple goods in the rural setting, where luxuries were relatively scarce and expensive. Further, her account reveals the frequency with which women bought fabrics and sewing needs. Her fabric purchases suggest that she either contracted her services out or that she had a very large family to clothe. Her entries in McCampbell's ledger also indicate that she frequently worked as a washerwoman to support herself and her family. Her account is credited $1.00, "by 1 days washing," on June 19, 1876, and again on July 3 and July 11.[73] On September 9, she is credited 50 cents "by cash for washing," and on

September 25, she is credited 50 cents "by 1 days washing for Senoir."[74] Evidently, Shaw kept herself busy washing garments for Refugio townspeople in 1876 and 1877, proving to be a reliable and frequent customer in the W. E. Campbell & Bros. store records.

Common to both McCampbell's and McAlester's store ledgers is the evidence these particular collections reveal about the class dynamics present in the small communities of McAlester and Refugio, especially regarding women. In both cases the store owners used the status distinction of "Mrs." or "Miss" on the accounts of some store customers, while in other cases such titles are noticeably absent. In McAlester's records, for example, the following accounts appear without titles: Salina Red, Vicy (col'd), Aunt Violet (col'd), Sallie Humphries, Rosa Yount, Ellen Sanders, Nancy Byington.[75] It should be noted that the majority of women in McAlester's ledger merited the distinction—so why not these women? A common attribute of all these accounts is that these women worked either as cooks for McAlester or as the more dubious category "hired girls." This is not to say that all of McAlester's female employees appeared in his ledgers without titles but, rather, that chances were pretty good that those without distinctions worked as common laborers for the store owner. Similarly, in McCampbell's records both Ann Shaw (col'd) and Eliza Peters appear without titles and both worked as laborers in the community. While McCampbell included the names of the prominent townspeople (and principal employers) in a separate ledger, all of the female accounts listed in this ledger included the title of respect.[76] Evidently, class and, to some degree, race were the primary determinants of who merited titles of respect in ledgers and who did not. In this respect, McCampbell inscribed his perception of the class hierarchy of his community into his ledger records.

A similar and equally revealing case regarding racial distinctions can be found at the Clark & Hyde Mercantile in Nacogdoches, Texas. This is the same store frequently visited by hotel keepers Mrs. Anna Hyde and Mrs. Susan Durst as well as dressmaker Mrs. Arkansas Sleet. Throughout the Clark & Hyde ledgers (and without fail), these female customers were given the distinction "Mrs." In fact, most women who made purchases at the store were recorded in the account ledgers with "Mrs." before their names—unless they were a "Miss," like Miss Elsie

Ingraham.[77] Two exceptions to this rule were Letty Hyde and Ellen Rolligan. Letty Hyde made frequent visits to the store for both fabric and food items and would, no doubt, be considered a regular. Ellen appears less frequently in the store's ledger but did make multiple visits.[78] Neither of these women is described as "Mrs.," and yet, according to the census, both were married. Lettie was married to Paul Hyde, listed as a black farmer in the 1870 census and as a mechanic in the 1880 census. Ellen Rolligan was married to Henry Rolligan, also a black farmer in the region.[79] Why did these women not merit the distinction "Mrs."? In all likelihood, this oversight was because they were black. In a ledger that did not otherwise distinguish race, distinctions were made all the same.

Over a decade later, at the Gauntt Brothers store in Athens, Texas, store customer Rosie Richardson appears in the early pages of an account ledger dated October 1, 1887, without any marital distinction beside her name.[80] Other females appearing in the ledger—including Mrs. Lerue, Mrs. Owen, Mrs. Reynolds, Mrs. Davis, Miss Davis, and Miss Williamson—did merit such distinctions. Richardson typically settled the few staple items charged to her account with cash. The clue to this particular discrepancy lies many pages later in the ledger, where there is an entry dated March 1, 1888—Rosie Richardson is distinguished as "(col.)."[81] There are too many examples in records spread across Texas and Indian Territory for this phenomenon to be considered mere coincidence. In their account records, store merchants chose not to add marital distinctions to their African American female clientele, and this both diminished their status in relation to their female white customers and affirmed the racial hierarchies so prevalent in the nineteenth century.

Store records provide valuable evidence of the types of work that women performed in frontier communities and suggest that women were seldom able to challenge the imposition of an accepted realm of "women's work." During the nineteenth century, the perception of women's work expanded to include such fields as teaching and nursing. By the turn of the twentieth century, the feminization of the teaching profession had long been underway. Much credit can be given to the early efforts of Catharine Beecher who, in the early to mid-nineteenth century, turned teacher training and placement into a personal campaign. She initiated a program to raise funds for the recruitment and training of teachers who would bring their moralizing mission west to staff common schools. In 1846, she wrote, "The plan is, to begin on a small scale, and to take women already qualified intellectually to teach, and possessed with a missionary zeal and benevolence, and, after some further training, to send them to the most ignorant portions of our land, to raise up schools, to instruct in morals and piety, and to teach the domestic arts and virtues."[82]

Mrs. Elizabeth Fulton Hester, wife of store owner George Benjamin Hester, responded to Beecher's call and moved to Indian Territory in 1856 to perform work as a teacher and a missionary in the Chickasaw Nation. Born in Georgia, Elizabeth Fulton was the daughter of Reverend Defau Tallerand Fulton, a Methodist missionary from Virginia. Reverend Fulton sent his daughter to Southern Masonic Female Seminary where she graduated in 1855. Elizabeth (Lizzie) Fulton initially came to the Choctaw Nation to serve as a governess for the children of Arlan and Sarah Ann Harlan, an elite family in the Nation (Sarah Ann Harlan was part Choctaw). After teaching the Harlans' children, Fulton accepted a position teaching at Robinson's Academy, a Chickasaw boys' school located near the town of Tishomingo. She married George B. Hester in 1858. After the Civil War, Mrs. Hester became a teacher in a National School provided by the Chickasaw legislature. It is in this context that Elizabeth Fulton Hester came to be known as the "first citizen of Muskogee in benevolence."[83]

Account ledgers from F. B. Severs mercantile firm in the Creek Nation indicate not only that female teachers frequented his store but also that they had their payments from the Nation applied directly to their store accounts. Abbie Berryhill, for example, on 25 November 1872 purchased:

a ring	$3.00
a pair of earrings	$2.50
nine yards of calico	$1.50
two and a half yards of Delane fabric	75¢
buttons	10¢
trimming	$1.00[84]

These are rather extravagant purchases for a woman teaching school in Okmulgee, Muskogee Nation, but perhaps she had income other than her teaching wages. On December 5, 1872, Berryhill received a credit "by school draft" for $10.50; on February 13, 1873, she received another credit for $20.02, "by school draft 2nd grade." Miss Mollie Willison also had a $60.00 credit "by school draft" applied to her account on December 5, 1872.[85] On the same day, a number of men received similar credits to their accounts, including William Wilson for $45.66, C. H Davis for $100.00, Dorsey Fife for $48.90, Archie Doyle for $15.00, David Yarger for $20.00, Lou Atkins for $100.00, and Robert Rawson for $100.00.[86]

In discussing women's experiences on the frontier, historian Julie Roy Jeffrey maintains that at least two sorts of single women decided to teach in the West. The first wanted jobs to earn money and pass a few years until they married. Such aspirations did not challenge the cult of domesticity, since ultimately these teachers would end up married and would shift their attention to the needs of the family home. The second group of women who found themselves in the teaching profession tended to come from the East as part of the crusade to civilize the West. Teaching was their vocation, not a temporary stop on their way to marriage. Although some of these women married, it was an occurrence "incidental to the main purpose of sending teachers west."[87] Mrs. Elizabeth Fulton Hester clearly fell into the latter category. Who knows what drew Abbie Berryhill and Mollie Willison to Okmulgee, the capital of the Creek Nation? Perhaps it was a combination of motivations that inspired them to teach among the Creek Indians. Appearing in the ledgers for G. B. Hester's store in Old Boggy Depot, Choctaw Nation, Miss Mary Chiffey, though not a teacher herself, opened her home up to Chickasaw children who attended school in the small settlement. The children of several Chickasaw families who had no school near their homes attended the day school at Old Boggy Depot and were boarded and cared for by Miss Chiffey, a young Chickasaw woman, described as "an earnest Christian and member of the Presbyterian Church."[88]

Another reason some women took up the profession of teaching was widowhood and the subsequent need to raise a family. Such was the case of Mrs. Harriet (Hattie) Olivia Coleman Withers who moved to McAlester as a young widow after her husband's untimely death. According to her family history, Mrs. Withers traveled to McAlester from Denton, Texas, where her husband had been the editor of the local newspaper. She arrived with her daughters, Edna and Lillie, sometime in the early 1890s, to teach and run the Presbyterian Mission School. The first entry in McAlester's ledgers places the Withers family in the McAlester area in late 1891. On 1 December 1891, Mrs. Withers purchased $6.43 worth of beef from the store. She followed up this order three weeks later, purchasing on Christmas Eve a sack of flour for $1.65 and 25¢ worth of oleo.[89] The Withers family appears throughout the ledgers in the 1890s. An account entry from May 16, 1899, indicates that on that date Hattie's daughter, Miss Edna Withers, commenced work for J. J. McAlester, although what she did is not specified.[90] Thus, at least two generations of working women from the Withers family appear in the pages of McAlester's store ledger in the Choctaw Nation.

Married, single, or widowed women in the Texas and early Oklahoma worked. Women in these regions modified their notions of domestic ideology, particularly those notions that confined the woman's role to the home, in order to meet the reality of life in their small and often isolated rural communities. The contrast between idealized domestic roles and the actual lived experiences of women was not simply a western phenomenon, however, but was true for settings throughout the United States, both rural and urban. Women challenged restrictive notions of domesticity perhaps by choice (no doubt this was the case for some) but often by necessity. Ledgers reveal that women frequented general stores with their purchases appearing under their own account or more often under their husband's accounts. In some locations, women were significant purchasers in their own right. At the Clark & Hyde mercantile firm in Nacogdoches, women not only patronized the store in significant numbers but female hotel owners and dressmakers held substantial accounts with the store owners, who undoubtedly appreciated and welcomed their business. However, in areas where their overall population numbers were few, like the small mining community of McAlester, women maintained only a marginal presence in store ledgers.

In McAlester, favorable demographics allowed women to capitalize on the demand for their traditional domestic skills such as cooking, washing, and sewing. This proved a mixed blessing. Work was available to women in frontier settlements, although such work tended to be limited in scope for most—but certainly not all—women in the West. After all, where does store owner, rancher, and banker Anna Martin fit into this paradigm? Martin's experiences diverged from both those of traditional women's work and the idealized notions of domesticity. To be sure, Martin operated her deceased husband's store out of necessity, but her success in the ranching and banking industries demonstrated her determination and willingness to take commercial risks. In many ways, women in rural communities and frontier outposts proved to be pragmatic when it came to idealized notions of female roles—accepting middle-class expectations when these proved valuable and purposeful or ignoring them when necessary. While there are certainly remarkable exceptions, more often than not store records affirm that employment opportunities outside the home paralleled women's tasks performed inside the home. While the frontier social conditions did not liberate women from tradition, women reshaped their domestic roles and created a hybrid drawn from both idealized femininity and the reality of rural life in Texas and Indian Territory.

Chapter 4
Recording Race

"Turbulent" hardly seems an adequate term to describe the volatility of race relations in late-nineteenth-century America. From a southern perspective, this was the period of Reconstruction, terror campaigns, lynch law, Redemption, and de facto and de jure segregation. From a western perspective, this was the period of migrations west, Indian wars, and the Dawes Severalty Act. For Texas and Indian Territory, a region that straddled both the South and the West, this was indeed a volatile time. Across the nation, the challenge of the late nineteenth century was to negotiate new ground rules for governing race relations in the postbellum environment. On the period of Reconstruction, Elliott West has observed, "Never had our presumptions about race been so jangled and divergent. And never had we faced such fundamental decisions about the arrangement of our racial parts." Despite federal policies that addressed basic equity issues and assimilation, long-standing attitudes on race prevailed, not just in the South but in all parts of the nation. In the summer of 1865, President Andrew Johnson sent Carl Schurz to the South to assess conditions. Testifying before Congress on the state of race relations in the immediate postwar period, Carl Schurz asserted that "the relations between the white and black races, even if improved by the gradual wearing off of the present animosities, are likely to remain long under the troubling influence of prejudice."[1]

In the 1870s and 1880s, America was still recovering from the Civil War and still grappling with its social and economic ramifications, in particular the numerous calamities (namely, poverty, dislocation, and violence) afflicting the roughly four million former slaves living in the South. All the while, the nation looked covetously at former, and soon-to-be-former, Indian lands in the West for possible expansion and development. The belief in and pursuit of "progress," so endemic to the Gilded Age, seemed to necessitate the destruction of Indian tribal power and the appropriation of Indian property.[2] In western outposts, racial tensions existed not only between whites and African Americans but also among Mexican and Chinese Americans and American Indians. The lofty goal of Reconstruction was to overcome the racial and regional divisions of the nation. Of course, the challenge of the period was to meet these idealistic goals at a time when racial boundaries were sharpened, strained, and deeply contentious.

Critical to the Reconstruction impetus was the national policy toward bridging the divides in America through economic and social "consolidation." Federal authorities attempted to integrate into the national economy all Americans, regardless of region or skin color, as both consumers and producers. It should be noted that the motivations behind this consolidation imperative were political and economic; by no means was the government, either sincerely or rhetorically, attempting to consolidate the races. To be sure, few in America would have supported such a policy. Attempts to integrate the hegemonic social or cultural mores of the white middle class filtered through such institutions as the Freedmen's schools for ex-slaves and the agency and boarding schools for American Indians. Elliott West contends that economic integration for freedmen and Indians came—at least ideally—through forty acres and a mule, sharecropping, and allotment.[3]

In keeping with this intellectual framework, general stores also enabled such economic integration. In effect, store merchants provided a forum for bringing outsider groups—specifically Mexican and African Americans and American Indians—into the national economic agenda. Through credit, minority groups could become important consumers who could help prime the burgeoning industrial economy of the North. Of course, credit was a mixed blessing. Poor African American sharecroppers often found themselves trapped in debt cycles with their economic fortunes tied to white store owners who, all too willingly, offered them available credit and consumer goods.[4] In cotton-growing regions where sharecropping and tenancy flourished, store owners "furnished" their customers with the clothing, supplies, and simple luxuries that the borrowers needed to get through until harvest time.

Customers then settled accounts with either their produce, which the merchant marketed, or with the cash they earned by selling their product directly to dealers. Often, the furnishing merchants performed multiple roles and served as landlords, storekeepers, cotton dealers, and lenders.[5]

General store records from nineteenth-century Texas and Indian Territory provide important clues into the success of national economic consolidation efforts. They also offer valuable insight into the deep racial chasms that characterized the last decades of the nineteenth century. Much like Radical Reconstruction itself, the initiatives of the national government designed to integrate all Americans into a cohesive economic whole challenged the deep-seated racist attitudes held by many Americans and, as a result, garnered little success. In a profoundly divided nation, the institutions that brought the races together served also to divide them, both determining and reinforcing the racial hierarchies of the day. Store data sharpen our understanding of white efforts to punctuate racial categorization—to "make" and affirm race—even in personal logs. The data provide evidence of the grounds on which minority groups were integrated into market relations and the cross-linkages of race and class. While such evidence sheds light on the day-to-day experiences of all persons—white, black, Mexican, and Indian—residing in this region, it also illuminates how these persons ultimately lived both together and apart.

In entry after entry, ledger records provide evidence that maintaining racial distinctions was a high priority for those responsible for recording sales data. Operating and owning a general store in Jacksonville, Texas, William McKinney and W. A. Brown distinguished race in their account books in a number of different ways. In some instances, the store owners included the words "Negro," "col," or "Freedman" beside the names of their African American clientele. On October 31, 1874, for example, the merchants listed the following transaction in their ledgers: "John Tilery (Negro), To one pair boy's shoes $1.50." In another example, an entry from the store's 1877–78 sales ledger was recorded as "Nelse Snead (col), 1877: April 28, one satchel $1.50, May 1, one plow point $1.00." Finally, "Freedman" appears beside George Anderson's name in the account ledger for 1882.[6]

While there is no evidence these customers had access to such records, the use of such qualifiers would hardly come as a surprise to

African Americans living in the South during this period—most were used to being reminded of their racial status. Given the problem of illiteracy among former slaves, it is unlikely that many of the store clientele could have read the ledgers even if they had gained access to them.[7] Further still, the procedures and prices of merchants who extended credit, furnished goods (often with the expectation of payment in produce), and then proceeded to present their customers with a final tally of debts was a process often shrouded in secrecy. As Ayers notes, "Everyone knew merchants' ledgers often hid shady bookkeeping, always to the merchants' benefit."[8] Receipts could have alleviated much of the mystery; however, most sharecroppers had no expectations of receipts and little hope for such disclosure by merchants. In defense of this system, some southern merchants who issued credit to African American customers declared that "secrecy was necessary to keep debt-ridden Negroes from running away."[9]

Another clue to identifying race in the McKinney & Brown account books (later Brown & Dixon) emerges in ledger entries for Sam Lacy recorded in 1883. On February 22, 1883, Lacy acquired a number of items from the store, including staples such as potatoes, garden seeds, coffee, snuff, a bucket, calico fabric, a box of caps, ladies shoes, a pair of pants, plow points, and twenty-seven yards of domestic fabric. This was a fairly substantial order by any standard of the day but especially in relation to others in the ledgers. The store owner entered the following qualification beside Lacy's name in the ledger: "Secured by Sandy Chandler, limits $25."[10] Sandy Chandler was one of a handful of African American customers who "secured" accounts at the McKinney & Brown store for new African American customers. Indicative of his spending habits, Chandler made the following extensive purchase on May 23, 1881, from the store: two pairs of gloves, several yards of ribbon, two ties, a cord and fan, a tuck comb, two handkerchiefs (one silk), a pair of hose, a parasol and some candy.[11] Chandler was obviously capable of large purchases.

What exactly was entailed in securing an account is not clarified in the ledgers; however there are a number of likely possibilities. The first is that Sandy Chandler assumed responsibility for Lacy's account; in other words, if Lacy skipped town, Chandler would cover Lacy's debt at the store. Perhaps, "secured" meant only that Chandler vouched for Lacy's character, providing a character reference for Lacy to the store owners. A long-standing and frequent customer of the store, Chandler would have established credibility with the store owners as being reliable. Possibly, Lacy worked on Chandler's land, and Chandler was effectually securing the right of his employee to establish credit at the store, but this is a situation that is difficult to confirm since both are listed in the census as farmers.[12] The latter scenario seems even more likely given the specifics provided in an entry for Ellen Edwards, who is listed in the ledger as "(Col.) Secured by Sandy Chandler lives with him."[13] Perhaps, "securing" an account entailed components of all these possibilities—covering the debt, vouching for character, and generally assisting an employee in attaining credit.

Implied in a system where one black farmer "secured" another's ability to make purchases at the local store is some form of social hierarchy. After all, what distinguished Sandy Chandler—and others like him—as being either capable or willing to vouch for the debts of others? Would there not have to be some vested interest on the part of those securing others to take on such a responsibility? According to the McKinney & Brown records, African American client March Kessentiner rendered such support for at least two of the store's account holders in the early to mid-1880s.[14]

Mr. Kessentiner secured the account held by John Pinkard in 1883. Three years earlier, Pinkard appeared in the census as a servant residing in the home of John W. Marshall, a white farmer successful enough to have two servants living in his home.[15] Pinkard's account in 1883 included basics typically associated with farm labor such as bolts for plows, nails, a hoe, shot, garden seed, potatoes, bacon, a pair of overalls, and brogan shoes. Demonstrating that his purchases extended beyond mere necessities, Pinkard's account was debited fifty cents on May 12 for "cash for whiskey."[16] In 1885, Kessentiner also secured the account of Mandy Bryant, who appeared in the census as a farm laborer. At the time of the census, she and her three small children resided with her father, Cesar Buford, no spouse was listed as residing in the household.[17] Like Pinkard, Mandy purchased mainly staple goods from the store—soda, sugar, coffee, spices, garden seed, flour, and domestic and cottonade fabric.[18] As is clear from these customers' accounts, "conditional" status predicated the terms of their participation in commercial relations. For the most part, both Pinkard and Bryant exercised restraint in their buying patterns. They did so, in all likelihood, because they were poor; indeed, one measurement of poverty is the inability to establish credit on one's own.

Not only did Perry Bolden secure the accounts of other African Americans in the McKinney & Brown books, but he also proved to be one of the more reliable—indeed more substantial—customers recorded in the ledgers during the first decades of the store's operation.[19] Bolden appeared early in the firm's records, purchasing, for example, two pairs of shoes, fabric, mattress ticking, and tobacco in August 1876.[20] Bolden's substantial purchase order on August 16, 1876, stands out from a sea of rather meager entries that were more typical of the area's residents, most of whom acquired only a handful of items at a time. While Bolden obtained the usual basics, he also included with his large orders many non-necessities among his purchases, a luxury not afforded many of his fellow African Americans. Bolden included with purchases on April 30, 1881, for example, a box of candy for twenty-five cents, bulk candy for ten cents, and a doll for forty cents.[21] Assigning class distinctions to the past is problematic, especially when so little is known of these customers, but still, factoring in his willingness to secure other customer's accounts, his large purchase orders, and his ability to acquire specialty items, Bolden emerges as a figure of some importance to the store owners. This is particularly compelling because Bolden was African American and this was post–Civil War Texas. According to historians of Texas of the period, violence and oppression played significant roles in reducing black political power and generally in limiting any claim by blacks for social and economic equality.[22] Active and determined white vigilante groups, lynchings, and terror all distinguished Reconstruction Texas; and inevitably, those who most threatened the racial status quo had the most to fear. Decades after these purchases appeared in store records, a local newspaper published an important piece of evidence that sheds light on both Perry Bolden's standing in the community and economic status—his obituary. The obituary reads as follows: "Uncle Perry Boling or Bolden (col.) died last Monday at his home ten miles east of Jacksonville, aged 85 (?). For about two years he has been blind and very feeble. Uncle Perry was born in Tenn., but came to Texas and to this county in 1866, living here until the time of his death. He owned a farm and other property through years of hard and honest work."[23]

Fear of black vigilante groups prompted town leaders in the community of Melrose, Texas, to organize "a Committee of Safety." Store owner L. T. Barret (from Hardeman & Barret General Merchandise) assumed a leadership role in the committee, serving as its secretary. Amid Barret's extant business correspondence and personal documents, which are located at the East Texas Research Center in Nacogdoches, local historian and researcher Gladys Hardeman uncovered the minutes of the Committee of Safety, which met at the Methodist Church in Melrose, on October 25, 1865.[24] Members produced a declaration of principles that outlined the concerns of the Committee (and perhaps the larger white Melrose population):

> As we desire to propagate the Principles of Justice, Honor, and Morality, the bases [sic] upon which depends the wellbeing of Society, Locally and Politically, and to guard against violation of such virtues and to protect our Families, ourselves and our neighbours against outrages that may be committed and which doubtless will be Committed (unless prevented by sufficient oposition [sic]) by the Negroes who are now wild and will ere long become desparate [sic] with excitement Consequent upon the declaration by the Federal authorities that they are Free, and being deluded as they the Negroes are with the idea that at a period not far in the future that a division or partition of our property (the white mans property) will be made with them forced by the power which the Federal authorities can exercise over us.[25]

The Committee expressed fears of wild out-of-control blacks who were deluded with the notion of federal land redistribution—the promise of forty acres and a mule. In an effort to control former slaves, the Committee resolved to "not allow Negroes under the Control to have in their possession Firearms of Ammunition and that they [sic] said Committee and each member thereof shall do every thing in their power to dispossess Negroes of Fire Arms and Ammunition." According to the resolution, blacks could use firearms, "when under the immediate

Control of proper white persons."[26] Operating through a secret society, prominent members of the white landowning class in Melrose sought with this new organization to place limits on the new freedoms afforded African Americans in the South with the defeat of the Confederacy and the end of slavery. There was clearly a deep distrust of the freedmen in the community of Melrose; consequently African Americans would need to work especially hard to make real their newfound freedoms.

Returning to the purchasing of Perry Bolden, in 1883, the store patron acquired from the McKinney & Brown store a spelling book for fifteen cents.[27] His eldest son, Perry Bolden, Jr., had made similar purchases in 1881, obtaining spelling books on two different occasions.[28] Sandy Chandler also acquired educational materials from the store, purchasing an arithmetic book, two spelling books, and pencils in 1878.[29] These purchases, as meager as they were, demonstrated a commitment to learning and suggested a desire to "improve" themselves and their families. Indeed, many African Americans deemed education as the most important avenue to a better life; accordingly, they expended much of their energies on education for themselves and their children, in addition to the "hard and honest work" they exerted in the fields. Even these small expenditures on education distinguished these Texas blacks as being extraordinary. As Eric Foner has demonstrated, an indispensable aspect of the meaning of freedom for blacks was the ability to acquire an education. Indeed, the historian notes that "white contemporaries were astonished by their 'avidity for learning.'"[30]

As in other parts of the South, educational opportunities for Texas freedmen initially were provided by the Freedmen's Bureau, specifically through Freedmen's schools. After 1870, however, administration of schools opened to black students was transferred from the Freedmen's Bureau to Texas state authorities and a state superintendent, until 1872, and then officially to the newly established public school system that was instituted by the Republicans in the early 1870s. Costs for tuition and books then fell on the shoulders of the freed slaves themselves. Despite limited incomes and high rates of poverty, freed men and women demonstrated remarkable resilience and dedication in finding the means to fund their children's education. As a result, illiteracy rates among school-age children dropped steadily. According to one Texas historian, "Illiteracy among freedmen over ten years of age in Texas fell from over 95 per cent in 1865 to 89 per cent in 1870 and to 75 per cent in 1880."[31] The almost zealous drive to educate their children continued among former slaves long after the Freedmen's Bureau closed its doors in the late 1860s; indeed, ledgers from McKinney & Brown indicate that education remained an important priority among African Americans throughout the last decades of the nineteenth century.

Ledger entries from the Hardeman & Barret General Merchandise firm, located in the community of Melrose in Nacogdoches County, Texas, also demonstrate the commitment by many agriculturally dependent African Americans to invest in their children's education. In September 1870, for example, Jesse Powers, a fifty-three-year-old "mulatto" farmer, purchased a picture primer. The same year, a seventy-year-old black farmer with six children, Starling Kyle, charged to his account four First Readers and three spellers. Thirty-five-year-old black farmer Jake Buford charged three spellers to his account in 1870. And finally, George Garret, a thirty-six-year-old black farmer, included two spellers among his store purchases in 1870.[32] The numerous examples of black farmers acquiring spellers and primers—either for themselves, or more likely for children—affirms that education was a priority for many Texas blacks in the post–Civil War period. Living under the continual threat of violence and the weight of economic oppression, African Americans not only persevered in the cumbrous environment of Reconstruction Texas but found a way to finance the education they so valued.[33]

Without doubt, readers were the most popular schoolbooks to appear on customers' accounts during the period. According to an inventory list from the McCampbell & Bros. store in Refugio, Texas, the most popular readers lining the store's shelves were McGuffey's readers. At the time of the inventory, the store had thirty-three McGuffeys in stock, exceeding by a large margin the store's two Holmes readers, McGuffey's nearest competitor.[34] Given the proliferation of the popular readers in the nineteenth century, it makes sense that they would appear so abundantly in the inventory for McCampbell's store. It has been estimated that from the time of the readers' first publication in 1837 until 1920, some 122 million copies of McGuffey's texts were issued, and 60 million were reportedly sold between 1870 and 1890 alone. They were unrivaled in their success, and no other school texts bearing a single person's name sold near as many copies as McGuffey's readers.[35] Designed to shape and mold the values of middle-class children, the readers espoused the values of hard work, perseverance, dependability, honesty, frugality, patriotism, generosity, and Christian piety.[36]

While not as common in customers' accounts as McGuffey's readers, elementary spellers also frequently appeared amid the purchases recorded in ledgers. Initially published in 1783 under a different title, Webster's *The Elementary Spelling Book* was by far the most popular speller of the nineteenth century.[37] Like McGuffey, Webster used his spellers to impart moral lessons to his predominantly young audience. Taking advantage of their captive audience, both authors sought to mold and train their reader's character; thus, moral neutrality was by no means their goal.

The social imperatives presented in these schoolbooks reflected those of white middle-class Americans, yet those who received these moral lessons were a much more heterogeneous group. In the small rural communities of Texas and Oklahoma, persons of all classes, races, and ethnicities were exposed to the message presented in these texts. That was the idea: to spread middle-class norms and values to schoolchildren in all parts of the nation. Whether such groups took them to heart, however, is another matter entirely. Middle-class reformers believed that those in the lower classes were especially in need of moral guidance. As noted before, records from the Hardeman & Barret store and McKinney & Brown's ledgers indicate that African Americans included readers, most likely McGuffey's, among their household purchases in the early 1870s.[38] Outside of the usual household necessities, few items rivaled spellers or readers in their popularity with African American customers.

Despite this explicit interest in educational materials, the spending habits of African Americans recorded in the store ledgers largely paralleled those of white farmers. For the most part, fiscal restraint rather than lavish spending characterized the purchasing patterns of the majority of African Americans in the cotton-producing regions of Texas. Studies examining the spending habits of African Americans in other parts of the postbellum South have likewise found that African

Americans exercised caution in their spending.[39] Poverty and fear of debt kept them from spending irresponsibly, and instead, they expended both their energies and their meager savings on trying to get ahead, not falling behind. The fact remains that it was exceedingly difficult for African Americans to get ahead in Reconstruction Texas. The state proved to be anything but the "land of milk and honey." As one former slave who migrated from Virginia noted, "I got to Texas and try to work for white folks and try to farm. I couldn't make anything at any work. I made $5.00 a month for I don't know how many year after the war."[40] Since money was clearly tight for many former slaves, frivolous spending was simply not an option.

If fiscal conservatism was the general rule, what should be made of African Americans who did not exercise such pecuniary restraint? The purchases made by Charles Menefee from the Hardeman & Barret store in Melrose extended well beyond necessities, even into the realm of modest luxuries. In the summer of 1870, Menefee, a twenty-eight-year-old black farmer with a large family, charged to his account:

a set of jewelry	$1.00
a harmonica	15¢
a set of tumblers	75¢
two vials of shoe cologne	50¢
a ladies' hat	$1.50
another ladies' hat	$1.75
a pair of bracelets	37¢
a strand of beads	35¢[41]

Granted these were inexpensive luxuries, but given that so many African Americans lived in poverty in East Texas, these are compelling purchases and worthy of further consideration.[42]

At the McKinney & Brown store in Jacksonville, Sandy Chandler's account also reveals expenditures on luxury items rather than just basics. As noted, on one trip to the store, he bought two pairs of gloves, several yards of ribbon, two ties, a cord and fan, a tuck comb, two handkerchiefs (one silk), a pair of hose, a parasol, and some candy.[43] The purchases totaled $5.75 and were subject to an additional 10 percent interest charge by the store owners.[44] In addition to these small extravagances,

Chandler's ability to secure accounts suggests that he had likely attained at least measured economic success and possibly middle-class standing in the rural community of Jacksonville. March Kessentiner, who, like Sandy Chandler, secured credit for other African Americans at McKinney & Brown, acquired on one visit to the store in June 1881, a set of goblets, knives, forks, spoons, cups, plates, a variety of fabrics, including lace and twelve yards of linen.[45] Again, the order went well beyond a few staples. In consumption terms, these examples indicate that Menefee, Chandler, and Kessentiner diverged, however slightly, from the fiscal cautiousness of many of their African American counterparts.

These extravagances, which suggest perhaps some gesture toward gentility and middle-class refinement, need to be considered in the context of white middle-class attitudes toward such genteel expressions by African Americans during the period. There were ample examples of middle-class African Americans in both northern and southern cities who adopted all the forms of respectability that middle-class whites also brought into their own lives in the nineteenth century. However, whites tended to heap disdain and ridicule upon any attempts by blacks to display their refinement. Examining the connection between race and class, one scholar has asserted that rather than praising blacks for their genteel behavior, aristocratic whites tended to chastise blacks for their middle-class pretensions.[46]

It is in the context of white ridicule that some historians have argued that dress and gestures toward refinement were in themselves politicized acts of transgression. According to Shane White and Graham White, reactions by whites to black dress, demeanor, and gestural language suggest that they recognized "a highly political subtext of struggle, a determination to renegotiate the social contract."[47] Certain behaviors challenged social boundaries, in fact, so carrying a parasol or taking an afternoon stroll along a city promenade could become politicized acts undertaken by African Americans, assertions of both dignity and resistance. Seen in this light, perhaps the purchases made by Sandy Chandler and March Kessentiner at the McKinney & Brown store go beyond mere middle-class aspirations and in fact intimate something far more significant: a desire for genteel goods that mounted a challenge to the social status quo and that tested the boundaries of freedom itself.

Since clothing often served as a battleground between white chastisement and black efforts to express individuality and freedom, it is worth examining the clothing purchases made by a handful of male African American customers at the Hardeman & Barret store in 1870. Identified in the ledgers as freedmen, two customers made significant purchases of ready-made clothing in June 1870. On June 7, Peter Barret (F.M.C.) bought a shirt, coat and pants, cravat, and suspenders from the store, totaling $9.40. Three days later, Dick Gray (F.M.C.) purchased a linen coat for $5.50, a pair of tweed pants for $3.50, and two "fancy" shirts for $2.50. In July, Henry Gray (F.M.C.) acquired from the store an alpaca coat for $3.50, "Cam Jeans" pants for $2.00, and "Casimer" (cashmere) pants for $6.00. Gray followed up these purchases in August by acquiring a "fancy" shirt for $2.75.[48] These customers did not opt for the cheapest clothing items that were available on the store shelves but, rather, chose more extravagant purchases. For these African American customers in East Texas, the meaning of freedom during Reconstruction included the ability to purchase, even lavishly—a social expression with both personal and political connotations in the context of a turbulent (even dangerous) period of race relations. By seeking equality through the lens of consumption, African Americans challenged white assumptions of expected behavior. As one scholar observed, "From slavery to long after emancipation, whites expected blacks not only to be inferior, but also appear inferior."[49]

Living in largely agricultural regions, the majority of McKinney & Brown's and Hardeman & Barret's customers, both white and black, engaged in farming, particularly sharecropping—hardly remarkable in a region where the principal crops were cotton and corn.[50] In post–Civil War Texas, most blacks became sharecroppers, and most found that they had limited opportunities either to save money or acquire land.[51] Frustrated with the opportunities afforded them in rural settings, some blacks chose to move to urban centers to seek employment. While nonagricultural employment among blacks in the last decades of the nineteenth century increased steadily, Texas maintained a lower percentage of urban workers, both white and black, than any other state because of its limited urbanization and industrialization. Discrimination also played a critical role in limiting employment opportunities for blacks in the cities. As a result, most blacks migrated into pursuits associated with personal and domestic services such as servants, laundresses, nurses and midwives, restaurant and saloon keepers, hairdressers, and barbers.[52]

According to ledgers for the Wolf General Merchandise store in Austin, African Americans also found work for city businesses as general laborers in a variety of capacities. Lem Chambers, for example, worked as a general laborer for one of the city's wholesale grocers, Brueggerhoff & Heidenheimer. He is listed in the *General Directory of the City of Austin, Texas for 1877–1878* as "Lemuel Chambers (co'd), lab [laborer] Brueggerhoff & Heidenheimer."[53] The Wolf Merchandise Firm was located just down Congress Avenue from Chambers's employer, and it attracted numerous customers from the immediate vicinity.

Not all city residents found themselves in the city's directory. There are few African Americans or women listed in the directory, in fact, and in part this is because the directory's focus was on listing businesses and skilled laborers. Spouses were often not listed. So why is Lemuel Chambers listed? The luxury items he acquired from the Wolfe store suggest that he either made a comfortable living or spent as though he did. In March 1873, Chambers's entries included:

Port wine	$1.00
salmon (canned)	70¢
ham	$1.35
wine	$1.00
cigars	$1.00
a half gallon of wine	$1.00
a bottle of whiskey	85¢

In January, he purchased a pipe for 50¢, brandy for $1.20, oysters and lobsters for 30¢ (canned).[54] From the scant examples available, it appears that Chambers had a rather expensive palate. Between his inclusion in the city directory and his expensive purchases, Chambers seems to have done quite well for himself, especially in relation to his sharecropping counterparts in rural Texas. Although Chambers does not appear in the 1870 census, the 1880 census provides pertinent information regarding his circumstances at the time of his was making his purchases from the Wolf store. Evidently, he was only twenty-two years old in 1873 (twenty-nine in 1880), and the census reveals that he continued to work as a store laborer since his occupation was listed as "porter in store." Since his wife, Caroline, was only eighteen in 1880, it seems likely that he was unmarried in the early 1870s.[55] Thus, his purchases may mean he was able to spend his disposable income on himself, typical of many young men both black and white in similar circumstances.

A critical component to discussions of race in nineteenth-century America is the issue of class, and store records suggest an important link between race and class in Texas. Few stores better exemplify this connection than those from William McCampbell's general store in Refugio, South Texas. The surrounding county reflected an increasingly complex and rapidly changing racial makeup of this cattle and cotton-farming region. In the late 1800s, Texas experienced a shift in racial demographics as Mexicans from the south migrated further north seeking work. By the turn of the century, Mexicans composed a large percentage of the labor force in both South and Central Texas. In the last decades of the nineteenth century, demographic trends saw East Texas (with both black and white populations) and South Texas converging. Mexicans gradually moved north, and southern whites and blacks followed the western expansion of the cotton frontier into Central Texas.[56] Ledger accounts from the W. E. McCampbell & Bros. store not only mirror the region's racially heterogeneous population but also demonstrate that, in regions with diverse racial compositions, white Texans tended almost to overemphasize and demarcate racial and class distinctions, leading one to question the stability of such racial categories.

The following examples are typical of the entries found in McCampbell's account ledger for 1876–77: "Lewis Roy (Col'd), 1876, July 13: 1 pair boots, . . . Marianna (Mex), 1876, June 8: 1 lb candles 25¢, 4½ lbs flour 25¢, ½ lb leaf tobacco 40¢, . . . Lee (Col'd), 1876, January 4, 1 lb candles 25¢."[57] Like many of their contemporaries, William and Thomas McCampbell distinguished race in their ledger books, and these two went a step further by splitting their account holders into separate ledgers based on criteria (seemingly) associated with employment status. Laborers, who were usually black or Mexican, ended up in one ledger (account ledger 1876–77), and employers, who were typically prominent white town residents, ended up in another (ledger 1877). Dates for the year 1877 overlap in these two ledgers. Daybooks, which listed all the sales recorded on a given day, included customers from both ledgers until the store owners split the transactions into the separate account ledgers. On June 11, 1877, for example, sales were made to A. J. West, R. R. Barber, B. F. West, and Joe Toups, and these all appear in the 1877 ledger. Sales were also made on this date to Arcadia (Mex), Telesferro (Mex), and Ann Shaw, and these names appear in the 1876–77 account ledger.

Class also seems to have been a factor, and certain telling characteristics differentiate the two ledgers. First, not only are customers distinguished by race in Ledger 1876–77, but a number of them appear without last names. It is significant that the same cannot be said of customers who appear in Account Ledger 1877. For example, Ledger 1876–77 includes the accounts of Phillisana (Mex), Nig (Col'd), Pancho (Mex), Mary (Col'd), Germo (Mex), Zano (Col'd), and Trinidad (Mex). What can be made of racialized entries that fail to include last names? If the store owners were so familiar with these customers that they did not require last names, why was it so important to note their race? Rather than simply suggesting a lack of respect toward these customers, the practice implies a need both to determine and to reinforce racial categories. Race clearly contributed to the merchants' character assessment of their clients—which was also tied in large part to occupation. Typical entries in Ledger 1877, on the other hand, included both first and last names—examples include Felix Dubois, Dick West, Dr. John S. Ragland, Henry B. Heard, George Maley, and H. V. Barrow.[58]

As a general rule, the store owners also recorded women differently in the two account books. Examples of the few women who appear in Ledger 1877 are Mrs. Kate Duncan, Mrs. Susan Dugat, and Mrs. Eliza Buck. All these women's accounts included quite significant purchases, including expensive pistols, jewelry, and table settings.[59] Examples of women in Ledger 1876–77 ledger include Ann Shaw, Mary, Elvira Peters, and "Scott's Mexican woman," whose accounts, perhaps not surprisingly, included more modest purchases.[60] The fact that Elvira Peters's name changed to Elvira Edwards during this period indicates that marital status alone did not account for the differences in titles. Rather, the differences appear to be related to a character assessment made by store owners. Single or married, Ann Shaw or Elvira Edwards surely merited the distinction of "Miss" or a "Mrs." The exclusion of such distinctions suggests that the store owners reserved these titles for specific women, perhaps those in the non-laboring classes. According to the ledger, both Shaw and Edwards received credits on their account "by washing" or performing some other unspecified labor for town residents.[61]

Figures from both ledgers are tied together in the daybooks, which recorded daily sales, and interactions between the two groups can also be traced in entries from the account ledgers, particularly Ledger 1876–77. Under the account of Henry Neel (Col'd), a credit is issued "By amount to a/c B. F. West of $1.80." West also applied credits to the account of Telesforo Caberro (Mex) and Henry Fields (Col'd), which suggests they were all probably his employees.[62] B. F. West was a prominent Refugio property holder, a "cowhunter" according to McCampbell's Ledger 1877, and a frequent and reliable customer of the store.[63] R. L. Dunman's name appears in the same ledger as West's. His occupation was also noted as cowhunter, and it is significant that he served on the same city council as William E. McCampbell, the store owner himself. Both men were elected to the city council (to serve in different capacities) in 1875. Dunman credited five dollars to the account of Hanibal Greenwood in Ledger 1876–77 on June 2, 1876. W. B. Doughty, another prominent town figure, issued a credit to Zano's account in March 1877.[64] In the ledgers the two classes overlapped, usually through the issuing of credits on particular accounts listed in Ledger 1876–77.

As ardent as racial attitudes and divisiveness might have been in the town of Refugio, Texas, the rationale behind the two ledgers probably had more to do with work status—laborers versus employers—rather than racial status. Still, there were certainly qualitative differences between the two books. The informality of Ledger 1876–77 diverges from the respectful tones of Ledger 1877. Of the hundreds of transactions listed in the ledgers, only a couple of account holders' names surface in both books. These are Viggo Kohler and J. S. Rafferty, neither of whom had racial distinctions behind their names. Both these customers went from Ledger 1876–77 to Ledger 1877.[65] What merited Kohler and Rafferty's change in status and consequent shift in ledger status is unclear. If class and race were essentially linked in these ledgers, what does such evidence say about the perception of laboring whites? Does presence in a ledger largely reserved for racial minorities suggest that some laborers were considered less "white" than some of their counterparts?[66] Most of the store's customers remained firmly in the ledger to which they were originally assigned, an apt metaphor for a period in which boundaries of race and class proved to be—for racial minorities at least—more fixed than fluid.

In examining the terms on which minority groups entered commercial relations, the question remains as to whether such groups faced price discrimination in their purchasing, especially in comparison to white customers. Obviously, some items do not lend themselves to direct comparisons, because differences in quality were usually not recorded in the ledgers. Such goods include shoes, clothing, and fabrics. This said, a handful of items do allow for some comparison of prices charged to whites and African American store customers. From the McCampbell & Bros. store, there were several goods purchased in similar quantities, obtained by customers in both Ledger 1876–77 and Ledger 1877. In March 1877, for example, a bottle of Wild Cherry Balsam was sold to Refugio town councilman Robert P. Clarkson for one dollar. The same product was sold to Henry Elliot, recorded as "(col'd)," for the same price two months earlier. Elliot also purchased one cake of tar soap for twenty-five cents and shortly thereafter, Mrs. Kate Duncan paid the same price for the same product. According to Ledger 1877, Zach Ballard paid one dollar for five plugs of tobacco in August 1877, and Ledger 1876–77 records that Charlie McCampbell (col'd) paid the same price for the same measure of tobacco in April. Finally, A. H. Barber purchased a box of caps for twenty cents in October, and George Hall (col'd) paid the same price for caps in November 1876.[67] These few examples suggest, rather than a race-based pricing policy, that customers in each ledger paid the same price for comparable items.

Perhaps the explanation for the McCampbells' fair pricing strategies lies in the fact that these store owners needed the business of their minority customers as much as these customers needed access to goods and credit. At the Hardeman & Barret store in Melrose, a comparison of prices for items such as spellers, slate pencils, and spools of thread sold to both white and African American customers also demonstrates that prices did not vary between the different racial groups.[68] Historian Ted Ownby finds a similar phenomenon in Mississippi stores during the same period. He notes that not only did black customers have considerably less cash than white customers (which, consequently, led to them settling their accounts less often) but blacks were far less likely to become store owners themselves—in large part because of their inability to access credit.[69]

There are likely two explanations for racially unbiased pricing strategies at these Texas stores, and both derive from merchants' need both to obtain and to retain customers. First, merchants were vulnerable to competition from other dry goods operators—this was true for virtually all the stores studied here. In Refugio, for instance, Major James Wiley Ratchford and George Robertson Ratchford, George Vineyard, and Ben C. Ellis operated general mercantile firms in the 1870s, which all competed for customers with the McCampbell & Bros. store.[70] One scholar has argued that many country stores often faced intense competition and, thus, were unable to establish territorial monopolies. He cites the instability of the staple crop economy as another factor that undermined merchants' economic control over their clients and left them vulnerable to economic ruin.[71] Store owners in Refugio, Melrose, Jacksonville, and Nacogdoches all faced similar conditions such as competition and reliance on the vagaries of the market, and perhaps these factors curtailed any desire to practice unfair pricing policies with regard to their African American customers. An additional point should be made on the issue of credit, which directly affected so many African American store customers. Since customers who relied on credit were subject to interest rates set by merchants (at the McKinney & Brown store, for example, this included a published 12 percent interest rate on carryover balances and an occasional 10 percent charge on large orders), they indeed paid higher costs than those who paid with cash and who were not subject to interest.

Store ledgers affirm the ubiquity of racial segregation in Gilded Age Texas, particularly for African Americans but also for Mexican Americans. A state previously dependent on slave labor, Texas in the postbellum period was clearly adjusting to life after slavery. Ledgers from this same period in territorial Oklahoma indicate that also in Indian Territory race proved to be a contentious and fractious issue. On the one hand, the "removed" southern tribes of Indian Territory shared with their southern neighbors a commitment to slave labor. On the other hand, not all in Indian Territory supported the peculiar institution; in fact, slavery proved to be a divisive issue among many tribal members, both before and during the Civil War.[72]

Indeed, Indians in Indian Territory faced a multitude of racial questions in the postwar period. Deemed outsiders and pushed to the peripheries of white society, Indians increasingly found themselves being pulled into the federal vision of national consolidation, an invitation that they, like African Americans, could not really choose to decline.[73] In frequenting and establishing accounts at their local dry goods store, Indians in pre-statehood Oklahoma also participated in a market economy—and, by extension, in the national economy. As in Texas, distinctions of race surfaced in ledgers from Indian Territory, again testifying to the complex racial divisions evidenced during this period.

Politics and power in Indian Territory split along different lines, racially, than in other regions. After all, the government in Indian Territory was largely administered through representatives of the Five Tribes; consequently, political, economic, and social status in Indian Territory was linked directly to one's relationship with tribal officials. American Indians in Indian Territory were not minorities to whites in the 1870s and 1880s, though this was quickly changing. In the postbellum period, white civilization encroached on Indian Territory, fractioning and undermining tribal power from both inside and outside the borders of Indian Territory. Racial politics in the region were not based on simple dichotomies between whites and Indians, or whites and blacks, but also between Indians and blacks and, significantly, between different Indian groups.

Indians residing in Indian Territory increasingly sought to define both their race and the region as separate, not just from whites but from blacks as well. In creating Indian Territory, whites established both geographic and racial boundaries between themselves and Indians. As one historian argues, Indians similarly desired to create a space of racial integrity separate from both whites and blacks: "a red man's country."[74] In doing so, Indians established laws designed to keep not only whites out of Indian Territory but also African Americans. Moreover, such laws restricted access by whites and blacks to the most critical component of tribal identity and power: citizenship.[75]

It is important, at this point, to step back in order to understand the status of freed blacks in Indian Territory in the immediate aftermath of the Civil War. As in other parts of the defeated South, northern Republicans imposed civil and political rights for blacks in Indian Territory, during the period often referred to as Radical Reconstruction. However, unlike in other southern states, federal officials required that tribal governments not only emancipate black slaves but also incorporate or adopt them into Indian nations. The Seminoles were the least resistant to the latter requirement; however, there is ample evidence that the other tribes in Indian Territory, including the Choctaws and the Creeks, mounted concerted resistance to the notion of full citizenship or equality for African Americans.[76] Ultimately, struggles over citizenship, tribal sovereignty, and the perception of an overreaching federal government marred race relations in Indian Territory during this era. Suffice to say, Indian Territory was not a more favorable setting for racial harmony than either Texas or any other part of the South in the late nineteenth century.

Despite concerns over white interlopers, it was easier for whites to marry into a tribe than blacks, and many whites took full advantage of this opportunity. The expectation of tribal leaders was that whites who crossed this boundary through marriage would "renounce their whiteness" and embrace being Indian.[77] Ledger records from white store owners who married into tribes provide evidence of the racial divisions and class divisions that existed in Indian Territory in the 1870s and 1880s. Such data attest not only to the importance of citizenship in demarcating identity and power in Indian Territory but also to the need to create and identify boundaries of race between American Indians and African Americans living in the region.

The pressure to open Indian Territory up to white settlement came from a variety of sources, including railroad officials, speculators of all kinds, farmers, and white interlopers already operating inside the region.

For those seeking to exploit the territory's economic potential, Indian Territory was seen more and more as an impediment to regional and national progress.[78] Booster newspapers operating within Indian Territory endorsed all those who sought to elevate and refine the territory's potential, sharply criticizing those who stood in the way of progress. As noted, the *Oklahoma Star* praised store owner, cattleman, and mine owner James Jackson McAlester for his entrepreneurial spirit.[79] Ultimately, it was allotment that proved the death knell of tribal sovereignty in Indian Territory. With the General Allotment Act, the Curtis Act, and the dissolution of tribal governments in 1906, the job was complete. As historian Brian Dippie wrote, "Then Indian Territory, the 'shrunken residue' of the millions of acres that once constituted Indian country, was wiped off the map."[80]

Store ledgers from the period provide some insight into the pressures from white encroachment that were building within Indian Territory in the years preceding allotment. Out of necessity, white store owners fostered relationships with tribal members, and consequently, tribal officials figure prominently in various account books from the region. The nature of relationships that developed between store owners and tribal members ranged from impersonal economic and political business partnerships to social, very personal relationships. Like their counterparts to the South, store owners distinguished race in their account ledgers, demonstrating that the racial distinctions so prominent in the nation as a whole transcended the boundaries of Indian Territory. Further still, distinctions were made between high-ranking tribal members and non–tribal members, affirming the social hierarchies within the region and the desire of those in power to maintain a racial hierarchy based on citizenship.

Store owners J. J. McAlester and F. B. Severs gained access to Indian lands and resources through marriage into the Choctaw and Creek tribes (respectively), and both became wealthy as a result. Many white Americans held mixed views on intermarriage between whites and Indians. On the one hand, intermarriage allowed access to Indian resources and furthered the assimilation process that had been underway since the time of Thomas Jefferson. On the other hand, racial mixing was not condoned in late nineteenth and early twentieth centuries, especially because some expressed concern over the "passing" of the so-called Anglo-Saxon race.[81] Still, there was a deep gulf between white attitudes concerning the intermarriage of whites and Indians and the intermarriage of whites and blacks. The latter was deemed almost the worst of all social taboos. It would seem that ambivalence best characterizes American perceptions of white–Indian relations, although there were plenty of inherent contradictions within those perceptions. Whites often perceived American Indians as "uncivilized" and inferior, and yet many enterprising young white men sought American Indian wives as an avenue to land and lucrative economic opportunities in Indian Territory.[82]

Discussing the complexities of racial intermarriage Brian Dippie observes the double standard applied to Indian–white marriages: "it was the Indian who was invited to join in the affairs of the nation, even to intermarry with the white race, while the black was consistently shunned."[83] Indians sought to protect their own racial boundaries within Indian Territory, and this entailed not only excluding blacks but requiring that whites either stay out of Indian Territory altogether or relinquish their whiteness by marrying into the tribe.[84] To some degree, many tribal officials welcomed into their tribes entrepreneurial-minded whites who might advance the economic fortunes of the region (under the condition that they embraced their new Indian identity). These same tribal officials did not see similar economic benefits accruing through marriages between Indians and blacks. Barred from political and economic opportunities, most African Americans in the South lived in abject poverty and were unable to provide tribal officials with the promise of economic progress. Indian leaders sought to strengthen the prospects of their respective nations and, as one historian observed, "nation-building in Indian Territory meant racial separation, notions about 'blood purity,' and the power of race in the making of place."[85]

The fact remains that whites could not get ahead in Indian Territory without at least marginal tribal support. Evidence of the fortuitous relationships forged by J. J. McAlester with important members of the Choctaw Nation appear throughout the account ledgers from his dry goods store. For example, the second entry in McAlester's 1870–72 Daybook is the sale of a pair of socks, a handkerchief, and a hat to Billy Pusley on October 8, 1870.[86] Billy's father, Joshua Pusley, was a prominent Choctaw farmer who owned coal leases in the Nation. McAlester established a business partnership with the Pusley family through which he gained access to the region's rich coal beds. Choctaw law forbade whites from extracting resources from their land, but tribal members did not face such restrictions.[87] As part owner of the Osage Coal and Mining Company, McAlester reaped the benefits of selling the coal resources and transporting them out of the area via the MK&T railroad. Finally, through his marriage to Rebecca Burney, McAlester received full citizenship in the Choctaw tribe and legal access to the Nation's coal reserves.[88]

Like his contemporaries in Texas, McAlester distinguished race in his ledgers by the now familiar practice of including a racial distinction in brackets after the account holder's name. In the case of African Americans, McAlester used (Cold.) to distinguish race in his books. William Yates's account in the 1874–75 ledger, for example, reads as follows:

William Yates (cold.), 1875–January 16

2 bottles of Wizard Oil	$1.00
one bottle of pills	25¢
one pair child's shoes	$1.00
two pair child's hose	70¢
Turner's Wonder [medicinal product]	50¢[89]

Reflecting the prevalence of coal miners in the region, the accounts of both George Trumbo and Richard Goram were listed in McAlester's ledgers with the distinction "(cold. miner)" behind their names.[90] In 1876, McAlester recorded the purchases of two of his female employees in the following manner: "Vicy (cold. cook or nurse), July 10–Bacon $3.20, calico $1.00, thread 10¢, snuff 50¢," and "Aunt Violet (cold. cook), May 27–One pair shoes $2.00, handkerchief 50¢."[91] The informality of these entries is evocative of the manner used to record the accounts of black and Mexican laborers in the ledgers from McCampbell's store in Refugio, perhaps because both of these women were evidently employees of the store owner.

Related to the unique circumstances of operating a store in Indian Territory, McAlester's account records indicate that he developed a hierarchy of status, which related to one's standing in the Choctaw Nation, at least as this was to be perceived by the store owner. Of note, racial overtones were prevalent in McAlester's constructed social hierarchy. For example, the store owner, himself a member of the Choctaw Nation, described Noel Cass, Dixon McKinney, and "Webster" all as "(Indian)."[92] Yet he did not distinguish as Indian any of the prominent Choctaw families he did business with, specifically the Pulseys, the Folsoms, or the Meshemahtubbies. Further, in his 1875–78 ledger, McAlester distinguished tribal members from non–tribal members by referring to the former as "citizen." James Anacher, who purchased a bottle of lung balsam for $1.00 on November 25, 1875, for example, is denoted in the ledgers as "citizen." McAlester also recognized Judge Ellis Folsom, Salone Owens, G. W. Riddle, Sam Moore, Washington Wade, Eastman Pusley, and Wade Hampton as "citizens."[93] However, both Isam Jefferson and William Moore appear in the ledger with "(Indian)" following their names.[94] Why the discrepancy? Probably, the generic "Indian" simply implied that Jefferson and Moore were not members of the Choctaw Nation and they maintained affiliation with another tribe.[95]

Given that McAlester himself occupied a position of wealth and prestige among the Choctaws and that status and racial distinctions were so important to tribal officials, the prevalence of social distinctions— identifying tribal citizens and Indians—in the store owner's ledgers are hardly unexpected. Of course, the practice of identifying citizens and Indians in his ledgers in itself does not suggest that McAlester either discriminated against or deemed his "Indian" clientele in any way inferior. Rather, the records provide evidence that he affirmed the social and racial distinctions witnessed in the region as a whole. Citizenship was a critical component of establishing Indian identity. In example after example, store records affirmed perceived racial distinctions. In doing so, they also helped constitute racial identities and, in Indian Territory, this included citizenship. In addition to distinguishing citizens from non-citizens, the level of one's Indianness also proved to be a divisive issue. Distinctions between full-bloods, mixed-bloods, and intermarried citizens also divided those living in the Choctaw lands. According to one Oklahoma historian, full-bloods were more politically inclined, while mixed-bloods and intermarried citizens such as McAlester usually devoted themselves to money-making. Despite their commercial focus, these groups were by no means politically aloof, choosing instead to influence politics from behind the scenes.[96] Many traditional full-bloods perceived both the close ties and the business focus of mixed-bloods and whites as a threat to tribal lands and sovereignty. Racial perceptions may have also played a role in shaping full bloods' distrust of white-mixed blood relations. Particularly in the years before statehood, whites chose to intermarry with mixed-blood Indians—perceiving them as morally and intellectually superior to full bloods.[97]

McAlester's customers obtained a wide range of goods from the store, demonstrating both the sophistication of the store owner's stock and the diverse tastes of his clientele. Judge Ellis Folsom's account included the purchase of a reader and an arithmetic book on January 3, 1876, suggesting that education and self-improvement were priorities among citizens of the Choctaw Nation. Wade Washington similarly bought educational materials, charging a slate, a pencil, and a grammar book to his account in the early months of 1876. The purchase of an accordion for $8.50 by Wade Hampton, another citizen of the tribe, suggests that McAlester's customers did not restrict their purchases to necessities or staples.[98] At the cost of $8.50, Hampton's accordion would have been an expensive strain on the budgets of many of his contemporaries. Certainly, not all of McAlester's clientele engaged in such extravagant spending. Staples such as tobacco, coffee, bacon, corn, and flour appeared most frequently on customers' accounts. Both Sam Moore (citizen) and William Moore (Indian) purchased three steel traps on the same day in 1875, indicating that hunting and trapping were still important to many in the Choctaw Nation. Three months later, William Moore received a credit on his account "by furs," which settled his balance.[99]

"Basics" is probably the best way to describe the items purchased by customers of Choctaw store owner W. N. Jones, who operated a general store in Cade, Indian Territory, in the early 1870s. Maintaining a position of wealth and prominence in the Choctaw Nation, Jones served as principal chief of the Choctaw Nation and maintained a large cattle ranch that employed, according to one source, "a great many Indians to handle his cattle and ponies."[100] Jones recorded customer accounts in his ledgers in both English and Choctaw, sometimes employing a mix of both. A typical entry from his ledger reads as follows: "Henry Buhring: 1874, January 17, two shirts for $3.00 each, one pair pants $4.00, February 7, one plug tobacco $1.00."[101] Items that most frequently appeared on customer accounts were tobacco, calico fabric, flour, finished clothing items, boots and shoes (recorded in the ledgers as "sholosh," the Choctaw word for shoes). One notable exception is the account of Simeon Levi, who is distinguished in the account book as "Dr. To W. Jones." Levi purchased from the Jones store an assortment of spelling books and a quire of writing paper on April 28, 1873.[102] Judging from the relatively few accounts listed in the ledger and the heavy emphasis on staple goods, it appears that this general store was a modest operation, established to service the basic needs of the region's largely ranching clientele.

Operating a dry goods store in Okmulgee, the capital of the Creek Nation, retailer Frederick Benjamin Severs in his ledgers did not differentiate "Indians" from "citizens" of the Creek Nation as McAlester did. However, there are some important similarities between the two. Like McAlester, Severs gained citizenship into the tribe through marriage and his relationship with Chief Samuel Checote. Clearly, the store owner developed strong ties to influential members of the Creek Nation. Between fostering key relationships with tribal leaders and capitalizing on lucrative business ventures, Severs emerged as a man of wealth and prominence among the Creeks. The pages of his account ledgers are chock-full of the names of important tribal leaders, including the Creek Chiefs Checote, Pleasant Porter, and Moty Tiger.[103] On Severs's relationship with tribal leadership, his niece Sarah Trent stated, "In this business, [his general store] he made the acquaintance of the Chiefs and leading Creek men and extended them many favors, which formed an everlasting friendship." Further, she continued, "In 1857, he was adopted by the Creek tribe—he was their beloved white brother." On his interracial marriage, Trent observed, "In 1860, he married Anna Anderson, a beautiful half-blood Creek Indian, she was educated in Tallahassee, Mississippi."[104] It's a fascinating description with Miss Trent's precision in noting that Severs's wife was beautiful, half-Creek, and educated.

While Severs did not indicate distinctions between Creek members and non-members in his ledgers, he did distinguish the race of his African American customers. On September 29, 1869, for example, a "Blk Woman" settled with the store owner a $2.25 balance on a pair of shoes, and a week later, Tom, a "Blk Man," purchased a half gallon of molasses.[105] In other entries, the store owner used the distinction "cold." to identify his black customers; for example, Macher "Cold. Man" purchased a pair of shoes on December 14, 1869, and Andy Fields (Cold.) charged two bars of lead and four dollars cash to his account, he also paid (Solomon cold.) fifty cents, recorded as a debit on his account.[106] A few general observations can be made regarding these entries. The most obvious point is that Severs recognized racial distinctions in his ledgers, or at least, he distinguished African Americans. Second, the majority of entries for black customers did not include last names, mirroring the informal tone employed by store owners in Texas ledgers. Finally, Severs's African American customers tended to stick to staples in their purchasing patterns, rarely acquiring more than a few items—surely, shoes and molasses can hardly be considered luxury items.

F. B. Severs's general store in Okmulgee, Creek Nation, was a long way from the McKinney & Brown store in Jacksonville, Texas, and even farther from William McCampbell's merchandise firm in Refugio, Texas, yet distinctions of race appear in ledgers from all three stores, especially in the form of shorthand qualifiers identifying customers as African American. It is important to keep in mind that ledgers were not written for public consumption; in fact, it was unusual for more than a few people to view such records, specifically store owners and, if they could afford them, their clerks. So why was distinguishing race so important to these store owners?

In all likelihood, the answer lies in the period itself. In late-nineteenth-century America, few issues divided the nation more than that of race, particularly in the South (or in the regions neighboring the South). In accordance with federal economic initiatives, *all* Americans were to be integrated into the national economy, and indeed, general stores provided an excellent forum for such economic inclusion. Customer records from Texas and pre-statehood Oklahoma indicate that persons of all racial categories frequented stores, established credit, and purchased both luxury and staple items. Perhaps in such an environment, store owners felt that such distinctions needed to be clarified more than ever, even in their business logs. However, it is one thing to shop together; it is another thing to bridge intense racial divisions entirely. Addressing this point, Ted Ownby includes in his study of consumerism in Mississippi the recollections of one farmer who noted that "the store was a place where races mixed well." That said, these "mixed" environments could be wrought with tension for African Americans had "to look out for trouble," as they often fell prey to racist comments or worse. Mississippian Charles Evers, for example, remembers that he and his brother hated having to go to the store because "Soon as we'd go in the white men standing around there would start picking on us and trying to make us dance. 'Dance, nigger!' The owner of the store was worst of them all."[107]

Ledgers also indicate that some store owners developed social hierarchies in their records, drawn from both racial and class distinctions. At the McKinney & Brown store, a handful of black customers, like Sandy Chandler and Perry Bolden, "secured" the right of credit for other blacks. In Refugio, store owner William McCampbell divided his customers' accounts into separate ledgers, probably denoting one's employment status, although race seems to have been configured somehow into the equation. While in Indian Territory, McAlester distinguished "Indians" from "citizens," a distinction confirming that not only was race important in this region but it was tied to the related issues of identity and citizenship. In effect, account ledgers demonstrate the persistence of social divisions in late-nineteenth-century America, particularly in regard to race. This persistence is hardly surprising given the time period. However, store records provide evidence that during the volatile period of the 1870s and 1880s, when economic relationships between different racial groups underwent reconfiguration or consolidation, the need to reinforce racial distinctions manifested itself in literal form. Whether it was at a dry goods outlet located in rural Texas or one situated in the heart of Indian Territory, store owners were sure to record not only their customers' names and purchases but also the color of their skin.

Figure 1. Lyne T. Barret. L. T. Barret operated a store in Melrose, Texas, with his partner Blackstone Hardeman, Jr. A former Confederate, Barret also served as the secretary for the Committee of Safety, an anti-black vigilante group. Courtesy of the East Texas Research Center.

Figure 2. Blackstone Hardeman, Jr., in about 1860. With a fine Texas pedigree, Blackstone Hardeman, Jr., partnered with L. T. Barret to form the Hardeman & Barret mercantile firm in Melrose, Texas. Courtesy of the East Texas Research Center, Stephen F. Austin State University, Nacogdoches.

Figure 3. Nacogdoches, Texas, about 1882. The Clark & Hyde mercantile store was located here. Mrs. Anna J. Hyde also operated a boardinghouse in this community. Courtesy of the East Texas Research Center, Stephen F. Austin State University, Nacogdoches.

Figure 4. Capt. George Benjamin Hester. Hester established a mercantile business in the community of Old Boggy Depot in the Choctaw Nation. He and his wife, Elizabeth Fulton Hester, engaged in philanthropic work organizing churches and schools and performing missionary work in the Chickasaw and Choctaw Nations. Courtesy of the Research Division of the Oklahoma Historical Society.

Figure 5. James Jackson McAlester. Retail merchant, cattleman, coal mine owner, land speculator, and politician, J. J. McAlester migrated to the Choctaw Nation with a geologist's map of the region's rich coal potential. Courtesy of the Research Division of the Oklahoma Historical Society.

Figure 6. Mrs. Rebecca McAlester. Through his marriage to Rebecca Burney, a Chickasaw woman, J. J. McAlester gained citizenship in both the Choctaw and Chickasaw tribes as well as access to Indian Territory lands and resources. Courtesy of the Research Division of the Oklahoma Historical Society.

Figure 7. McAlester's lavish home in McAlester, Oklahoma (named after the store owner). Reflecting their elite status, this was a fitting home for one of Indian Territory's most prominent couples. Courtesy of the Research Division of the Oklahoma History Society.

Figure 8. F. B. Severs's Cash Store. Frederick Benjamin Severs operated a dry goods store in Okmulgee, the capital of the Creek Nation, Indian Territory. Courtesy of the Research Division of the Oklahoma Historical Society.

Figure 9. Mrs. Anna Martin and her sons, Max (seated) and Charles (standing). German store owner Anna Martin migrated to the Texas Hill Country in the 1850s. In a rags-to-riches life arc, she parlayed her role as a merchant and creditor into the position of bank president. Courtesy of the Museum of American Finance, New York.

Figure 10. Anna Martin's dry goods store and home located in Hedwig's Hill, Texas. She catered to a predominantly German clientele. Courtesy of the Museum of American Finance, New York.

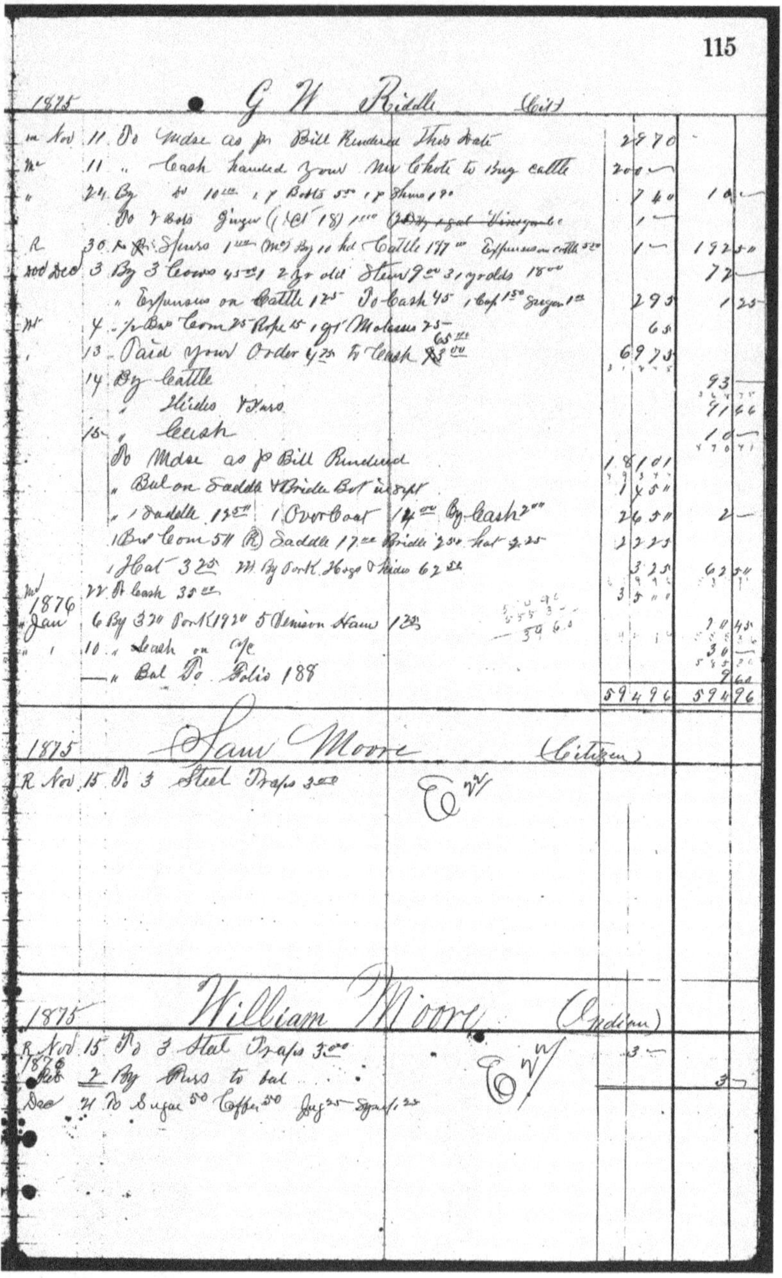
115

1875 G W Riddle (Cit)

Nov 11 To Mdse as pr Bill Rendered This date 29 70

11 " Cash handed your Mr Chote to buy cattle 200

1875 Sam Moore (Citizen)

Nov 15 To 3 Steel Traps 3.00

1875 William Moore (Indian)

Nov 15 To 3 Steel Traps 3.00 3

Figure 11. A page from J. J. McAlester's store ledgers in Indian Territory (Daybook no. 153, page 115). In his ledger records, the store owner differentiated citizens of the Choctaw Nation from "Indians." Courtesy of Western History Collections, University of Oklahoma Libraries.

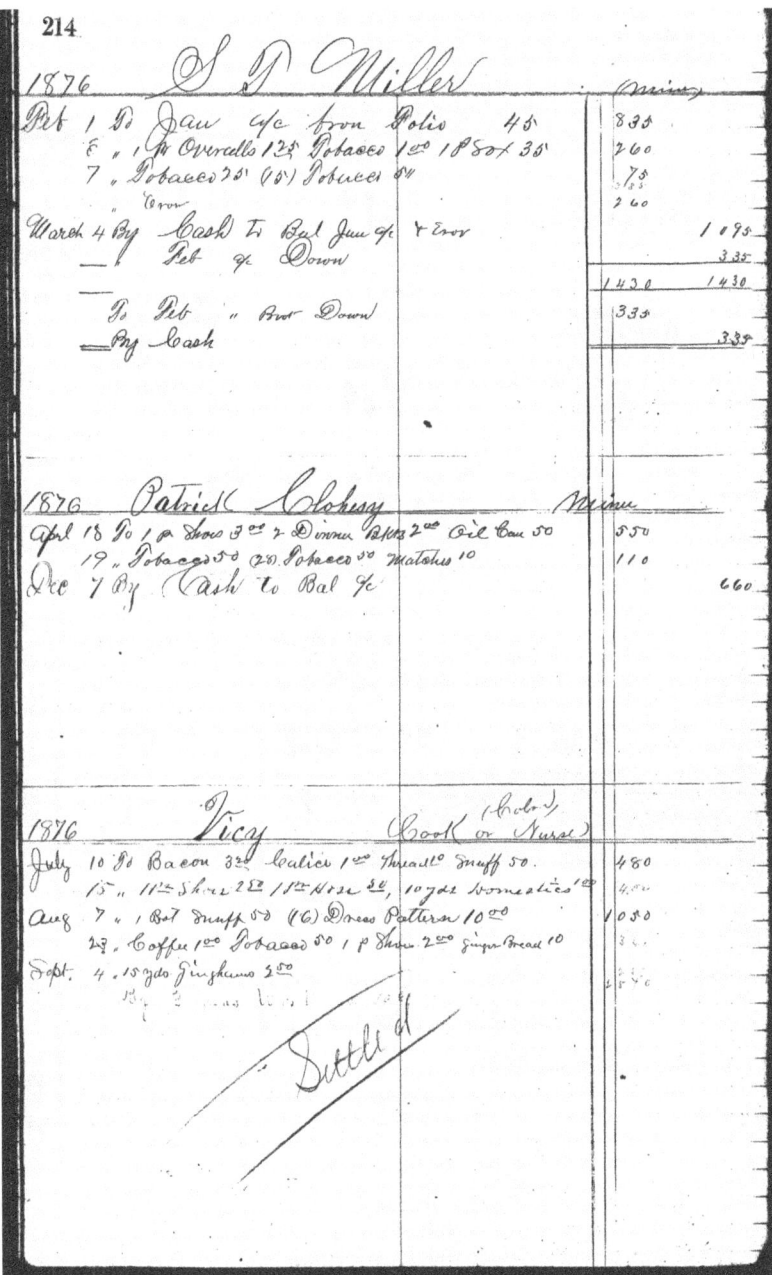

Figure 12. This page from J. J. McAlester's store ledgers in Indian Territory (Daybook no. 153, page 214) highlights the preponderance of coal miners mentioned in the ledgers. McAlester distinguished not only occupations in his ledgers but also race; for example: Vicy, a "colr'd" cook or nurse. Courtesy of the Western History Collections, University of Oklahoma Libraries.

Figure 13. Ad from *Nacogdoches News* (July 20, 1877) for Mrs. A. J. Hyde's Boardinghouse in Nacogdoches, Texas. Mrs. Hyde was a frequent and valued customer of the Clark & Hyde mercantile store. Courtesy of East Texas Research Center, Stephen F. Austin State University, Nacogdoches.

Chapter 5

The German Imprint

IN A LETTER RELAYING THE EXPERIENCES of her life on the Texas frontier to an interested New York banker, store owner Anna Martin added in a postscript the following apology: "Excuse my poor English as I have lived all my life in a German settlement and all my dealings were most with Germans. We don't speak anything else in our home, only German. But I love my adopted Fatherland and my sons are good loyal Americans."[1] Ledger entries from Martin's general store indicate the preponderance of Germans in the small settlement of Hedwig's Hill; in fact, virtually all of the customers listed in her store records from the 1880s were of first- or second-generation German descent. Unlike the divisions of race and class that distinguished store owners from their clients at other stores in Texas, Anna Martin had more in common—socially and culturally—with her customers than she had differences.

In a period that featured so much social upheaval and divisiveness, Hedwig's Hill was a community built on cohesiveness, continuity, and shared culture and value systems. This largely immigrant settlement paralleled similar pockets of ethnic clustering that occurred throughout nineteenth-century America in both rural and urban settings. Rather than melting into some amorphous American identity, these nascent communities retained much of their own particular cultural identities, while concurrently exchanging their rituals, language, and values with persons from different backgrounds and ethnic origins. As such, German-owned stores provide another layer to the already complex fabric of commercial relations on the southern plains.

By the last decades of the nineteenth century, Germans were the largest European immigrant group in the state. In 1887, the roughly 130,000 Germans in Texas constituted the second largest ethnic group in the state (second only to African Americans) and made up well over half of the European migration.[2] Germans began arriving in Texas in the early 1830s, though significant immigration did not occur until a decade later. Texas offered the new immigrants a fresh start and, most important, the promise of land for farms and ranches. Although briefly interrupted by the Civil War, steady German immigration continued into the postbellum period, climaxed in the 1880s, and dropped off by the end of that decade. It was during the 1880s that a large number of immigrants first began arriving in Indian Territory to work as laborers in the coal mines. With their families in tow, immigrant miners ultimately left a lasting impression on the coal regions of southeastern Oklahoma, where annual ethnic festivals still enliven certain times of the year and attract visitors to the small communities. Although the early period of German migration has drawn considerable interest by historians, postwar migration has garnered less scholarly attention, despite the fact that it exceeded the antebellum migration in terms of both population and influence. The peak periods of postwar migration were between 1870–74 and 1879–83.[3] Thus, by 1890, the German imprint on the state of Texas was well established.

Although Anna Martin's family settled in a small agricultural hamlet, many German immigrants to Texas chose cities and towns rather than rural areas. Cities such as Galveston, which served the Germans as a welcoming port, acquired a large percentage of Germans from the 1840s onward. During his visit to Texas in the 1850s, Frederick Law Olmstead estimated Galveston's German population at thirty-five hundred, roughly one-third of the city's population at that time. As he moved further inland, Olmstead estimated that San Antonio's German population was approximately three thousand residents, again roughly one-third of the city's population.[4] Olmstead was a travel writer and cultural critic, and his observations are worth noting. "In social and political relations," he wrote, "the Germans do not occupy the position to which their force and character should entitle them. They mingle little with the Americans, except for the necessary buying and selling." He continued, "The manners and ideals of the Texans and of the Germans are hopelessly divergent, and the two races have made little acquaintance, observing one another apart with unfeigned curiosity, often tempered with mutual contempt."⁵ In short, Olmstead focused on the differences, rather than any cultural similarities, between the Germans and other "Americans." Perhaps Olmstead's desire to stress the differences between Texans and Germans lay in his generally favorable views of Germans—whom he perceived as being proponents of antislavery, a view similar to his own. This positive assessment of Germans veered sharply from his attitude toward pro-slavery Texans, whom he viewed with some contempt. For Olmstead, Germans represented a distinct cohesive group in the heart of the Texas Hill Country. With this in mind, it can be said that the advantage for immigrants of shopping at German-owned stores was that they did not enter commercial relations as outsiders. Indeed, both German store owners and their clients shared their "otherness" status.

The high number of German immigrants in Texas towns and cities mirrored national patterns. According to immigration historians, while many German immigrants remained in northeastern cities, the majority migrated inland to the region often described by demographers as the "German Triangle," comprised of the three midwestern cities of Cincinnati, St. Louis, and Milwaukee. As in Texas, Germans constituted the largest immigrant group in America during the decades following the Civil War, representing approximately 25 percent of the total immigrant population nationally during the 1870s and 1880s. While German immigrants tended to cluster in centers in the Midwest, historian Roger Daniels concedes that there were "occasional German-bloc communities elsewhere" citing Anaheim, California, as an example. He notes that about one German-born person in four was engaged in agriculture in 1870, and at that date Germans comprised more than one-third of all foreign-born farmers in the United States.⁶

Immigration to the United States was hardly a new phenomenon in the post–Civil War period. After 1880, however, economic and demographic changes in Europe propelled a new wave of immigrants from regions other than northern and western Europe (the most common source of immigrants to the United States in the previous decades of migration, the first waves of migration). After 1880, a second massive wave of migration brought immigrants from eastern and southern Europe, particularly Italians, Greeks, Slavs, Slovaks, and Russians, plus smaller contingents from Canada, Mexico, and Japan. Persons from northern

Europe continued to migrate after 1880, but change was clearly underway. By the 1890s, more than half of all immigrants came from the new regions, as opposed to fewer than 2 percent in the 1860s. Most of the new immigrants to the United States in the late nineteenth century lacked the capital to buy land for farms or ranches in the West; consequently, the majority found themselves settling in eastern cities. There were labor opportunities for those willing to make the trek past the urban centers of the East. In the end, thousands of immigrants were able to find their way west—including to Texas and Indian Territory.

It was not only Texas that saw an influx of European immigrants settle within its borders, pre-statehood Oklahoma also experienced such demographic shifts, albeit immigrants to Indian Territory generally migrated in the decades after the Civil War. Recall, it was the rich coal beds that initially prompted J. J. McAlester to migrate to Indian Territory in the early 1870s. Coal production developed in conjunction with the MK&T railroad, which reached McAlester's store in 1872. An intricate web of contracts, networks, professional affiliations, and personal relationships linked McAlester to the interests of both the MK&T (or Katy) and the Osage Coal and Mining Company, businesses prominently featured in the store owner's ledgers in the 1870s and 1880s. McAlester and three business partners, Joshua Pusley, Tandy Walker, and Dr. Daniel M. Hailey, relinquished their individual coal leases (acquired in McAlester's case through marriage) for royalties in the Osage Coal and Mining Company, which was owned by the Katy. The railroad company claimed that the coal company was a separate operation, even though many of the mine's directors were also MK&T directors.[7] In the early 1870s, the mining company entered into an agreement with the Choctaw Nation, which essentially permitted the company to do whatever was required to facilitate mining operations. The MK&T tracks reached the Crossroads area in 1872, prompting the small community to rename itself McAlester in honor of the man who first discovered the region's economic potential.[8]

The changing migration patterns in the United States is evidenced in the ledgers from McAlester's store in Indian Territory. Most of the names listed in the account records suggest that the miners were of American, English, Scot, Welsh, and Irish descent. Indeed, the railroads and coal companies recruited new immigrants from the British Isles to work in the mines located deep in the heart of Choctaw territory.[9] Miners were the most common profession listed as purchasing the basic foodstuffs in McAlester's ledgers. On February 17, 1875, for example, miner Enoch Cartlidge, purchased a fifty-pound sack of flour for $1.75; he made a similar purchase a couple of weeks later, on March 1, 1875. As a critical staple, flour was one of the most popular items at the store. Miners Paddy McLaughlin, Mike Dunn, U. A. Keith, J. J. Wooten, and C. C. White, all purchased fifty-pound sacks of flour in the early months of 1875.[10]

One of the most striking features of coal mining in the district after the 1880s was the proliferation of immigrants from all parts of Europe, including eastern Europe. In his study of coal mining in Oklahoma, Michael Hightower observes that, "Harsh and unsafe conditions in the mines made it difficult to attract workers, so agents were often sent to the eastern states and Europe to convince men to migrate to the Indian Territory. Sometimes agents in Europe were paid for each worker that they sent to the Choctaw coal fields."[11] Hightower asserts that in 1889 the mining population numbered two thousand and included Czechs, Slovaks, Slovenes, Hungarians, Belgians, Italians, French, English, Swedes, and Germans.[12] Later census records from 1910 and 1920 affirm the demographic shift that took place during the last decades of the nineteenth century, as more foreign-sounding surnames appear in the ledger records, including Italian miner Antonio Caffro and German miners Frederick Tronier and his son Otto.[13] Paralleling immigration trends in other parts of the United States, nearly two-thirds of the eight thousand coal miners who migrated to early Oklahoma in early twentieth century were foreign-born. Similar to the German migration to the Hill Country in the mid-nineteenth century, most miners brought their entire families with them, and their women and children found employment around the mines. Towns like Krebs, Hartshorne, Alderson, LeHigh, Coalgate, Wilburton, and Stringtown, Oklahoma, developed distinctly immigrant populations in their coal-mining heyday; indeed, Krebs still honors its immigrant past with an annual Italian festival that attracts thousands of visitors to the small community.[14]

Texas was a popular destination for German immigrants of the period. Part of the impetus for migration to central Texas after 1865 was the promotional activity pursued by railroad communities who actively sought settlers to the region. In creating a Bureau of Immigration in 1869, the Texas government under Republican control enthusiastically pursued a "Come to Texas" policy, at least until the fiscally conservative 1876 constitution prohibited state funding for such booster campaigns. From the mid-1870s, the campaign to attract European settlers fell squarely on the shoulders of private organizations and businesses.[15]

After the Civil War, with the collapse of the slave labor system and the breaking up of former plantations, new lands opened up. Further, transient Anglo-Americans proved willing to sell their lands to German migrants and seek opportunities elsewhere.[16] From 1881 to 1885, for example, 5,106 Germans departed from Bremen, Germany, alone and traveled to the Texas port of Galveston.[17]

Much like the Anglo-American immigrants who were attracted to Texas through the *empresario* system, German immigrants were initially drawn to West Central Texas by the offer of a vast land grant, obtained through an association called the *Verein zum Schutze deutscher Einwanderer in Texas* (the Society for the Protection of German Immigrants in Texas), generally known in both English and German as the *Adelsverein*. Comprised of an assortment of wealthy princes and noblemen from numerous provinces throughout Germany, the Adelsverein acquired a huge tract of land, approximately two million acres, from the Republic of Texas, allocating it for the purpose of German settlement. The association then used enticements to draw settlers to the new colony. Future settlers would pay a fixed sum to the association and receive in exchange passage to America, a grant of land, and a free log house. The project was initially supervised by Prince Carl von Solms-Braunfels and later by the Baron von Meusebech. Beginning in 1844, German emigrants boarded ships destined for Galveston, then went by smaller ship to Indianola, the Adelsverein port on Matagorda Bay, and then proceeded inland. From 1844 to 1846, nearly ten thousand German settlers were shipped by the Adelsverein alone, including a number who wound up patronizing Anna Martin's store.[18] Anna's uncle, Louis Martin, was on the first ship of German immigrants to arrive in Texas under the Adelsverein plan on November 23, 1844.[19]

Houston, Austin, Indianola, New Braunfels, Gonzales, and Victoria, also, were among the towns and cities in Texas that benefited demographically from German immigration in the mid-nineteenth century.[20] German immigrants remained in such cities well into the 1880s, prompting one scholar to observe that "one should look to the urban scene in Texas for some of the deepest continental cultural imprints." Regrettably, there is little in-depth scholarship tracing the cultural influences of Germans in preindustrial towns and cities in Texas.[21] This oversight is particularly unfortunate, given that approximately 57 percent of the German population in Texas in 1870 engaged in non-agricultural occupations.[22]

Ledger records from Charles Wolf's store in Austin provide some insight into Germans' encounters in larger Texas communities (although "large" is a relative term, given that the population of Austin was 4,428 in 1870).[23] According to his obituary, Charles Wolf was born in Germany and emigrated to Texas as a teenager with his father in 1860.[24] After apprenticing as a clerk, Wolf opened a small merchandise store on Fifth Street, two years after the end of the Civil War, and the store remained open until his death in May 1913.[25] Described as a prominent business "pioneer" in the city, Wolf garnered respect from his community for his "likeable," "industrious" and "charitable" character: "Scores are in this city—many scores are outside of this—who will at all times proclaim Charles Wolf as having been the best man with the biggest heart and the freest purse that ever came to their assistance."[26] In the end, Wolf's hard work paid off. At the time of his death, Wolf's estate was valued at $300,000, which was ultimately divided between to his wife and four children. The specifics of his "remarkable will" (as the newspaper put it) merited citywide interest in local newspapers in the weeks following Wolf's demise.[27] With such a large estate, less fortunate Austin residents likely relished in the details of how the other half lived.

Wolf recorded sales transactions that took place at his store between the years 1872 and 1875. Compared with Martin's predominantly German clientele in Hedwig's Hill, Wolf's customer base was a much more heterogeneous group. It was at Wolf General Merchandise store in

Austin, for example, that Lem Chambers (the African American porter discussed earlier) in 1873 purchased extravagances such as Port wine, brandy, cigars, and canned oysters and lobster, and seamstress Regina Brinkman in 1874 purchased three pairs of scissors, likely reflecting the professional needs of her business in "embroideries and worsted beadwork."[28] Reflective of the town's ethnic demographics, plenty of Germans frequented the store. A quick overview of surnames appearing in Wolf's ledgers include Blomeke, Friedberger, Freissis, Froehlich, Greideweis, Goerken, Haske, Klein, Krause, Kruger, Kleinschmidt, Plueger, Wolf, Seligman, Stroehmer, and Scholz.[29] Add to the mix customers with the surnames such as Hill, Benford, Bell, Cox, Summers, Hancock, Miller, and Gibson, and the end result is quite an ethnically diverse lot.[30]

Of course, not all of those who passed through Galveston settled in cities and towns; some opted to establish their homes in the rural agricultural areas of Central Texas, such as Hedwig's Hill in Mason County. If Wolf's store addresses the "urban" experience, a handful of extant ledger records from general stores in nineteenth-century Texas tell the story of the rural German immigrant experience. These ledgers feature Germans who first ventured to Texas with the early migrations that took place primarily during the 1840s and 1850s. The ledgers follow their experiences into the latter decades of the nineteenth century. The collections include ledgers from Hermann Fisher's store located twenty miles northwest of New Braunfels, Texas, in the Hill Country of northern Comal County and a loose collection of ledger information from Hermann Ernst's account book from his store in Industry, Texas (the first German town founded in Texas in 1838). However, neither of these collections furnishes as valuable a window into the lived experiences of the German immigrants on the Texas frontier as the ledger collection from Anna Martin's store in Hedwig's Hill. The fact that Martin also recorded her life experiences in her letter to Chapman provides an invaluable firsthand account of life in both early Texas and the small immigrant community of Hedwig's Hill.

Many of the Germans who settled in the region arrived in Texas in the mid- to late 1840s.[31] It was a volatile period, and the term "frontier" aptly describes this inchoate stage in Texas history. Evidently, Martin's first experiences in Texas were marred by fear. In her letter to the banker, she provided the following description of those early years: "It was horrible for a young girl just growing to womanhood who had seen all the nice things young girls had in Germany and then taken abruptly away in the wilderness of Texas without any future where we could not go a step from the house fearing the Indians would all kill us." In the years during and after the Civil War, the situation apparently worsened: "From 1861 to 1865 and till the seventies, we had a horrible time here on the frontier. All the bad element running away from the battlefields gathered here on the frontier and robbed and killed man and beast all around us. And the Indians we had to deal with also, but the Indians we knew were our enemies, but the others we did not know, friend or foe."[32] As daunting as the task seemed in the early years, life on the frontier fortunately improved for Anna and her family, as it did for many of the immigrants who arrived on American shores in the mid-nineteenth century.

After landing in ports along the Texas coast, most German immigrants journeyed inland, some eventually making their way to the north slope of the Llano River in Hill Country and forming the community that came to be known as Hedwig's Hill. Once they established their homesteads in Hill Country, these immigrants truly "settled" in the area. Indeed, there is ample evidence of these first-wave immigrants in the records from Anna Martin's store in the late 1880s, forty years after their arrival. The story of Henry Julius Behrens provides a fitting example. In the fall of 1845, Henry Conrad Behrens with his wife, Sophia, their eight-year-old son, Henry Julius, and their three daughters sailed from Bremenshaven, Germany, aboard the *Gerhard Hermann*. They arrived in Galveston, Texas, on January 10, 1846.[33] The Behrens family traveled with other German families who also appeared some forty years later in the Martin store records, including the families of Conrad Pluenneke and Christian Leifeste. After taking a second smaller ship to Indianola, Texas, the Behrens departed for New Braunfels, Texas, on February 2, 1846, and shortly thereafter moved on to the new German settlement of Fredericksburg.

They stayed in Fredericksburg for a few years before moving to the north bank of the Llano River in 1849, where they created a new settlement called Castell. According to the son, Henry Julius Behrens, life in Fredericksburg was difficult, at best: "Some days [we] didn't have anything to eat and very little to wear. . . . We took a stocking each [he and another boy] and went to the camp [Ft. Martin Scott] which was a short distance. [We] picked up the grains of corn that oxen (and horses) had scattered while eating."[34] Such scraps served as family meals, sustaining the Behrens through their most trying periods in frontier Texas. Shortly after the family moved to Castell, the father, Henry Conrad Behrens, acquired a grant of land from the German Immigration Company in late 1849, but unfortunately, he did not live to enjoy his new land for very long, as he was killed by Indians in 1850. The tract of land was located four miles north of Camp Mason, near the area where, in 1853, the small community of Hedwig's Hill was established. Young Henry left the area briefly in the 1860s and served under Captain Davis in the Second Frontier District, Texas State Troops, stationed at Camp Davis in Gillespie County.[35]

Behrens evidently returned to Mason County after the Civil War, as he appears decades later in the pages of Anna Martin's general store ledgers. He purchased from the Martin store, for example, sugar, bacon, and a gallon of oil on March 5, 1888.[36] By the time of these purchases, Henry's relationship with the Martins had spanned thirty years. In 1857 he had begun working as a butcher for Charles Martin, Anna's husband, who had a contract to supply beef to Fort Mason. Henry's sister Sophie worked as a domestic servant in the Martin household during the same period. By the 1880s, Henry Julius Behrens had become a prosperous farmer and rancher; he established a community school in the mid-1880s that bore his name, the Behrens Community School.[37] In 1881, he traveled to Austin to purchase lumber for a new schoolhouse, to be located only a few hundred yards from his house. Operating out of the same building, Behrens organized a Sunday school in 1883 for the community's young people. From his meager immigrant beginnings, Behrens had by the 1880s achieved enough success to enable him to give something back to his community. Behrens's interest in developing educational facilities in his region suggests that community activism and moral improvement crossed ethnic as well as racial boundaries.

In many ways, the experiences of Henry Behrens and his family were similar to those of his German contemporaries who migrated to Texas in the mid- to late 1840s and early 1850s. The German community in Hedwig's Hill was defined by its commitment to the region and by the longevity of the members' relationships to one another—many of these families had met initially on the ship crossing the Atlantic. From landing to settlement, they experienced their new land together. As Anna Martin noted in her 1904 letter, written almost fifty years after her family arrived in America, she had lived all her life among Germans, "in a German settlement," where her "dealings were most with Germans." Hedwig's Hill was an oasis of German culture, a tightly knit German enclave, steeped in German traditions and values, but situated in the heart of Texas. Reflecting the pluralistic trends of the period, the immigrants who settled in the region left an indelible imprint on the region, both socially and economically, in their agricultural innovations and social rituals such as Christmas celebrations. They were both Germans and, as Anna noted, "good loyal Americans."

In many ways, Anna Martin's immigrant experience mirrored that of her long-standing friend and customer Henry Julius Behrens. Leaving her father behind for a few months, Anna traveled with most of her family from Bremen, Germany, to Galveston, arriving at the port on December 10, 1858, Anna's fifteenth birthday. They also took a steamer from Galveston to Indianola, leaving that location shortly after to venture inland to the small community of Hedwig's Hill in Mason County. Located on Matagorda Bay, Indianola emerged as the principal dropping off point for Germans entering the Hill Country of Central Texas in the mid-nineteenth century. From there, migrants moved overland to regions as far west and north as Mason County. Earlier in 1858, Anna's uncle Louis Martin had named the small settlement Hedwig's Hill in honor of his mother, Hedwig. Anna and her family resided with her uncle while they waited for her father to join them in America; he had remained in Germany for six months after his family's departure in order to settle his affairs.[38] Her father's small business had fallen on hard times. She wrote, "When I was nine years old, he [Anna's father] established business for himself in Solingen, the great steel manufacturing town." However, she continued, "In 1858, my father failed in his business. My mother who was from an aristocratic family, and all well to do, could not face poverty among her wealthy relations and friends so she left old Germany with her six children, of which I was the oldest, without telling anybody good-bye."[39]

Apparently, the Martins' hard luck story was not unusual in Germany in the middle of the nineteenth century. By the 1850s, the German economy was undergoing the first shift to industrial capitalism and, along with that shift unfortunately all the social and economic growing pains associated with such transformation. Historian Mack Walker has argued that a principal impetus behind much of the German migration to Texas in the mid-nineteenth century was a reaction against modernity, more specifically industrial capitalism, which had increasingly pressured small family farmers off their land and driven small independent artisans and merchants out of business. Modern industry and capitalism exposed the small German craftsman or family businessman to a scale of competition that threatened to overwhelm not only his economic independence but his dignity and social status as well.[40] It appears that the Martin family business could no longer compete in the rapidly changing economy where large industrial firms bankrupted small family enterprises. The Martins chose to move rather than risk losing their status. Perhaps on the Texas frontier, the small German craftsman or businessman could regain his place, dignity, and honor once again. Like the scores of other immigrants boarding ships to America, Anna's parents hoped to find prosperity and make a fresh start in their new land.

Walker relates the negative reaction toward industrialism to the context of the artistic Biedermeier movement popular in Germany in the mid-nineteenth century. Named for a form of artistic and cultural expression that celebrated stability, privacy, serenity, traditional values, and domesticity, the Biedermeier style reflected a reaction against the massive cultural and economic changes associated with industrialism.[41] The Germans who migrated to Texas in the 1840s and 1850s sought to return to a more traditional, preindustrial world. To be sure, by the middle decades of the nineteenth century, America could hardly be considered pre-capitalist. However, industrial capitalism affected different regions of the country in different ways. By and large, the

Germans who migrated to America during the Biedermeier period avoided the industrial centers of the Northeast and instead headed inland—either to smaller centers in the Midwest or to rural areas like the Hill Country in Central Texas. They did not expect to escape capitalism altogether, rather, they hoped to return to an earlier period of capitalist development, a period before large-scale industrial firms virtually swallowed up their small family enterprises.

Immigrants who arrived in the initial years of the Adelsverein and who later appear in Martin's ledgers from the 1880s include Jacob Bauer, George and Bernhardt Durst, Henry Hasse, Jr., John Keller, Fritz Kothmann, Christoph and Henry Leifeste, Conrad Pluenneke, Conrad Simon, and Conrad Wisseman.[42] Many of the other names in the store ledgers are names of people who arrived in America, like Anna Martin herself, in the late 1840s and early 1850s. As was the case with the Behrens family, some not only left Germany at the same time but traveled on the same ship. Jacob Bauer sailed to America with his parents, Melchior and Rosina Bauer, on the ship the *Element*, which landed at Galveston on October 22, 1846. Similarly, George and Bernhardt Durst traveled with their parents, John and Christina Margarethe Durst, and their siblings on the *Element*, landing in Galveston first, then proceeding to Indianola and Fredericksburg, before settling in the Hedwig's Hill community. Forty years later, Jacob Bauer and the Durst brothers ended up only pages apart in the ledger records for Anna Martin's store. Literally growing up with the community, these immigrants would have a lasting impact on the small settlement of Hedwig's Hill and the Hill Country region in general.

The German colony established by Friedrich Ernst in 1831 in northwestern Austin County predated both the founding of the Republic of Texas and the Adelsverein migration, the latter by more than a decade. On April 16, 1831, Ernst received a land grant from the Mexican government that enabled him to begin farming in the region. He planted fruit trees and began growing crops, including tobacco. Demonstrating a great deal of commercial initiative, Ernst produced cigars from the tobacco and sold them in the nearby towns of San Felipe, Houston, and Galveston. Enthusiastic about the potential of his new country, Ernst wrote a letter to a friend back in Germany that was subsequently published in a local newspaper. As a result of this letter, Friedrich Ernst is credited with starting the first steady stream of German migration to Texas. In the letter, Ernst detailed the positive attributes of his new land, describing the mild climate as similar to that of southern Italy with fields of wildflowers and rolling hills. For the industrious immigrant, Texas offered every married German a league of land, "the only expense being one hundred and sixty dollars for surveying and recording."[43] As Germans arrived in Texas, Ernst served as their principal benefactor; he assisted German immigrants in their new setting by opening up his home as a boardinghouse for travelers and providing loans. So significant was Ernst's role in assisting Germans in their new land that he earned himself the nickname "father of the immigrants."[44] Ernst founded the town of Industry in 1838, noted for being the first German town in Texas. While the town's founder died in 1848, the small community pressed on, shifting its economic focus from tobacco to cotton in the 1850s.[45]

Remnants of information concerning this small historic community are captured in ledger records from Hermann Ernst's general store, which operated in Industry during the 1870s and 1880s. The store actually opened for business in the late 1830s during the very earliest stages of German migration. Initially it was owned and operated by John G. Seiper (Hermann Ernst's brother-in-law, the son-in-law of Hermann's father, Friedrich Ernst). Seiper was named the community's postmaster in 1838, although the first written records of the post office in Industry date from December 23, 1840.[46] Hermann Ernst took over the management of many of his father's businesses when Friedrich died in 1848. After the death of John Seiper in 1855, Hermann also assumed operation of the community's general store. Born in 1827, Hermann was a mere toddler when his family traveled to Texas in 1831. He became so acculturated to his new land that his father, describing him in a letter in the 1830s, wrote, "My Hermann is growing remarkably and is turning into a real Mexican."[47] From his father's perspective, little Hermann absorbed much of the cross-cultural exchange between these newly arrived Germans and the locals.

As a retailer, creditor, and employer, Hermann Ernst occupied a position of importance in the small community of Industry. Through his store, Ernst established relationships with virtually all the area's residents, and his account records indicate that he served as a middle man between his largely cotton-farming clientele and outside markets. Many of his clients paid their store accounts with bales of cotton, which Ernst, in turn, hauled to Brenham, Texas, to be distributed and sold. Cattle were also brokered out of his store. On March 1, 1882, for example, three bulls and one heifer were sold to the store owner for $38.00.[48] Ernst also hired laborers and paid them through his account ledgers.

Like many of his counterparts in other areas of Texas and Oklahoma, Ernst played a prominent role in the local economy, which he parlayed into a position of elevated social importance within the community. He assumed responsibility for the administration of Industry's modest educational system. For example, through the store he was in charge of paying the local schoolteacher, who was paid $1.50 a year for each child taught. The store owner paid the teacher, a year in advance from October 1 to September 30 in 1875 and 1876. School repairs and school taxes were also assessed and charged to customers' accounts through the store. On January 17, 1876, Ernst recorded an entry for "Schoolhouse repair (on each child)"—Louise and Adolph $1.00.[49] In December 1881, Simmons School House assessed a tax of $1.50 for each pupil, which was subsequently applied to customers' accounts. Still in the 1880S, schoolteacher T. R. Simmons was paid for teaching through Ernst's store; he received a $14.75 credit for teaching school, recorded on his account in November 1883.[50] Clearly, German immigrants placed a high priority on providing their children with an education—even in rural settings, a situation not unlike that of many of their contemporaries in the American Indian and African American communities (or, for that matter, myriad ethnic communities across the country).

Hermann Ernst's ledgers also provide insight into the lives and consumption practices of his largely German clientele. Between 1846 and 1850, Ernst F. G. Knolle and his brother Frederick purchased a large tract of land adjacent to the Ernst league, establishing themselves as prominent landholders and cotton producers in the region. In 1857 Knolle and another investor, Andreas Buenger, constructed the town's first cotton gin.[51] Buenger received credit on his account at the store for cutting hay in the surrounding area. On July 7, 1882, Ernst credited

Buenger's account $10.00 "for cutting 10 acres of hay at $1.00 per acre."[52] And Knolle made regular purchases from Hermann Ernst's store. For example, on December 18, 1869, he purchased a coat, a pair of boots, sugar, pepper, and two pocket handkerchiefs.[53] E. Knolle (Sen.) bought ten yards of calico on April 24, ten bottles of lye, soda, and medicine on May 9, and six cups and saucers on June 19, 1876.[54]

The presence of both Hermann Ernst and E. Knolle in ledgers recorded several decades after they arrived in the area suggests that, like those who settled in Hedwig's Hill, the German immigrants in the Industry area tended to remain in the region, establishing long-standing communities and relationships with their fellow expatriates. Other key inclusions in Ernst's ledgers are the transactions made by Madam L. Stoehr, Hermann's mother. Stoehr deposited $270.00 with the store and received 10 percent interest from her son; in this capacity, Ernst's store served as a regional bank.[55] Stoehr received a $10.00 credit from the store for "1 oxe" on October 30, 1872.[56] Ernst employed his son Wilhilm to work for him in January 1878. The transaction is recorded in his ledger as of January 1878: Wm. Ernst "bargained to work for one year at $8.00 a month."[57]

During Frederick Law Olmstead's visit to Texas in the early 1850s, the travel writer expressed a favorable impression of the Germans in Texas, in part, because of his belief that the immigrants held an antislavery political position. In truth, the politics of Germans in Texas both before and after the Civil War was rather complex in regard to slavery as well as to a host of other contentious issues. Despite Olmstead's perception, Germans did not unvaryingly oppose slavery and the subsequent secession, although most of them did. Friedrich Ernst, the "father" of German migration, adopted a cautious approach to the issue of slavery and counseled his countrymen to do the same. He believed it unwise for Germans to take a defiant stand against slavery, fearing "that the slaveowners might become antagonistic toward the German immigrants and deny them political rights."[58] Like the majority of German immigrants in Texas, Anna Martin's husband, Charles, opposed the Confederacy and faced strong retribution as a consequence: "My husband was a strong Republican and was often threatened to be killed. If a stranger came to our door I greeted him always in fear that they came to kill my husband." Martin continued, "These kind of people killed my uncle and brother-in-law, hanging them on a mesquite tree with their own rope, on a trip to Mexico where they wanted to get provisions for us, our ports being all blockaded."[59]

According to his biographers, the German store owner Charles Schreiner fought for the Confederacy during the Civil War: "His service with the Texas Rangers had undoubtedly instilled into him a love of Texas and an appreciation of the Southern cause, even though he was not and never had been a slave owner." Schreiner operated a mercantile firm in Kerrville, Texas, located deep in the heart of the Hill Country. He served in the Confederate army for three and a half years before returning to his home in Central Texas. He was the only one of four Schreiner brothers to fight for the South—indeed, the majority of his German counterparts sided with the Union army, even if they did not join the fight.[60] What is not clear in the Schreiner case is whether the store owner chose the Confederate side because of a true commitment to the southern cause or because he felt pressure or threats from secessionist neighbors. At least one historian has argued that many Germans joined the Confederacy because they were intimidated by the actions of local Texas rebels.[61]

Despite the exceptions such as Charles Schreiner, most Germans immigrants did not find unity with their fellow Texans—many of whom were from the South—on the highly divisive issues of the Civil War. Thus, in veering from the southern cause, the bulk of Germans immigrants left an important political imprint on the Texas countryside during the war years (doing so, even in the face of violent retaliation). It is worth noting that Schreiner, whose store and business interests were in Kerrville, quite south of Hedwig's Hill, served as a trusted advisor and friend to Anna Martin, suggesting that Germans and their cultural ties were not isolated to small enclaves but rather spanned across the region of Central Texas.[62]

Perhaps it is not surprising that German farming practices heavily influenced the agricultural development of the areas settled by the new immigrants, particularly in the Hill Country. From the earliest periods of migration, the western German settlements were characterized by numerous kitchen gardens, which featured an array of vegetables both consumed and sold by the settlers, including varieties of vegetables not grown in the usual Anglo-Americans gardens such as kohlrabi, mustard, parsley, and leeks.[63] Another agricultural variation more common among German settlers than their southern Anglo-American counterparts was the practice and preponderance of haymaking; Terry Jordan attributes such differences to their respective agricultural heritages. Evidently, the draft animal of choice of the German western settlements was the ox, which again differentiated Germans from the area's Anglo-American settlers. Oxen were cheaper to purchase than horses, the draft animal of choice for most non-Germans, and the cost of keeping oxen was less than the cost of keeping horses. Jordan observed that, "In the antebellum period, and even as late as 1870, the ox was in almost universal use among the Germans, in contrast to the Anglo-Americans of the same area, who relied much more on the horse."[64] While economic considerations played an important role in the discrepancy, it is also significant that the ox had been the traditional farm draft animal of Germany, proving that the traditional farming practices of their homeland crossed the ocean with the settlers. Affirming the presence of oxen in Industry, they appear on the above mentioned transaction of Madam Stoehr, and M. Schulz received a $14.00 credit from the Ernst store for an ox on January 25, 1875.[65]

In Mason County, cattle ranching eventually developed into the region's primary agricultural activity. This was especially true for the 1880s, the period covered in the ledgers from Anna Martin's store. In fact, Prince von Solms-Braunfels had predicted the suitability and profitability of cattle to the region as early as the 1840s, noting in his earliest correspondence that "Cattle should take the first place among domestic animals."[66] Cattle ranches were first established in the area not by Germans or Anglo-Americans but by New Spain settlers around San Antonio in the mid- to late eighteenth century. By the time the Germans arrived in the Texas Republic, Anglo and Spanish herding practices had converged, ultimately shaping the nature of ranching in southern and Central Texas. Recognizing the suitability of the land on which they settled and, no doubt, drawing from what they observed among Mexican and Anglo-Americans, the German immigrants entered in the business of cattle ranching shortly after their arrival. The physical environment of Mason Country was well suited to raising cattle. With the area's gently sloping ground (natural topography that allowed for protection from the cold), open ranges, and abundant grasses, little effort was needed on the part of the immigrants to raise cattle successfully. Although the physical environment lent itself to ranching and the new immigrants eagerly pursued the venture, however, the development of the cattle industry in Mason County was a gradual process, beginning in the 1840s and continuing to the present day.[67]

The German impact on the Texas frontier was by no means restricted to the realm of agriculture. From the arrival of immigrants in the mid-nineteenth century, German cultural influences shaped the development of Hill Country in Central Texas. Anna Martin described Hedwig's Hill as a "German settlement," and German rituals, routines, values, and language strongly influenced the *Kulturebe* (cultural heritage) of the community.[68] While ledgers from Anna Martin's store indicate that many of her customers stocked up on staples of the German diet such as sauerkraut, mustard, and vinegar for pickling, the great majority of items listed on their accounts were interchangeable with those of non-German consumers at general stores not only throughout Texas and Oklahoma but across the nation and overseas. Indeed, staples such as tobacco, sugar, flour, bacon, coffee, and fabrics appear most frequently on customer accounts at the Martin store.[69] Moreover, the purchasing of items like sauerkraut was not restricted to German immigrants. Account entries from the Gauntt Bros. store in Athens, Texas, reveal that non-German consumers also purchased the flavorful German cabbage. In 1887 and 1888, for example, J. G. Stewart, William Davis, and store owner William [Bill] Gauntt all acquired large quantities of sauerkraut from the store.[70] Such evidence suggests that German immigrants to Texas did not simply produce items for their own consumption. German commodities were sold at general stores around the state, including stores not owned by German immigrants. Moreover, commodities such as sauerkraut were popular with Germans and non-Germans alike. Even at the level of eating and general food choices, the German imprint was felt in the daily lives of both Germans and non-Germans living in the Hill Country and other parts of Texas.

Records from German-owned stores in Texas demonstrate that cultural influences had a decidedly seasonal element to them, particularly when it came to the Christmas holiday. Entries from Martin's store show the importance the German immigrants of Hedwig's Hill gave to carrying on their holiday customs, reflected in their Christmas purchasing. A number of historians whose research focuses on the subject of Christmas in America argue that, through a selective reworking of older European customs, Americans by the late decades of the nineteenth century recast the Christmas holiday to fit American culture, most especially American middle-class culture.[71] Over the course of the nineteenth century, the middle-class emphasis on social order, moral probity, and Protestantism refashioned Christmas from its more secular and less genteel roots to a more ordered and "respectable" holiday, both religiously and socially. Victorians remodeled the Christmas holiday to fit their own social norms. As one historian observed, "Santa Claus, the exchange of presents, a decorated evergreen tree, and Christmas cards—all were major new elements added to Christmas by the Victorians."[72] The new elements that formed the basis of the Americanized version of the holiday drew upon older European icons and rituals, particularly German traditions. On the transformation of the European figure of Santa Claus, historian Penne Restad wrote, "Through this American saint, parents schooled their children in the subtle inflections of the dawning Victorian era, coaching them on the fundamentals of pluralistic Protestantism, demonstrating their affection, and domesticating the new forces of the marketplace by buying toys and other gifts."[73]

As one might imagine, given that so many Texans migrated from southern states, southern influences also shaped Texas holiday rituals, proving at least as important as European cultural traditions. Indeed, ledger records from Texas stores suggest that holiday rituals in the state drew heavily upon both European and southern traditions, sometimes creating an interesting hybrid of the two. Southerners placed their own stamp on the American Christmas season, for example. Unlike their Yankee brethren, southerners saved their fireworks for Christmas instead of the Fourth of July.[74] Prior to the 1830s and 1840s, fireworks had also been a part of Christmas celebrations in the North; however, part of the process of making Christmas more sacral and more ordered in the North, at least in the eyes of middle-class reformers, involved extirpating public fireworks displays and encouraging private celebrations in the home.⁷⁵ Such reforms were far less successful in the South. For southerners, noise and public spectacle were all part of the fun. In fact, once the last fireworks fizzled out, more adventurous southerners resorted to the use of black powder and anvil for their noisemaking celebrations. As one southern historian observed, anvil shooting was part of every Christmas affair: "Country stores, school and church grounds boomed with thunderous impacts of these black-powder charges, and evidence of this primitive custom has lingered in many farmyards."⁷⁶

Besides fireworks and black powder, a variety of holiday food selections and gifts appeared frequently on southern shopping lists, including oranges, apples, dolls, nuts, oyster crackers, coconuts, Roman candles, Jew's harps, rattlers, and a variety of specialty candies such as kisses, rolls, and candy trunks.⁷⁷ In keeping with the southern flavor of its economy and culture, in Texas shopping lists often mirrored those in other parts of the South. For example, a number of account entries from William Wadsworth's general merchandise firm in Matagorda, Texas (located just inland from the Texas Gulf Coast), indicate that southern traditions heavily influenced regional holiday consumption patterns. On December 21, 1885, W. S. Stewart purchased two dozen apples, three rubber dolls, and a dozen fire crackers; F. L. Rugeley charged a toy pistol to his account. On Christmas Eve, George Bedford purchased two boy's hats and a dozen fire crackers; Harry Sirrell purchased one pound of candy; Jonathon H. McCain purchased one pound of stick candy; C. D. Bruce purchased half a dozen fire crackers and one pound of candy; A. C. Bruce purchased a dozen apples, one pound of candy, and half a dozen fire crackers; and H. Cookenboo purchased two dozen apples, three packages of fire crackers, and two pounds of candy.⁷⁸ Clearly, candy and firecrackers were popular Christmas purchases with Matagorda residents.

The impact of Christmas on general consumption patterns in rural outposts in Texas and early Oklahoma varied significantly depending on both the location and the economic fortunes of the population. Those living in poverty could ill afford to partake in the lavish spending that was becoming increasingly associated with the Christmas holiday, a celebration both defined and perpetuated by the middle class. This was true for both rural and urban poor. An examination of ledger entries from the McKinney & Brown store in Jacksonville, Texas, during the month of December in the late 1870s and early 1880s, suggests that area residents were either not willing or not able to spend their hard-earned dollars on goodies for the Christmas holiday. In fact, Christmas seems to have had little impact on the shopping patterns of many of the store's clientele. For example, the purchases for Dr. J. T. Simpson in the week leading up to the Christmas holiday from the McKinney & Brown store include: on December 19, an undershirt, coffee, and a bottle of snuff; on December 20, six yards of cotton strip fabric; on December 21, ticking fabric and a spool of cotton; on December 22, coffee; and on December 26, two pounds of shot.[79] Simpson's purchases were not unusual. Although specialty items like apples and peaches appeared on the account of store owner W. A. Brown, most of his customers did not veer from their usual shopping habits during the holiday season.[80] Items usually associated with Christmas shopping such as toys, candles, and firecrackers appeared only sporadically on the shopping lists of those who frequented the store during the month of December. The fact that many store customers did not engage in extravagant Christmas spending should not be interpreted as lack of enthusiasm for the holiday itself. Indeed, it seems likely that many living on a tight budget celebrated Christmas on their own terms and chose perhaps to buy practical items for their family or gave homemade gifts.

The Christmas holiday performed important cultural work in communities throughout Texas and Indian Territory, particularly in newly established settlements such as Jacksonville and McAlester. Even though spending habits did not alter much, Christmas still left its mark on lives of town residents. The town hosted a public holiday celebration in 1874 during which a "committee of gentlemen" presented every child in the community with a Christmas present. After the gift-giving celebration, all the town residents came together under a community Christmas tree, exchanged "Merry Christmases" and happy good nights and then dispersed to their homes. Reporting on the success of the 1874 Christmas celebration in Jacksonville, the *Texas Intelligencer* observed, "We believe this was the first public Christmas tree ever given in our town, and we heartily rejoice at its success; for all occasions of this kind bring out the better side of human nature, serve to develop kindly generous feelings, and bind closer the golden links of friendship and love."[81] In effect, the holiday celebration presented an opportunity for town leaders to demonstrate their generosity, promote community cohesion, and elevate the level of civic boosterism.

The small coal mining community of McAlester also celebrated the Christmas holiday with a community tree. In 1876, the *Oklahoma Star* encouraged town residents to come out and join in the festivities. The Christmas holiday provided civic leaders with the opportunity to cement social cohesion and celebrate community spirit. Meanwhile, J. J. McAlester took advantage of the holiday to advertise to potential customers that his store was well stocked with Christmas goods, including drums, hobby horses, wax dolls, whistles, rattle boxes, and stick and fancy candies.[82] At a national level, the Americanized celebration of Christmas provided an opportunity for social unity and contributed to the effort of creating a cohesive national identity because the holiday festivities pulled together disparate groups into a collective whole. At the local level in communities such as Jacksonville and McAlester also, the festivities performed a similar role.

As early as the 1830s, the German holiday ritual of gift giving among family members inspired Americans to incorporate such a custom in their own holiday celebrations. In *Christmas in America*, Penne Restad describes George Ticknor's visit to Dresden in 1835, where Ticknor observed the German holiday ritual firsthand. So impressed was he with what he saw, Ticknor wrote, there "was nothing very valuable or beautiful in what was given, yet it was all received with so much pleasure by the parents and the elder brother, that the children were delighted, and kissed us all round very heartily."[83] In accordance with traditional customs, the Christmas tree was usually decorated secretly by the parents or the older children on the afternoon of December 24. Then, after the family dinner, a little bell was rung or the children were told that *Weihnachtsmann* had come and had prepared a tree and left presents for them.[84] The children could then proceed to the Christmas room and gleefully see what goodies awaited them under the Christmas tree. Early evidence of the German Christmas tradition in Texas can be found in the writings of Friedrich Hermann Seele, who traveled to Texas in the winter of 1843. In recollecting his first holiday celebrations in the state, Seele described his visits to German homes, which featured not only Christmas trees but also an array of presents for the household's children.[85]

Old World holiday traditions came to Kerrville, Texas, with the arrival of the community's first Christmas tree. According to one local account, this was quite different from the later adaptations. It generated enormous excitement in the small Hill Country town: "It was hung with red apples and stick candy, brought from San Antonio, cookies cut in the shapes of animals and birds, decorated with red, white, and blue sugar, nuts wrapped in silver and gold paper and long chains made of strips of bright paper. With homemade tallow candles to light the tree, it appeared very wonderful, and people came from miles around to see and enjoy its splendor."[86] The holiday symbol performed dual functions in the community—serving as a link to the Old World and creating an occasion for social cohesion in the New World.

While all family members exchanged gifts, German parents usually gave much more to their children than they received; thus, for the most part, nineteenth-century Germans shared present-day perceptions of the holiday—Christmas was for kids. Ledger entries from Anna Martin's store reflect the emphasis her German clientele placed on gift giving, especially when it came to their children. In addition to a number of grocery items, for example, on December 17, 1885, D. Kothmann purchased two dolls, two toy pistols, and a toy monkey. Conrad Pluenneke, who served the Hedwig's Hill community as both doctor and preacher, on December 19, 1885, bought two children's hats, two yards of ribbon, two dozen apples, one cap, toys, two dolls, one dozen plates, candy, and a set of cups and saucers. On December 21, 1885, A. A. Reichenau charged candy, a toy gun, slippers, a doll, and "Xmas" candles to his account. On the same day, John Keller purchased candy, three Winchesters center fire (rifle cartridges), fire crackers, a toy, a dozen Christmas candles, two pounds of currants, and a bottle of wine. On December 22, 1885, cattle raiser Jakob Bauer acquired a doll, four trumpets, three French harps, mixed candy, fire crackers, and eighteen apples. And finally, another resident cattle rancher, Fritz Kothmann, purchased eight dozen apples, toys for $1.00, mixed candy, stick candy, seven different types of picture books, lemons, two yards of satin, and toys for $2.25.[87]

Account entries from Anna Martin's ledgers provide ample evidence of the kinds of specialty items acquired before the Christmas holiday by her predominantly German clientele. The presence of firecrackers on customer accounts suggests that Germans in the region shared some holiday rituals with their American neighbors. Still, the fact that so many of Martin's clientele not only made special Christmas purchases but focused their purchases on their children—who were so fundamental to traditional German gift giving—indicates that continuity, rather than change, largely shaped Christmas in Hedwig's Hill in the mid-1880s. The small German settlements of the Hill Country had yet to experience the adoption of an Americanized version of the holiday, one that would be drawn from a myriad of cultural influences, including, but not limited to, northern Europe. And while the immigrants living in Hill Country began absorbing outside cultures from the moment they stepped off the ships in Galveston harbor, they clearly remained largely committed to their German cultural traditions well into the last decades of the nineteenth century.

For the German immigrants of Hedwig's Hill, Christmas was not only a celebration of the present but a cultural link to the past—and by extension, the old country. Christmas was a significant event in the German communities of Central Texas. The consuming rites of German immigrants residing in the Hedwig's Hill community show that they attached deep significance and importance to the Christmas holiday and generally stayed true to their traditional holiday customs. While Christmas in Hedwig's Hill was very much a German affair, it appears that residents incorporated at least some Anglo customs, particularly the southern purchases like firecrackers and gunpowder. Still, many of the traditions that would eventually be considered American Christmas customs can be traced to northern Europe, especially Germany and Holland, including Santa Claus (*Sankt Nikolaus*), Kris Kringle (*Christkindlein*), and the Christmas tree (*Tannenbaum*).[58] In addition to these holiday icons, a German Christmas included such rituals as hanging advents wreaths; lighting candles and leaving them in the windows, "so the Christ Child, who might be wandering in the dark streets, would know he was welcome to enter"; and most important, decorating a Christmas tree—and placing gifts under the tree, to be opened by family members on Christmas Eve.[59]

Anna Martin faced enormous challenges on the Texas frontier in providing for her family after her husband's sickness, infirmity, and ultimate death, and unfortunately her upper-class upbringing in Germany had not prepared her for such challenges. There can be no doubt that, like many of her German contemporaries, Anna needed to adapt to the conditions of her new environment. And yet, the continuity of the Hedwig's Hill community is considerable. Among her customers there were Germans who had traveled to America on the same ships; they had developed new communities together and maintained ties with each other for forty, fifty, and sixty years after their arrival. Whether they were part of the Adelsverein program or in one of the later waves of migration, the German immigrants cited in Martin's ledgers followed remarkably similar paths in establishing new homes in Central Texas.[90] These immigrants left an indelible imprint on their new surroundings, affecting, from the outset, the region's social and economic development. To a lesser degree (in terms of demographics), European immigrants left a similar cultural impression on the small coal-mining communities of southeastern Oklahoma, beginning in the 1880s and continuing onward. In the Hedwig's Hill community of Texas, however, German influences were felt in the realms of agriculture, consumption patterns, diet, and holiday rituals. German immigrants engaged in a system of cultural exchange with those outside of their community, profoundly shaping the emerging cultural identity of the Hill Country in Central Texas while remaining committed to their own ethnic heritage.

Chapter 6

Commodities from Local, Regional, and National Perspectives

IT SHOULD BE CLEAR BY NOW THAT store records provide a remarkable perspective on the day-to-day lives of persons living in Texas and Indian Territory in the 1870s and 1880s. Ledgers detail not only who engaged in commercial relations (the merchants and their clients), but what types of goods were purchased by those who frequented general stores. Shifting the focus to the goods recorded in ledgers enables us both to see what was available locally and to draw comparisons with purchases made by consumers in other regions of the country. The focus in this chapter is exclusively on the commodities themselves in order for us to address a number of important questions: Do such commodities help to define this region in any meaningful way? How do consumption patterns in Texas and Indian Territory differ from those in other regions of the country? Does the sale of any commodity in these regions provide new insight to any long-standing historical questions? Do commodities from these regions reflect larger national trends? Does local purchasing shed any light on the larger social questions of the period?

At a national level, there can be no doubt that alcohol was one of the most contentious commodities available to consumers during the 1870s and 1880s. Many people considered the elimination of the sale of alcohol the most pervasive social issue of the day, especially women, Christian reformers, and employers. For women, the issue generally came down to the threat that the consumption of alcohol posed to the family. Both women and Christian reformers abhorred the effects of drinking on working-class families, pointing to the link between drinking and violence. Employers, on the other hand, argued that alcohol consumption led to less productivity in the workplace. The concern over alcohol in late-nineteenth-century America was serious enough for Frances Willard, president of the Woman's Christian Temperance Union (WCTU), to describe the temperance campaign as a war: "There is a war about this in America, a war of mothers and daughters, sisters and wives. There is another sort of war and I want to have the boys and girls follow me as I talk to them and I think I can make you understand me. There is a war between the rum shops and religion. They stand against each other, insurmountable and unassailable foes."[1] A war? Surely such language points to the contentiousness of the product and the high intensity that some reformers brought to the temperance movement.

The spirit of reform captivated middle-class Americans in particular, as alcohol consumption and the social problems associated with it increasingly became the subject of national debate. One of the many ramifications of this debate was that it inspired middle-class women to participate in social reform movements, a political role for women that was relatively rare before this period. Such female activism was by no means welcomed by all, especially in the more traditional southern states. In the 1820s, temperance became a mass movement and advocates promoted the idea of moderation when it came to alcohol use, but this stance hardened over time so that by the 1870s and 1880s temperance meant total abstinence from alcohol.[2] With battle lines drawn, exponents on both sides of the issue lobbied legislatures at the local, state, and national level to adopt their position. Not surprisingly, ledger records provide insight on both the popularity of this controversial product and the effects of temperance crusades in early Texas and Indian Territory during the period.

Two events that transpired during the same week in 1874 demonstrate that the West had a rather divided mind on the subject of alcohol consumption. On February 24, 1874, the ladies of Manhattan, Kansas, as part of a much larger national women's crusade embarked on a campaign to close down the saloons in their community. They sent postcards to saloon keepers in Manhattan, which threatened that they [the Ladies Committee Temperance] would enter the saloons and use prayers, pleading, and singing in an effort to close down the salacious businesses. Similar campaigns were waged in other east Kansas cities including

Fort Scott, Leavenworth, and Lawrence. These efforts made little headway against saloon owners in the short term, but they planted the seeds for long-term success, and Kansas enacted prohibition in 1880.[3] While there was clearly success by the late nineteenth century for the temperance advocates in midwestern states such as Kansas, the same could not be said of the urban industrial centers of the Northeast. In fact, temperance reform faced stiff opposition in cities from Democratic-leaning ethnic communities who favored the continuing sale of alcohol. Thus, temperance success was initially achieved in small rural centers and not in industrializing urban centers with large immigrant populations.

This said, successful temperance campaigns similar to the Kansas efforts were slow to materialize in Texas. On February 28, 1874, four days after the ladies of Manhattan initiated their assault on local saloons, John Craft made two purchases of whiskey from the J. L. McInnis store in Webberville, Texas; his first purchase cost fifty cents and his second seventy-five cents.[4] It is quite unlikely that, after leaving the McInnis store, Mr. Craft met with spirited opposition from the ladies of the Webberville community. And why should he? After all, he was merely conducting a legal sales transaction at the local store. Similar transactions took place in a wide range of towns, cities, and rural outposts across nineteenth-century Texas. For example, during the same month of February, H. Boldebuck purchased a half gallon of whiskey from the Charles Wolf mercantile firm in Austin. Shortly thereafter, Jesse Delona purchased a full bottle of gin from the same Austin store.[5] While temperance reformers directed their attacks at saloons, general stores discreetly provided alcohol to customers willing to make the investment, and there were plenty of buyers. As one southern historian observed, no other place, including the saloon, afforded a man the golden opportunity to get drunk while accomplishing the shopping for his household.[6] To the chagrin of many temperance advocates in the region, Texas was wet. It remained so for the next several decades—statewide prohibition was not successfully enacted until 1919.[7] Scholars focused on identifying why men consumed alcohol, particularly in rural settings, have stressed the role alcohol plays in rituals of male bonding. Men gathered together to swap stories, share common complaints, combat boredom, and generally to celebrate their gender unity; not surprisingly, a general store equipped with ample kegs of whiskey provided an excellent forum for such bonding.[8]

Despite the obvious popularity of alcohol among both urban and rural Texans, temperance reform made important inroads in the state during the 1870s and 1880s. Through organizations like the United Friends of Temperance and the WCTU, reformers relied on moral suasion to preach against the effects of alcohol on the family. Dr. William Carey Crane, a prominent member of the United Friends of Temperance, reported to his organization in 1871, "Less than two years ago there was not a council of temperance in this great State. Now there are nearly two hundred councils in existence. Then other organizations exerted some influence in special localities, and even now are doing good, but at this time, the order of the Friends of Temperance is a moral power in every quarter of the State."[9] Temperance concerns in the 1870s in Texas led to the inclusion of a local option clause in the Texas Constitution of 1876 (enacted by Redeemers), which clarified that a statewide prohibition law could only be put in place with the support of Texas voters; in other words, through a referendum.[10] When a referendum opportunity arose, Texas dry forces needed to be ready to act. Frances Willard visited the state on a speaking tour in 1882 in an effort to bolster support for local WCTU chapters in the southern states.[11] Women had particularly important roles in temperance campaigns. The temperance movement was profoundly vested in protecting the notion of domesticity—a drunkard, it was argued, threatened the sanctity and welfare of the family; thus, women attacked drinking establishments on behalf of their homes. The opportunity that temperance reform gave women to participate in public debate challenged traditional perceptions of whether it was appropriate for women to engage in such activities, and this debate regarding women's roles was especially true in the South.

A recent history of early temperance activities in Texas traces the development and success of temperance campaigns in Texas in the 1880s up until the statewide referendum on prohibition in 1887, which ultimately failed. The author examines the impact and legacy of Frances Willard's visit to Texas in 1882, asserting that her visit was marred by the conservatism and paternalism of southern society. The fact that so many Texans lived in rural isolation impeded farm women's ability to participate in the larger temperance movement. Willard's influence in Texas was stunted also in part because she was a northerner. Given the freshness of events surrounding the war, southerners were deeply suspicious of northern reform movements, once again highlighting the cultural connection between Texas and the South. Nevertheless, Willard's visit infused life into the Texas temperance movement, a movement that had actually started pushing for a statewide prohibition amendment as early as 1881. Most gains in Texas were made at the local level, and a number of small towns and communities passed local option laws within three years of Willard's visit. Even if women's participation in temperance reform challenged nineteenth-century perceptions of their roles, women clearly performed an important function in early reform.[12] Although temperance advocates in the 1870s and 1880s did not successfully ban the sale of alcohol in Texas, their movement attracted enough attention to push their agenda into the public consciousness, fomenting both support and opposition among Texans.

Both federal and tribal law restricted the sale of liquor in Indian Territory. In 1890, when Indian Territory and the Unassigned Lands became two separate districts, the new Oklahoma Territory permitted the sale of alcohol while Indian Territory remained dry. Among the Choctaws, laws forbidding the sale of alcohol dated back to the early years of the nineteenth century, a fact that prompted historian Angie Debo to describe them as "the first people in the United States to enact a 'prohibition law.'"[13] Despite these early restrictions, however, these laws proved difficult for tribal administrations to enforce. According to Debo, "The Indian police experienced great difficulty in keeping liquor out of the Nation, especially after the coming of the Missouri, Kansas, and Texas Railroad. Certain wholesale merchants of St. Louis disguised shipments of liquor in almost every package."[14] Although J. J. McAlester received much of his stock from St. Louis merchants, his ledger records do not indicate that he sold alcohol through his retail establishment.[15] The same can be said of G. B. Hester's store in Old Boggy Depot, W. N. Jones's store in Cade, and F. B. Severs's store located in the Creek Nation. If any of these retailers broke the law by selling alcohol, they were not inclined to record such evidence in their books. Considering

Debo's assertion that laws governing the sale of alcohol were largely ignored by both merchants and railroad representatives, it seems clear that someone was selling liquor in Indian Territory. However, there is no clear evidence that any of these merchants engaged in such activities; if they sold alcohol, they did so clandestinely.

If the sale of alcohol was officially prohibited in Indian Territory, the same could not be said of Texas, where general store owners offered a wide variety of liquor options to their customers. The popular product could be sold in full gallons, half gallons, bottles, quarts, pints, flasks, and on rare occasion, barrels. Although whiskey was the spirit of choice for most store customers, retailers in some locations offered their clients a variety of liquor choices, including brandy, gin, ale, wine (both port and claret), and champagne.[16] Further, just as temperance reformers cautioned, ledger records indicate that there were a number of store customers who not only purchased alcohol but did so frequently and in large quantities. At the Rowlett store in Nacogdoches, for example, Ben McLain purchased a bottle of whiskey on September 4, 1869, a quart of whiskey on September 10, and a pint of whiskey on September 12.[17] The purchases of Judge Goodlaw in the spring of 1873 from the Wolf mercantile store in Austin would have alarmed most temperance advocates. Goodlaw bought whiskey by the bottle, gallon, or half gallon on February 28, March 2, 5, 8, 10, 15, 17, and 24.[18] There appears to be nothing moderate about Goodlaw's consumption habits.

Given the obvious popularity of alcohol in late-nineteenth-century Texas, it is significant that a number of stores, either in whole or in part, opted out of selling alcohol to their customers. At the Clark & Hyde mercantile firm in Nacogdoches, alcohol does not appear in the hundreds of accounts listed in the store's two surviving ledgers. The same can be said of accounts at the Gauntt Bros. store in Athens, Texas.[19] Is it possible that these stores' customers were not interested in purchasing the controversial product? Further, amid the numerous accounts listed in the Brown & Dixon company records from Jacksonville (ledgers that spanned several decades), alcohol is also very noticeably absent from the purchases charged to customers' accounts. An exception to this pattern is the entry made on John Pinkard's account on May 12, 1883, which reads "cash for whiskey—50¢."[20] A similar anomaly occurs in the account records from William McCampbell's store in Refugio. Generally, alcohol does not appear under customers' recorded purchases; however, an exception emerges in the account of Mrs. Susan Dugat from May 16, 1877. Like Pinkard, Mrs. Dugat's account was debited one dollar for "cash for whiskey."[21]

A few possible scenarios might explain these unusual entries. The first is that apparently both W. A. Brown and William McCampbell required their customers to pay for alcohol with cash. If this was the case, it is strange that there are not more indications of people needing to make such charges to their accounts; after all, in the 1870s Greenback era, hard currency was an elusive commodity available to only a few. One wonders about the multiple "cash charges" assessed to Lon Dixon's account for amounts such as thirty, fifteen, sixty, or twenty cents in the spring of 1885.[22] Could these be cash charges for whiskey? It is not clear from such examples that either of these stores provided the whiskey that Pinkard and Dugat purchased, only that they provided the cash for the whiskey.

Perhaps, it was pressure from the temperance camps that explains why store owners either did not sell liquor or were reluctant to record such transactions in their ledgers. For example, there was a vibrant temperance movement in the community of Jacksonville in the 1870s. According to the *Texas Intelligencer*, a lovely temperance display was set up by the good citizens of Jacksonville outside the Masonic Hall during the 1874 Christmas season. In addition to a decorated pulpit, organizers and presenters—including the Good Templars, the Friends of Temperance, and the children of the Band of Hope—gave speeches, played music, and marched in procession for the onlookers: "light after light was springing into existence and adding to the beauty of the scene." The editors noted, "There is always a charm and glamour which hang about the words and deeds of lovely women, and we can only say that these fair champions of Temperance did their devoirs nobly—and many a manly heart beat high as its owner listened to their earnest appeals for a cause which is so worthy of manly support."[23] Did the effectiveness of such campaigns lead W. A. Brown to curtail the sale of alcohol at his store? Possibly. While some stores in both urban and rural centers sold alcohol freely and in large quantities to their customers, other stores seemed averse either to selling alcohol or to keeping a paper trail of such transactions. Moreover, some store owners no doubt supported temperance but may have sold whiskey for "medicinal purposes." Regarding the sale of this contentious product, it is difficult to assess the full impact of the temperance campaign in explaining the presence of alcohol at some stores and its absence from others.

Account entries from Texas stores with a largely German customer base serve to complicate the matter of alcohol consumption even further. As a general rule, Germans immigrants tended to be staunch opponents of prohibition legislation, and the situation was no different in Texas. German immigrants proved a significant voting bloc for the anti-prohibition forces during the 1887 temperance referendum. This pro-alcohol stance often resulted in Germans being the subject of vehement attacks by both nativists and prohibitionists. As one historian observes, "They drank beer publicly, they were often Catholic, and they or their parents were of foreign origin."[24] However, the fact that Germans were also perceived as being solid and respectable middle-class citizens compounded matters for the prohibitionists, especially since many of the German immigrants had ties to the state that went back much further than those of their xenophobic critics. During the period, the prevailing stereotype of Germans was that they were notorious alcohol consumers, and ledger records from both Fischer's Store in Comal County and Ernst's store in Industry support such perceptions. Both whiskey and wine found their way onto customers' accounts at Hermann Ernst's store in Industry, as in the case of Emil Knolle, whose purchases on August 10, 1879, included both items. By far the spirit of choice at Hermann Fischer's store, whiskey frequently appeared on the accounts of the store's largely German clientele. Apparently, neither store maintained a cash-only policy; thus, customers were able to charge alcohol to their account at both locations.[25]

However, the same consumption patterns do not hold true at Anna Martin's store in Hedwig's Hill. Unlike at Ernst's and Fischer's stores, whiskey is noticeably absent from her customers' accounts. Wine, however, appears on a handful of accounts recorded during the mid-1880s. For example, Mrs. Simon charged a bottle of wine to her account on November 16, 1885, Charles Martin purchased a gallon of wine from the store on March 15, 1886, and Gottlieb Brandenberger purchased two bottles of wine on August 18, 1887.[26] It should be noted that some historians have argued that Victorians did not consider wine to be in the same league as spirits such as whiskey, rum, or gin. Consequently, wine frequently graced the tables of respectable, otherwise temperance-supporting, middle-class Americans.[27] With regard to beer, many of Martin's store customers may have brewed it themselves rather than pay the retailer to do so for them. Still, it is peculiar that whiskey does not appear on customers' accounts, especially in relation to its popularity in other German stores. This period in Martin's ledgers coincides with the prohibition campaign of 1887, however. Perhaps, the prohibition debate "tempered" Martin's sale of alcohol. Another possibility is that, like many women in the middle class during this period, Anna Martin favored temperance and intentionally chose to curtail the sale of certain "hard" liquors, at least in her establishment. Finally, perhaps selling whiskey was thought to be "unladylike," prompting Martin to avoid such a characterization.

In the 1870s and 1880s, middle-class norms kept respectable women solidly in the temperance camp at a time when opinions on the subject became deeply divisive, often splitting groups along class and ethnic lines. The widely held public perception was that refined women did not drink, but recent evidence suggests that, whether it was medicine in tonics, hidden within recipes, or fine dining, middle-class women consumed alcohol, albeit usually in private spaces.[28] And even if it was not socially acceptable for women to drink, the same could not be said of other vices. According to H. Wayne Morgan, drug addiction—more specifically, opiate consumption—was significantly more socially acceptable than drinking among middle-class women of the period. Morgan cites the findings of one doctor in 1891, who observed, "As a rule, women take opiates and men alcohol, both seeking the same pleasurable results. A woman is very degraded before she will consent to display drunkenness to mankind; whereas, she can obtain equally if not more pleasurable feelings with opiates, and not disgrace herself before the world."[29] It appears that escapism through inebriates divided the nineteenth-century middle classes along gender lines.

Although an infrequent occurrence in terms of the sheer number of stores and purchases themselves, a handful of ledger records indicate that African Americans also made purchases of alcohol at general stores. As noted, general laborer Lem Chambers, for example, was able to make rather expensive liquor purchases at the Wolf Merchandise store in Austin, including brandy and Port wine.[30] At the Hardeman & Barret store in Melrose, Texas, during the peak years of Radical Reconstruction, African Americans were also able to make liquor purchases. For example, Dick Gray (F.M.C) purchased a bottle of whiskey on October 10 and a quart of whiskey on October 15, 1870.[31] In the post-slavery era, the ability to purchase alcohol, like many other individual choices, became closely associated with notion of freedom for many African American consumers. Attempts to restrict black access to alcohol by whites can conversely be seen as both a demonstration of power and an affirmation of the racial hierarchy. The politicization of alcohol and its correlation to racial politics in Texas became apparent during the temperance referendum of 1887. Both wet and dry forces launched campaigns designed to win the support of the shrinking black vote during the 1887 referendum. In the end, 74 percent of the black vote opposed prohibition, in part because blacks perceived prohibition as a threat to their personal liberty. The racist rhetoric employed by the drys also seriously undermined their appeal to black voters.[32] Thus, the sale of alcohol in the state of Texas in the 1870s and 1880s tended to divide the population along lines not only of class, gender, and ethnicity, but also of race.

It would be presumptuous to assign an addiction problem to any of the general store customers in Texas and pre-statehood Oklahoma who purchased "medicinal" products; nonetheless, it should be noted that addiction to opiates was a very real social concern in the late nineteenth century, a problem prevalent in both rural and urban environments. While salt-of-the-earth farmers hardly conjure up images of serious opiate abusers, the reality was that rural settings proved especially susceptible to the problem of drug addiction. There are a number of explanations to account for the problem of rural vulnerability to opiate addiction. Doctors were overworked and often spread too thin to administer drugs to rural people; consequently, many in rural areas diagnosed their illnesses themselves and self-medicated. Obviously, the general public knew very little about the dangers of habitually taking opiates, and it is not clear that the medical profession fully understood the dangers either. Whether it was to escape the rigors of the workday or to alleviate the doldrums of rural isolation, people consumed opiates for many of the same reasons that they drank alcohol. Further, cheap mail delivery increased the amount of all consumer items, including medicines, available to those living in outlying rural communities. Particular opiates such as laudanum and paregoric were popular among rural families who used these items to alleviate pain and tranquilize crying babies, the aged, and the infirm. One historian asserts that "many people, especially women, were taking maintenance doses of opiates without knowing it, just as many upright temperance supporters used tonics that contained alcohol."[33] Since the story of much of the Texas and Indian Territory is largely a rural story and the sale of medicinal products seemed to have a particular impact on rural regions, the sale of such products at general stores merits some attention.

Of the various medications listed in store ledgers, the frequency of paregoric in account records suggests that this opiate was particularly popular among consumers in this region. Paregoric, a milder form of camphorated tincture of opium, was generally used to relieve the pains associated with colic in babies, although adults could also find relief in the mild opiate.[34] The liberal usage of paregoric by concerned parents to pacify their crying babies prompted stern warnings from many in the medical profession. One doctor described paregoric as "the nemesis of the nursery."[35] Still, few in isolated farming communities areas knew of the dangers associated with the substance and proceeded to administer the medication to their children, and liberally when they deemed it necessary. There are many examples of paregoric purchases in the ledgers, including its purchase by store owners L. T. Barret, A. C. (Lon) Dixon, and J. J. McAlester.[36]

While seemingly the most popular opiate listed in account records, paregoric was by no means the only habit-forming drug available to customers in the region. Laudanum, opium, morphine, and cocaine also provided pain relief for rural consumers, and each of these substances found their way into ledgers records from the period. Laudanum, an opium derivative sold in liquid form, was a particularly dangerous concoction. It was created by mixing opium and either water or alcohol.[37] Vials of laudanum were purchased by E. Taylor, Doctor George S. Hyde, and store owner William Clark from the Clark & Hyde mercantile firm in February 1873.[38] D. W. Dorsey made a similar purchase from the Hardeman & Barret store on April 20, 1870.[39] Sam Cartlidge included a bottle of laudanum among his purchases from McAlester's store on December 4, 1875.[40] "Gillette" purchased two bottles of laudanum from the Severs store in Okmulgee on January 8, and two more bottles on January 18, 1870.[41] Significantly, these examples represent only a small portion of the customer accounts that included these harmful, possibly hazardous substances.

Besides opiates, general stores sold other medicines to their clientele that, while not necessarily habit-forming, were potentially dangerous in their own right. Account entries from William Wadsworth's store in Matagorda, Texas, provide a number of representative examples. On October 26, 1885, Jonathon McNabb purchased a bottle of chloroform, and on the same day, George Bankston purchased a bottle of glycerin. William Baxter obtained a bottle of "nitro" from the store on October 30, 1885, as did D. P. Moon on November 4, 1885. In other examples, bottles of chloroform were purchased by James Williams and Mrs. C. Williams on November 5, 1885. A. A. Duffy acquired one ounce of arsenic and carbolic acid on December 1, 1885, assumedly not for ingestion. On December 3, 1885, Ed Savage bought a bottle of quinine (an extremely popular pain medication during the period) and a box of "capsules." On December 7, 1885, Mrs. Uzzell purchased nitro, castor oil, paregoric, and "Rx 5010."[42] Given the potent nature of her other purchases, one can only imagine what merited a prescription. Thus, within a period of six weeks, several transactions involving a number of possibly dangerous substances transpired at the Wadsworth store. And this was not the only store. Among the purchases of John Dagan from J. J. McAlester's store in January 1872, there was a bottle strychnia, derived from strychnine, which was used for myriad medical purposes. Again, the danger posed by the powerful drug, however, can hardly be overstated.[43] While it is true that folk medicine had long involved risky treatments with both positive and negative results, the increased availability of powerful substances such as laudanum, chloroform, and strychnine in the late nineteenth century presented the potential of new problems for rural consumers. If poorly administered, such products could lead to addiction or death.

In addition to the products listed above, a number of traditional remedies that were commonly found in country households offered their own share of risks to the infirm. The king of the medicinal "standards," according to southern historian Thomas Clark, was turpentine: "Everything from a cut finger to worms, backache, kidney trouble, sore throat, rheumatism, croup, pneumonia, toothache, and earache was treated with this cheap native antiseptic." Turpentine frequently appeared on the account records from general stores in Texas and early Oklahoma. In an effort to treat their children's sicknesses, caring parents forced their little ones to ingest heaping spoonfuls of sugar doused in the foul product. Needless to say, after ingesting turpentine, whatever poisons lay within were quickly purged. As Clark astutely noted, "Southern kidneys paid a heavy price for its frequent use."[44] Still in use today, castor oil—or castoria—was another common purgative employed by farm families, and it regularly appeared on store accounts in the region. Further, vermifuge (a medicine used to purge intestinal worms) frequently appeared under customer accounts; examples include entries from William Wadsworth's, Hermann Fischer's, and F. B. Severs's stores.[45]

Perhaps, more alarming as a purgative than either turpentine or castor oil was the calomel commonly used by country dwellers to purge buildup in their intestinal systems. On September 14, 1869, Mr. Cothran purchased a bottle of quinine, oysters, calomel, and castor oil from the F. B. Severs store in Okmulgee, Creek Territory, and future Creek principal chief Pleasant Porter purchased calomel and castor oil on January 5, 1870.[46] Apparently the drug was very popular, and store owners carried large quantities of calomel on their shelves, readily available for sale. Calomel was a mercury-based drug given in "rounds" of broken doses by store owners. The drug required much precision on the part of store owners so as not to inadvertently poison their customers. In reality, however, store owners were neither doctors nor pharmacists and the dosage amount was pure guesswork on their part. Thomas Clark surmised that "it was in the selling of opiates and calomel that the country stores perhaps made their most serious medicinal mistakes."[47] Again, neither store owners nor their clientele were fully aware of the dangers associated with the drugs they ingested to bolster their immune systems and remedy their health troubles.

In conjunction with these medicinal products, general stores carried scores of other medicines, elixirs, tonics, seltzers, powders, and pills that were purported to cure virtually all medical ailments. Promising to work miracles, such items sold under names like Wilholf's Chill Tonic, Ague Tonic, Balsam Wild Cherry, Harter's Ague Tonic, Pain Killer, Seidlitz Powders, Hanebury Drops, Thompson's Elixir Water, Smith's Tonic Syrup, Liver Medicine, Allen's Lung Balsam, Wizard Oil, Jaynes Expectorant, Turner's Wonder, St. Jakob's Oil, Elixir of Life, and Wonderful Eight.[48] Since the sale of these products preceded the passage of laws regulating medicines (specifically the Pure Food and Drug Act of 1906), the ingredients that enabled these products to remedy ailments is largely a mystery. Many bottled and packaged drugs drew upon the soothing powers of both opiates and alcohol; tonics were especially notorious for containing alcohol. Needless to say, consuming these miracle cures, once again, involved some degree of consumer risk—especially for children and those aspiring to "clean" living. One would think that the laws of supply and demand would weed out especially dangerous or altogether ineffective medicinal products, although this was clearly not always the case. Access to consumer information regarding the safety of administering these drugs was clearly limited in the predominantly rural communities under consideration here. No doubt, trial and error also played an important role in dictating consumers' choices. In the end, store customers in Texas and Indian Territory took their chances with the medicinal products they purchased, and indeed, sometimes desperate situations called for desperate measures.

While alcohol and medicines commonly appeared in store ledgers of this region (and in themselves reveal an intriguing picture of rural life), the more substantial and significant products recorded in account books were related to agriculture. Scores of products exchanged at general stores in Texas and Indian Territory confirm that these regions were primarily agrarian in nature and depended on cash crops like cotton and cattle for their economic viability. This was clearly the case in the principally cattle-raising communities of Hedwig's Hill and Refugio, as well as cattle, corn, and cotton-growing communities such as Webberville,

Athens, Fischer's Store, Industry, Matagorda, Manor, Cherino, and Melrose. In Melrose, for example, most of the customers listed in the store records for the Hardeman & Barret general merchandise store were farmers, specifically cotton farmers. Underscoring this point, the 1870 census indicates that of the 350 households listed for the East Texas community of Melrose, roughly 80 percent of the households listed were headed by "farmers."[49] Stores situated in larger towns like Jacksonville and Nacogdoches also drew on a predominantly cotton-producing countryside for their customer base. Cross-referencing ledger records with census data indicates that, by a large margin, the majority of customers listed in the McKinney & Brown records were "farmers." The same can be said of customers for the Clark & Hyde mercantile firm in Nacogdoches.[50] In such communities, the town maintained an intrinsic link with the surrounding countryside, both economically and socially. Only Austin, with a population over four thousand in 1870, provides an exception to the rule.[51] And while the main industry in McAlester was coal mining, this too can be considered a rural community in the 1870s and 1880s with strong ties to the surrounding coal-rich countryside.

Part of what made this region unique in the late nineteenth century was its location at the intersection of the two converging frontiers—cattle and cotton. These industries figure prominently in ledgers from stores operating in Texas and Indian Territory during this period. In a cash-short economy, many rural inhabitants relied on an intricate system of exchange with local retailers wherein they received credit from local store owners in exchange for their bales of cotton or year-old calves. Thus, ledgers are a testament to the integral relationship between store owners in the small communities of this region and the outlying agricultural hinterland.[52] Cotton- and cattle-related purchases appear in customer accounts at the McKinney & Brown store in East Texas as well as at Anna Martin's store in the Hill Country of Central Texas. At the McKinney & Brown store in 1881, for example, on November 12, Sandy Chandler received credit on his store account for cotton, on November 21, March Kessentiner received credit for a bale of cotton, and on December 12, Perry Bolden received credit on his account for one bale of cotton.[53] At Anna Martin's store in Hedwig's Hill, Henry

Kensing received $15.00 credit for two "one year old calves" on June 28, 1886. The following day, Fritz Lorenz received a $112.50 credit for fifteen "one year old calves."[54] Ledger evidence suggests that in both locations the role of credit was crucial to the choreography of commercial relations in Texas and Indian Territory in the 1870s and 1880s.

Most consumers in this largely agrarian region exercised considerable restraint in their purchasing; indeed, few could afford not to be cautious in their spending. The small communities of this region were mainly made up of farmers who struggled with the debt cycles and the uncertainties of a cash crop economy. Those who engaged in cattle or mining fared only marginally better. Ultimately, poverty and debt, or at least the fear of exacerbating already tenuous economic conditions, significantly influenced consumer spending at general stores in this part of the country. The story of the Texas and Indian Territory in the late nineteenth century is predominantly rural in nature and sustained by people of modest means, and there is the ongoing question of how this region—comprised mainly of farms, ranches, and small town sites—fits into the larger national narrative of the period. One could argue that America was still very much an agrarian nation in the 1870s and 1880s, although this period coincides with the "age of the city" when both northern and southern cities (Houston, New Orleans, Atlanta, for example) experienced accelerated urbanization. Demographically, America was in transition in the late nineteenth century. Between 1880 and 1890, for example, the urban population increased by 56 percent, the total U.S. population by 26 percent, and the rural population by only 13 percent—most urban growth was focused in the northeast region of the country.[55] While America was becoming increasingly urbanized during this time period, much of it remained rural until well into the twentieth century, and this was especially true for the South and the Great Plains. Therefore, the daily experiences of those living in this region of the country of the late nineteenth century fit comfortably in the larger rubric of rural culture in nineteenth-century America.

The picture that emerges from comparing studies of consumption patterns elsewhere is that purchasing in Texas and Indian Territory mirrored that of farmers residing in agricultural regions throughout the country. According to Ted Ownby, rural Mississippians rarely purchased expensive luxury goods. Far more typically, "customers who made large single purchases were not buying special goods but bulk quantities of subsistence goods like cloth, shoes, and salt." African American customers, Ownby argues, were especially prone to subsistence shopping: "The basic economic structure for rural African Americans consisted of the necessity for hard and steady labor with the hope for eventual land ownership, and a denial of the comforts and pleasures available in consumer goods."[56] Anthropologists William Hampton Adams and Steven Smith found that black sharecroppers who purchased items from Henry Long's general store in Waverly Plantation, Mississippi, tended to stick to basic food items and clothing such as sugar, rice, pork molasses, cloth, and shoes rather than specialty goods.[57] In short, basics tended to be the focal point for rural Mississippians, especially for African American sharecroppers.

In his study of a country store in rural Alabama, Kenneth Wesson finds similar fiscal conservatism in the shopping patterns among tenants and sharecroppers in this region of the agrarian South. Wesson examines John C. H. Jones general store in Fairfield, Pickens County, Alabama, a region primarily engaged in cotton production. As in the cotton-producing regions of Mississippi, a large portion of Jones's clients were African American sharecroppers. Referencing an 1873 account ledger, Wesson notes that, after whiskey, the most popular items sold at the Jones store were tobacco, sugar, and coffee. Bacon was also a popular product at the store, followed by flour, molasses, and cooking oil.[58] In terms of dry goods, Jones sold plenty of fabrics, ready-made clothes and shoes, building materials, farming equipment, guns and powder. Indeed, there was little difference in the types of goods sold at this Alabama store from items sold at the McKinney & Brown store in Jacksonville or at McAlester's store in the Choctaw Nation.

Perhaps it is not unexpected that sharecroppers in the South shared similar consumption patterns with their neighbors in Texas and Indian Territory, given that many in these regions also engaged in cotton production. However, similar patterns can be found in other rural regions where sharecropping was not the principal economic industry. For example, James Wettstaed's study of consumption patterns in an Ozark mining community suggests that miners generally limited their spending to basic staple items. Wettstaed asserts that the most frequently purchased items from Stone, Manning & Co. were fabrics, clothing, and food. He breaks purchasing down into these percentages: fabric (17.9 percent), clothing (23.3 percent), food (11.5 percent), and sewing items (9.7 percent). Breaking these categories down further, he notes, "The single most frequently purchased item was whiskey (4.4 percent of total purchases), followed in order by shoes (4.1 percent), tobacco (4.1 percent), salt (3.7 percent), coffee (3.5 percent), calico (3.1 percent), domestic (a type of fabric, 3.1 percent), and gunpowder (2.8 percent)."[59] Wettstaed considers items like tobacco and whiskey to be "indulgences." From the frontier perspective, "indulgences" might be too strong a word to describe these vices. Tobacco, for example, appeared as frequently on customer accounts in Texas and Indian Territory as items like salt and potatoes. To be sure, tobacco can hardly be considered a basic necessity; however, it appears that many consumers in the region considered it a staple. Store ledgers from the 1870s and 1880s indicate that tobacco was typically sold to consumers either by the plug, in twists, loosely by the pound, or in the case of snuff, by the container. Rolled cigarettes were just beginning to be introduced in this period, so they rarely appear in ledgers. An exception appears in ledgers from the Gauntt Bros. store in Athens. According to the store's records, both Will Sullivan and Wade Renfrow purchased packaged cigarettes in November 1887.[60] Rolled cigarettes, the standard of the twentieth century, were a little too modern and expensive to alter substantially the tobacco purchasing habits of the majority of residents in Texas and Indian Territory during this period.

Not surprisingly, there are clear similarities in the spending patterns of Ozark miners with their counterparts in the McAlester coal mining region. A few examples are enough. On January 21, 1875, miner Mike Dunn purchased from McAlester's store such staples as flour, sugar, and soap, and weeks later he bought more flour, cheese, lard, and a coffeepot.[61] That same year, U. A. Keith, a fellow miner, purchased sugar, tea, tobacco, flour, salt, thread, and denim.[62] Bowing to practical considerations, McAlester's advertising emphasized the staples in his stock. In the advertisements he placed in local newspapers, the store owner stressed that his dry goods store offered clothing, boot, shoes, hardware, queensware, tinware, hats, caps, blankets, fruit, and potatoes.[63] McAlester neither emphasized the availability of specialty goods in his stock nor his ability to acquire such goods. One has to believe, however, that if there had been a steady demand for luxury items from eastern centers, the store owner would have done his best to meet such a demand.

Necessity purchasing was not limited to those living in the cotton-producing and mining regions of the country. Doris Fanelli's study of consumption patterns in rural Delaware in the early nineteenth century suggests that the agrarian consumers in this region also focused their purchasing on basic needs—including fabrics, sewing items, and food products. Fanelli's conclusions are based on her examination of a daybook from William Polk's general store located in the community Saint George's, Delaware.[64] And finally, Elizabeth Perkin's analysis of consumption in frontier Kentucky also highlights the importance of staple items to consumers in this predominantly rural region. Items that appeared most frequently on customer accounts in Kentucky included dry goods such as cloth, ready-made clothing, and haberdashery, as well as food items such as tea, coffee, sugar, spices, and whiskey.[65] In all of these studies, the common premise is that people living in frontier environments tended to be fiscally conservative in their purchasing. In part this was a consequence of limited selection, but to a large extent, the emphasis on necessity buying reflecting the tight budgets of those involved.

While it is true that in Texas and Indian Territory during the late nineteenth century *most* rural people, *most* of the time, acquired basic necessities from their general store rather than expensive luxuries, there were significant exceptions to this rule. This study has provided countless examples of how consumption practices reflected important divisions of class, gender, race, and ethnicity in the area. As a case in point, store owners often extended their purchasing beyond common necessities. Whether it was for them or their families, merchants in our study region attained commodities befitting their status as the local elite. While interest in "scarce commodities" by rural inhabitants was not merely a product of the late nineteenth century, the increased proliferation of ready-made, mass-produced commodities profoundly expanded that interest.[66] Examples cited in earlier chapters include the purchases of Alfred B. Lewis from his store in Manor, Texas. Lewis purchased expensive ready-made suits from his store as well as a buggy for the impressive price of $145.[67] There were also the purchases of William Clark III from his store in Nacogdoches, Texas. The Clark family tended to focus their shopping on food delicacies and fine fabrics. It was Mrs. Clark who purchased a purchased a roll of wallpaper from the family store to decorate her walls in the popular design trend of the period.[68]

It was not only the store owners who expanded their shopping selections beyond basics. There are the examples of African Americans Charles Menefee, Sandy Chandler, and March Kessentiner. Menefee made purchases such as jewelry, shoe cologne, ladies' hats, bracelets, beads, and a harmonica for his family. While these were inexpensive luxuries, they were likely not essential to the family's needs.[69] Chandler purchased gloves, ribbon, a silk handkerchief, a parasol, and candy from the McKinney & Brown store in Jacksonville. Kessentiner acquired goblets, lace, and linen from the same store.[70] African Americans also focused their purchasing on the items necessary to attain an education. Examples include the acquisition of spellers and primers evidenced in the accounts for Jesse Powers, Starling, Kyle, Jake Buford, and George Garret.[71]

In the Hill County of Central Texas the Christmas purchases of German immigrants reflect their connection to Old World holiday rituals and their desire to continue those traditions in their new environment. At Anna Martin's store in Hedwig's Hill, her predominantly German customers made the following purchases in December: candy, apples, dolls, toy pistols, trumpets, French harps, a toy monkey, children's hats, ribbon, apples, toys, cups and saucers, slippers, fire crackers, Christmas candles, currants, wine, different types of picture books. Opting to make the holiday special for their families likely required some sacrifice, and again provides example of purchasing outside of staple items.[72]

Concern over debt and economic uncertainty meant that most farmers exercised restraint in their spending—a pattern that resembled consumer purchasing in other rural areas of the country. That said, ledger records indicate that consumers often went beyond staples into purchases that reflected their desire to project notions of refinement, comfort, social mobility, progress, or conversely, as in the case of German immigrants, tradition. One would expect luxury purchases like parasols, fine china sets, fancy fabrics, and jewelry to distinguish class among agricultural consumers, particularly because in those areas far removed from eastern supply centers. Such luxuries, however, were rare in countrified settings. In many ways, more common items prove to be equally telling indicators of consumer behavior and attitudes in this region during the 1870s and 1880s. The appearance of alcohol and drugs in ledgers not only highlights the very real social problems of addiction that plagued the nineteenth century but also enables a discussion of the prevalent attitudes regarding consumption of such items. For example, the greater social evil for respectable middle-class women was not opiate addiction but alcoholism (although the former was clearly a problem, particularly in rural areas). Ledger records provide insights on how these larger social issues affected consumers in this region. Temperance campaigns, for example, reached down from a national level and influenced those living in farming communities of East and Central Texas. Rural conditions proved especially conducive to drug addiction, partly because of isolation but also because of the lack of both medical knowledge and doctors. The polemics of such products were not limited to debates among middle-class reformers in the East but similarly found relevance in the lived experiences of persons residing in the small communities and outposts in Texas and early Oklahoma. For the most part, consumption patterns in Texas and Indian Territory reflected the agrarian nature of the region. Concern over debt and economic uncertainty meant that most farmers exercised restraint in their spending, although they did make exceptions for special items—perhaps, a new suit, a spelling book, or Christmas treats—goods that projected an image of who these rural residents were or, perhaps, who they wanted to be.

Conclusion

FROM THE PAGES OF LEDGERS RECORDED almost a century and a half ago, there emerges a broad and dynamic account of late-nineteenth-century America. Store records provide evidence of the day-to-day experiences and community life of persons living in Texas and Indian Territory. They detail the intricacies of commercial relations from a local, regional, and national perspective. The ledgers demonstrate that class, gender, race, and ethnic distinctions were determined and reinforced on a daily basis during commercial transactions carried out at general stores. The store records indicate that the social and cultural issues that affected Americans living in other parts of the nation during this period similarly impacted those living in remote regions of Texas and Indian Territory—in communities like Hedwig's Hill, Jacksonville, Fischer's Store, Okmulgee, and McAlester. The immigrants from Europe and southern and eastern areas of the United States who settled in these communities brought with them the problems, attitudes, and value systems prevalent in the regions from which they came. For these immigrants, there was no boundary that separated the West from other parts of the nation or, for that matter, from communities overseas.

The merchants who recorded transactions in these ledgers probably thought nothing of their historical significance, yet such evidence provides valuable insight into their social and economic experiences, as well as the experiences of their customers. As a group, store owners were an interesting sort. They were an amalgam of the cultural dispositions prevailing in late-nineteenth-century America. Some appear to have been brazen profit-motivated entrepreneurs, exhibiting the cutthroat capitalist drive commonly associated with the Gilded Age, while others displayed the high degree of moral probity, community responsibility, and social refinement generally associated with the middle and upper classes. In describing merchants, it is not enough to fall back on any standard Victorian description, as is often the case in histories of the West. Frankly, the term "Victorian" is too vague to capture adequately the nuances of this multifaceted group. In Indian Territory, store owners such as James J. McAlester and Frederick B. Severs capitalized on the region's economic potential, amassing great wealth and prestige in their respective communities. In the postbellum period, store owners like William Clark III and Lyne T. Barret transitioned from their role as a slaveholding elite to that of a merchant elite. Except for her gender, the rags-to-riches experiences of Anna Martin's life might easily be found in the pages of a McGuffey reader or a Horatio Alger novel, both quite popular with readers of the period. As a woman, Martin was by no means a typical nineteenth-century store owner, yet she, like her retailing contemporaries, possessed remarkable business savvy, and she engaged in economic activities beyond retailing such as ranching and banking. As members of the social and economic elite, store owners demonstrated a commitment to the moral and social development of their communities through their involvement in the establishment of churches and schools. In this regard, they reflected the kind of communal responsibility that was closely associated with the middle class. Other store owners displayed aspects of all of these qualities, again affirming the heterogeneity of the merchant class in this region.

Both Martin's and the McCampbells' store ledgers highlight the interconnection of the store owners with their clientele and the local economy; in both cases, ranching was the dominant economic activity in the region. In the communities under analysis, store merchants played a pivotal role in the economic fortunes of their store customers. Merchants not only supplied their clients with the goods necessary for daily survival. They also served as creditors, marketing agents, postmasters, and crucial links to more cosmopolitan centers in the East and overseas. In especially remote locations, store owners faced little or no competition, which enabled them to gain a monopoly over their clients' consumption choices. In other locations, merchants faced competition from other retailers, which forced them to compete for customers and limited their ability to exploit their clientele. In both cases, it was their extension of credit that placed store owners in control of the economic fates of many of their customers. This was an especially precarious situation for sharecroppers and tenant farmers—significant since both represented an enormously important, and growing, segment of the agricultural population of Texas in the last decades of the nineteenth century. In the early 1870s, census data from Melrose, Texas, confirms that the prospects of landownership for African Americans were highly improbable. For the most part, store owners dictated the terms on which their clients entered commercial relations. Because of the vagaries of the market, however, merchants were similarly dependent on their clients for their economic well-being. Indeed, theirs was a relationship of mutual economic interdependence. Despite this fact, merchants were hardly the social equals of their largely farming clientele. Store owners not only catered to the needs of their customers but also assumed the responsibility of advancing their respective communities' economic, social, and moral development—a privileged position, indeed.

In commercial terms, Thomas Clark's early study of country stores concluded that women maintained only a marginal, largely insignificant presence at general stores. As a consequence, the role of women as rural consumers has been largely overlooked by historians. Certainly in terms of real numbers, women frequented stores less often than their male counterparts. Moreover, accounts tended to be listed under the name of the male head of household, which further obscures women's experiences with general stores. But store ledgers reveal that women played an important role as consumers, particularly those women who were engaged in employment as hotel keepers or as dressmakers (examples of the few employment opportunities afforded women in the late nineteenth century). Ledger evidence also challenges notions of domesticity that limited women's work experience to housework and raising families. Women's contribution to both the visible and invisible economies of local communities can also be traced in store records. Women were drawn into employment from a number of circumstances that extended beyond the needs of their immediate families. In frontier outposts like McAlester, women worked because they had to, typically performing tasks traditionally regarded as women's work such as cooking, washing, and sewing. To be sure, work was available to women in frontier settlements, although such work tended to be limited in scope.

Ledgers from the McCampbell & Bros. store in Refugio not only provide evidence of the types of labor that women performed in small communities but also indicate that issues of race and class played a significant role in shaping the opportunities that were available to both women and racial minorities. During Reconstruction, issues of race were thoroughly divisive, not just in Texas but in all parts of America. General stores served as a common ground for persons of all races and ethnicities, effectively providing a forum for integration into the national economic mainstream. However, store records demonstrate that divisions persisted, even in the largely private ledgers and account books of store owners. These records suggest that divisions of race were determined and "made" during commercial encounters, reflecting the racialized perceptions of those in charge of recording transactions. The Committee of Safety concerns in Melrose, Texas, reveal that many former slaves in the region faced limitations on their newfound freedoms. Evidence from McAlester's store in the Choctaw Nation indicates that similar divisions of race and class prevailed in Indian Territory, partly because tribal leaders sought to establish a racial identity for Indians in this region separate not just from blacks but from whites as well. Again, the deep-seated racial attitudes plaguing the nation similarly affected those living in the counties of Texas and early Oklahoma.

As the largest ethnic minority in Texas in the 1870s and 1880s, Germans left an indelible cultural imprint on the areas in which they settled, particularly in the Hill Country of Central Texas. Although smaller in sheer numbers, European immigrants left a similar cultural impression on the small coal-mining communities of southeastern Oklahoma, beginning in the 1880s and continuing through the decades that followed. As a bank president, cattle broker, rancher, and store merchant, for example, Anna Martin contributed substantially to the economic development of Mason County and the Hill Country. Rich in detail, the ledgers from Martin's store in Hedwig's Hill are especially important in providing critical insights into the German experiences in Texas. Her German clientele both influenced and were influenced by their new environments, though they retained much of their particular cultural identity. While these ledgers confirm many prior observations made by historians regarding the German community in Texas, they also challenge earlier generalizations regarding this immigrant group. The residents of Hedwig's Hill exhibited remarkable resilience, maintaining their cultural traditions and remaining committed to each other and their region. Given that she did not sell a great deal of alcohol through her store, ledger entries from Martin's store also invoke questions regarding this German settlement and the issue of temperance. The evidence suggests that earlier perceptions regarding this group need to be amended to include possible exceptions to the generalization that Germans wholeheartedly supported the sale of alcohol. German influences were felt in the realms of agriculture, stock-raising, consumption, and holiday rituals, profoundly shaping the cultural identity of Central Texas.

Both the persons who frequented general stores and the goods exchanged not only reveal the consumption patterns of the period but shed light on some of the larger social issues associated with consumer goods. Alcohol was an especially contentious product among the middle classes in the nineteenth century. This was clearly the case in Texas during the 1880s, when the temperance campaign gathered momentum and culminated in the prohibition vote of 1887. When it came to alcohol consumption, standards of behavior generally split along class, gender, ethnic, and racial lines. While the temperance movement was certainly alive and well in Texas during the period, it garnered little success in abolishing the sale of alcohol from saloons—the usual target of reformers—or from the more discreet location of general stores. The prevalence of medicinal products in ledgers underscores the fact that rural consumers often had to deal with health issues on their own, partly because of the shortage of doctors in such areas. To be sure, consumption patterns in the predominantly agricultural regions of Texas and Indian Territory were not unlike those in other rural areas of the country—debt and economic uncertainly often led consumers to limit their spending to necessity items. In fact, for most general store customers, frivolous spending was the exception, not the rule.

From general store ledgers, the picture that emerges of this region is that of predominantly rural people living a simple life. For the residents of Texas and Indian Territory, this entailed making the most out of often challenging circumstances, avoiding unnecessary excesses, and doing all they could to get by. As consumers, most store customers exercised restraint in their purchasing, generally adhering to the basic needs of their households. There are notable exceptions that challenge the pattern of necessity spending, however. These exceptions include store owners who sought to establish themselves as the social elite as well as women who wanted to enhance the décor of their homes through little "extras" they were able to acquire from their local store. Able finally to pursue an education, many African Americans included in their purchases primers and spelling books, requiring a significant economic sacrifice given that many freedmen lived in poverty. Seeking to retain their cultural connections to their past, and replicating a tradition in their homeland, many German immigrants celebrated the Christmas holiday by purchasing special holiday gifts and treats for their families. As a record of consumption, ledgers provide direct evidence of which consumer items were deemed important enough to make it onto the shopping lists of persons who were often on a woefully limited budget.

Finally, ledger records connect the interests, values, and social concerns of local people to the national social and cultural concerns of the period. Such evidence enhances our understanding of how issues like domesticity, Reconstruction, immigration, and temperance played out at the local level. Indeed, the residents of Texas and Indian Territory wrestled with many of the same social and economic challenges as those living in other parts of the nation. Store records provide great insight into the complex relationships and power dynamics evidenced in small communities. Merchants may have held the upper hand through credit practices, but their dependence on their clientele for their own economic well-being bolstered the power of the customers—including women, blacks, American Indians, and German immigrants. Seemingly mundane names and figures in ledger books provide fascinating and important glimpses into the consumer experiences of persons living in this region in 1870s and 1880s, including unrivaled access to life at the community level. By all accounts, to access this rich period in American history, one need only open an account ledger from a general store.

Notes

Introduction

1. Account Ledger 1870–73, Hardeman & Barret General Merchandise (B-38), East Texas Research Center, Nacogdoches (hereinafter cited as ETRC), 101. Hoop skirts are a type of women's undergarments. When dresses are worn over the top, the shape of a triangle is created—a popular silhouette in the late nineteenth century.

2. For examples, see the account entries for Peter Barret, Peter Taylor, Dick Gray, Charles Byrd, Jr., and Reuben Chandler in ibid., 45, 76, 83, 98, 142.

3. Wendy Gamber, *The Female Economy: The Millinery and Dressmaking Trades, 1860–1930* (Urbana: University of Illinois Press, 1997), 190–228.

4. Carolyn Reeves Ericson, ed., *The People of Nacogdoches County in 1870: An Edited Census* (Nacogdoches: ETRC, 1977), 43. It seems safe to assume that the majority of married women in the county "kept house" in some capacity or another, even though the census failed to record such women as housekeepers. Evidently, the distinction applied only to women who engaged in "visible" labor outside their immediate households. Interestingly, the 1880 census taker for Nacogdoches County blurred the distinction. For the 1870 census enumerator, housewives were not the same as housekeepers. For a description of visible and invisible labor, see Jeanne Boydston, *Home and Work: Housework, Wages, and the Ideology of Labor in the Early Republic* (New York: Oxford University Press, 1990).

5. Ledger 1870–73, Hardeman & Barret, ETRC, 53, 140, 146, 160, 161, 185, 215.

6. For a definition of "free woman of color," see Irving Lewis Allen, *The Language of Ethnic Conflict: Social Organization and Lexical Culture* (New York: Columbia University Press, 1983), 49.

7. For examples, see Ledger 1870–73, Hardeman & Barret, ETRC, 21, 22, 23.

8. Nacogdoches County Genealogical Society (NCGS), *Nacogdoches County Families* (Dallas: Curtis Media, 1985), 340.

9. Linda Ericson Devereaux, "A History of Oil Springs," in *The Bicentennial Commemorative History of Nacogdoches* (Nacogdoches Jaycees, 1976), 150. See also C. K. Chamberlain, "Lyne Toliaferro Barret: A Pioneer Texas Wildcatter," *East Texas Historical Journal* 6 (March 1968): 8.

10. For perspectives on Reconstruction in Texas, see Barry A. Crouch, "A Spirit of Lawlessness: White Violence, Texas Blacks, 1865–1868," *Journal of Social History* 18 (Winter 1984): 217–32; Barry A. Crouch, *The Freedmen's Bureau and Black Texans* (Austin: University of Texas Press, 1992); Alwyn Barr, *Reconstruction to Reform: Texas Politics, 1876–1906* (Austin: University of Texas Press, 1971; reprint, Dallas: Southern Methodist University Press, 2000); James Smallwood, *Time of Hope, Time of Despair: Black Texans during Reconstruction* (Port Washington, N.Y.: Kennikat Press, 1981); Randolph B. Campbell, *Grass-Roots Reconstruction in Texas, 1865–1880* (Baton Rouge: Louisiana State University Press, 1998); James M. Smallwood, Barry A. Crouch, and Larry Peacock, *Murder and Mayhem: The War of Reconstruction in Texas* (College Station: Texas A&M University Press, 2003).

11. J. Evetts Haley, *Charles Schreiner, General Merchandise: The Story of a Country Store* (Austin: Texas State Historical Association, 1944), 10.

12. Thomas D. Clark, *Pills, Petticoats, and Plows: The Southern Country Store* (Bobbs-Merrill, 1944; reprint, Norman: University of Oklahoma Press, 1964), 21–23.

13. Given that the time period studied here covers the 1870s and 1880s, the proper designation of the region examined is not Oklahoma but Indian Territory. In 1890, Indian Territory and the Unassigned Lands (sometimes referred to as the Oklahoma District) were divided into two separate and distinct districts, Indian Territory and Oklahoma Territory. Ultimately, Oklahoma achieved statehood in 1907.

14. Hereinafter referred to as the Five Tribes.

15. Ann Smart Martin, "Makers, Buyers, and Users: Consumerism as a Material Culture Framework," *Winterthur Portfolio* 28.2–3 (1993): 143.

16. Donald Worster, *Under Western Skies: Nature and History in the American West* (New York: Oxford University Press, 1992), 15.

17. James Deetz, *In Small Things Forgotten: An Archeology of Early American Life* (New York: Anchor Books, 1977; revised 1996), 35.

18. Martin, "Makers, Buyers, and Users," 144.

19. Kenneth R. Wesson, "The Southern Country Store Revisited: A Test Case," *Alabama Historical Quarterly* 42 (Fall/Winter 1980): 157–66; Elizabeth A. Perkins, "The Consumer Frontier: Household Consumption in Early Kentucky," *Journal of American History* 78 (September 1991): 486–510; Alexander Moore, "Daniel Axtell's Account Book and the Economy of Early South Carolina," *South Carolina Historical Magazine* 95 (October 1994): 280–301; Christine Daniels, "'Getting His [or Her] Livelihood': Free Workers in Slave Anglo-America, 1675–1810," *Agricultural History* 71 (Spring 1997): 125–61; Aileen B. Agnew, "The Retail Trade of Elizabeth Sanders and the 'Other' Consumers of Colonial Albany," *Hudson Valley Regional Review* 14 (1997): 35–55; Michael V. Kennedy, "'Cash for His Turnips': Agricultural Production for Local Markets in Colonial Pennsylvania, 1725–1783," *Agricultural History* 74 (2000): 587–608; James E. McWilliams, "Work, Family, and Economic Improvement in Late-Seventeenth-Century Massachusetts Bay: The Case of Joshua Buffum," *New England Quarterly* 74 (2001): 355–84. Also see Dale L. Flesher and

Michael G. Schumacher, "A Natchez Doctor's Ledgers as a Source of History, 1804–1809," *Journal of Mississippi History* 58 (1996): 177–92; Deborah J. C. Meyer and Laurel E. Wilson, "Bringing Civilization to the Frontier: The Role of Men's Coats in 1865 Virginia City, Montana Territory," *Clothing and Textiles Research Journal* 16 (1998): 19–26.

20. Lynn Hunt, "Introduction: History, Culture, and Text," in *The New Cultural History*, ed. Lynn Hunt (Berkeley and Los Angeles: University of California Press, 1989), 12.

21. Clark, *Pills, Petticoats, and Plows*, 271–91; Edward L. Ayers, *The Promise of the New South: Life after Reconstruction* (New York: Oxford University Press, 1992), 81–103.

22. Ayers, *Promise of the New South*, 93.

23. See Elliott West, *The Saloon on the Rocky Mountain Mining Frontier* (Lincoln: University of Nebraska Press, 1979); Thomas J. Noel, *The City and the Saloon: Denver, 1858–1916* (Lincoln: University of Nebraska Press, 1982). For some recent articles on the culture of saloon life, see Elaine Frantz Parsons, "Risky Business: The Uncertain Boundaries of Manhood in the Midwestern Saloon," *Journal of Social History* 34 (2000): 283–307; Jon T. Coleman, "The Men in McArthur's Bar: The Cultural Significance of the Margins," *Western Historical Quarterly* 31 (2000): 47–68. For studies of brothels and prostitution, see Elliott West, "Scarlet West: The Oldest Profession in the Trans-Mississippi West," *Montana* 31 (1981): 16–27; Anne M. Butler, *Daughters of Joy, Sisters of Misery: Prostitutes in the American West, 1865–1890* (Urbana: University of Illinois Press, 1985); Jan Mackell, *Brothels, Bordellos, and Bad Girls: Prostitution in Colorado, 1860–1930* (Albuquerque: University of New Mexico Press, 2004).

24. Lewis E. Atherton, *The Pioneer Merchant in Mid-America* (Columbia: University of Missouri Press, 1939).

25. Lewis E. Atherton, *The Southern Country Store, 1800–1860* (Baton Rouge: Louisiana State University Press, 1949). Examples of sources that focus exclusively on Texas merchants and general stores include Charles G. Anderson, *Deep Creek Merchant: The Story of William Henry "Pete" Snyder* (Snyder, Texas: Snyder Publishing, 1984); Rose G. Biderman, *They Came to Stay: The Story of the Jews of Dallas, 1870–1997* (Austin: Eakin Press, 2002); Henry B. Crawford, "George W. Singer and Dry Goods Retailing on the West Texas–South Plains Frontier, 1880–1890," *West Texas Historical Association Year Book* 69 (1993): 18–33; Patrick Dearan, *Halff of Texas: A Merchant Rancher of the Old West* (Austin: Eakin Press, 2000); Donald R. Walker, *A Frontier Texas Mercantile: The History of Gibbs Brothers and Company, Huntsville, 1841–1940* (Huntsville: Texas Review Press, 1997).

26. Richard Wightman Fox and T. Jackson Lears, eds., *The Culture of Consumption: Critical Essays in American History, 1880–1980* (New York: Pantheon Books, 1983); Daniel Horowitz, *The Morality of Spending: Attitudes toward the Consumer Society, 1875–1940* (Baltimore: Johns Hopkins University Press, 1985);

Simon Bronner, ed., *Consuming Visions: Accumulation and Display of Goods in America, 1880–1920* (Winterthur: Henry Francis du Pont Winterthur Museum, 1989); William Leach, *Land of Desire: Merchants, Power, and the Rise of a New American Culture* (New York: Pantheon Books, 1993). For useful historiographical essays and bibliographies on consumption, see Martin, "Makers, Buyers, and Users," 141–57; Paul Glennie, "Consumption within Historical Studies," in *Acknowledging Consumption: A Review of New Studies*, ed. Daniel Miller (London: Routledge, 1995), 164–203; Ellen Furlough, "Gender and Consumption in Historical Perspective: A Selected Bibliography," in *The Sex of Things: Gender and Consumption in Historical Perspective*, ed. Victoria de Grazia and Ellen Furlough (Berkeley and Los Angeles: University of California Press, 1996), 389–409; Lawrence B. Glickman, "Bibliographic Essay," in *Consumer Society in American History: A Reader*, ed. Lawrence B. Glickman (Ithaca: Cornell University Press, 1999), 399–414. Other important works on consumer society in the late nineteenth and early twentieth centuries include Susan Porter Benson, *Counter Cultures: Saleswomen, Managers, and Customers in American Department Stores, 1890–1940* (Urbana: University of Illinois Press, 1986); Elaine Abelson, *When Ladies Go A-Thieving: Middle-Class Shoppers in the Victorian Department Store* (New York: Oxford University Press, 1989); T. Jackson Lears, *Fables of Abundance: A Cultural History of Advertising in America* (New York: Basic Books, 1994).

27. An important exception is Thomas J. Schlereth, "Country Stores, County Fairs, and Mail Order Catalogues: Consumption in Rural America," in Bronner, *Consuming Visions*, 339–75.

28. Ted Ownby, *American Dreams in Mississippi: Consumers, Poverty, and Culture, 1830–1998* (Chapel Hill: University of North Carolina Press, 1999).

29. Historians using material culture to examine the past have proved especially influential in my research, especially those who analyze the interplay of class and consumption in the mid- to late nineteenth century. Essays by Kenneth Ames exploring the Victorian era and Victorian sensibilities provide a sense of the idealized class dynamics present in midcentury America. Ames asserts that by studying the items that surrounded Victorians we can not only learn about prominent aspects of Victorians' everyday life but also come closer to understanding their thinking. Ames asserts that both rural and urban Victorians felt a fervent interest in acquiring goods that demonstrated both their gentility and respectability, items that were more readily available because of the proliferation of ready-made, mass-produced goods advertised through catalogues. Kenneth L. Ames, "Meaning in Artifacts: Hall Furnishings in Victorian America," *Journal of Interdisciplinary History* 9 (Summer 1978): 19–46; Kenneth L. Ames, "Trade Catalogues and the Study of Culture," in *Accumulation and Display: Mass Marketing Household Goods in America, 1880–1920*, ed. Deborah Anne Federhen et al. (Winterthur, Delaware: Henry du Pont Winterthur Museum, 1986), 8–14. See also Schlereth, "Country Stores,

Country Fairs," 347; David Jaffee, "Peddlers of Progress and the Transformation of the Rural North, 1760–1860," *Journal of American History* 78 (September 1991): 511–35; David Jaffee, "The Village Enlightenment in New England, 1760–1820," *William and Mary Quarterly* 47 (July 1990): 327–46; Neil McKendrick, John Brewer, and J. H. Plumb, *The Birth of Consumer Society: The Commercialization of Eighteenth-Century England* (Bloomington: Indiana University Press, 1982); T. H. Breen, "'Baubles of Britain': The American and Consumer Revolution of the Eighteenth Century," *Past and Present* 119 (1988): 73–104; Richard L. Bushman, *The Refinement of America: Persons, Houses, Cities* (New York: Alfred A. Knopf, 1992); John Brewer and Roy Porter, eds., *Consumption and the World of Goods* (London: Routledge, 1993); Cary Carson, Ronald Hoffman, and Peter J. Albert, eds., *Of Consuming Interests: The Style of Life in the Eighteenth Century* (Charlottesville: University Press of Virginia, 1994).

30. In discussing the influence of *Annales* historians like Roger Chartier and Jacque Revel, Lynn Hunt notes the interplay of economic and social factors with cultural concerns: "Economic and social relations are not prior to or determining of cultural ones; they are themselves fields of cultural practice and cultural production—which cannot be explained deductively by reference to an extracultural dimension of experience." Hunt, "History, Culture, and Text," 7.

31. Also influential to this book, although perhaps less obviously so, is Laurel Thatcher Ulrich, *A Midwife's Tale: The Life of Martha Ballard, Based on Her Diary, 1785–1812* (New York: Vintage Books, 1990). While it is certainly true that countless histories have been written from personal diaries, Ballard's diary lacks the description, analysis, and emotion found in many of the others. Ulrich overcomes the thin detail of Ballard's diary by weaving a comprehensive analysis of women's lives and work in the late eighteenth and early nineteenth centuries around the data provided in the diary. A typical entry from Ballard's diary, for example, reads as follows: "Clear morn. I pulld flax the fornon. Rain afternoon. I am very much fatagud. Lay on the bed & rested. The two Hannahs washing. Dolly weaving. I was called to Mrs Claton in travil at 11 O Clok Evening." Much like a ledger entry, Ballard's diary entries provide little in the way of detail or narrative, requiring Ulrich to patch together the people and relationships mentioned in the diary and to place the events in the larger context of the period. Ulrich, *A Midwife's Tale*, 38.

32. Walter Nugent, "Where Is the American West? Report on a Survey," *Montana* 42 (Spring 1992): 2–23. Also see David M. Emmons, "Constructed Province: History and the Making of the Last American West," *Western Historical Quarterly* 25 (1994): 437–59; Martin Ridge, "The American West: From Frontier to Region," *New Mexico Historical Quarterly* 64 (April 1989): 125–41; Clyde A. Milner II et al., eds., *The Oxford History of the American West* (New York: Oxford University Press, 1994); David M. Wrobel and Michael C. Steiner, eds., *Many Wests: Place, Culture, and Regional Identity* (Lawrence: University Press of Kansas, 1997).

33. Robert A. Calvert, "Agrarian Texas," in Walter L. Buenger and Robert A. Calvert, eds., *Texas through Time: Evolving Interpretations* (College Station: Texas A&M University Press, 1991), 197.

34. U.S. Bureau of the Census, *Tenth Census of the United States 1880, Population* (Washington, D.C.: GPO, 1883), 455.

35. U.S. Bureau of the Census, *Ninth Census of the United States 1870*, Vol. 1, *Population of Civil Divisions less than Counties*, Table III–State of Texas (Washington, D.C.: GPO. 1872), 270–74. For 1890, see Robert A. Calvert, Arnoldo De Leon, and Gregg Cantrell, *The History of Texas*, 4th ed. (Wheeling, Ill.: Harlan Davidson, 2007), table, 175.

36. Elliott West, "Reconstructing Race," *Western Historical Quarterly* 34 (Spring 2003): 7.

37. For a description of Victorianism, see Daniel Walker Howe, "Victorian Culture in America," in *Victorian America*, ed. Daniel Walker Howe (Pennsylvania: University of Pennsylvania Press, 1976), 3–28 (12). See Peter Gay, *The Bourgeois Experience: Victoria to Freud* (Oxford University Press; reprint, New York: W. W. Norton, 1984), vol.1, also *Education of the Senses* (1984); vol. 2, *The Tender Passion* (1986); vol. 3, *The Cultivation of Hatred* (1993); vol. 4, *The Naked Heart* (1995); vol. 5, *Pleasure Wars* (1998). In this comprehensive collection, Gay focuses on the life and social awareness of the Victorian middle classes in the nineteenth century. Thomas J. Schlereth, *Victorian America: Transformations in Everyday Life, 1876–1915* (New York: HarperCollins, 1991). Other important works on Victorian culture in America include Katherine Grier, *Culture and Comfort: People, Parlors, and Upholstery* (Rochester, N.Y.: Strong Museum, distributed by the University of Massachusetts Press, 1988); Kenneth L. Ames, *Death in the Dining Room and Other Tales of Victorian Culture* (Philadelphia: Temple University Press, 1992); Jessica H. Foy and Thomas J. Schlereth, eds., *American Home Life, 1880–1930: A Social History of Spaces and Services* (Knoxville: University of Tennessee Press, 1992). For a discussion of Victorian and the American West, see Robert Haywood, *Victorian West: Class and Culture in Kansas Cattle Towns* (Lawrence: University Press of Kansas, 1991). For an interesting discussion of Victorian gentility among those outside of white middle-class culture in the West, see Adrian Praetzellis and Mary Praetzellis, "Mangling Symbols of Gentility in the Wild West: Case Studies in Interpretive Archaeology," *American Anthropologist* 103 (September 2001): 645–54; Richard White, *"It's Your Misfortune and None of My Own": A New History of the American West* (Norman: University of Oklahoma Press, 1991; reprint, 1993), 307–19; Elliott West, *The Contested Plains: Indians, Goldseekers, and the Rush to Colorado* (Lawrence: University Press of Kansas, 1998), 241.

38. For counterarguments of Victorianism, see John Lucas, "Republican versus Victorian: Radical Writing in the Later Years of the Nineteenth Century," in *Rethinking Victorian Culture*, eds. Juliet John and Alice Jenkins (New York: St. Martin's Press, 2000), 29. Also see John Kucich and Dianne F. Sadoff, eds., *Victorian Afterlife:*

Postmodern Culture Rewrites the Nineteenth Century (Minneapolis: University of Minnesota Press, 2000); Gary Day, ed., *Varieties of Victorianism: The Uses of a Past* (New York: St. Martin's Press, 1998); David E. Shi, "Review of Stanley Coben's *Rebellion against Victorianism: The Impetus for Cultural Change in 1920s America*," *American Historical Review* 97 (October 1992): 1301–302.

39. For a definition of the "cult of domesticity," see Barbara Welter, "The Cult of True Womanhood, 1820–1860," *American Quarterly* 18 (Summer 1966): 151–75; Nancy F. Cott, *The Bonds of Womanhood: "Woman's Sphere" in New England, 1780–1835* (New Haven: Yale University Press, 1977). For more on domestic ideology, also see Gerda Lerner, "The Lady and the Mill Girl: Changes in the Status of Women in the Age of Jackson," *Mid-Continent American Studies Journal* 10 (Spring 1969): 5–15; Kathryn Kish Sklar, *Catherine Beecher: A Study in American Domesticity* (New Haven: Yale University Press, 1973); Carl N. Degler, *At Odds: Women and the Family from the Revolution to the Present* (New York: Oxford University Press, 1981); Linda K. Kerber, "Separate Sphere, Female Worlds, Woman's Places: The Rhetoric of Women's History," *Journal of American History* 75 (June 1988): 28. Kerber's article traces the development and challenges to separate sphere arguments. For interpretations beyond domesticity and separate spheres regarding women's lives and roles in the nineteenth century, see Suzanne Lebsock, *The Free Women of Petersburg: Status and Culture in a Southern Town, 1784–1860* (New York: Norton, 1984); Christine Stansell, *City of Women: Sex and Class in New York, 1789–1860* (New York: Alfred A. Knopf, 1986).

Chapter 1

1. Customer Ledger 1876–77, Brown & Dixon Company Records, ETRC. (The name of this store changed from McKinney & Brown to Brown & Dixon in the mid-1880s. W. A. Brown remained the principle store owner throughout this period.)

2. *Cherokee County Banner*, 11 February 1916, 185, in *The Saga of Cherokee County, Texas*, compiled by Helen Crawford (1987), ETRC.

3. Neil Foley, *The White Scourge: Mexicans, Blacks, and Poor Whites in Texas Cotton Culture* (Berkeley and Los Angeles: University of California Press, 1997), 28.

4. *Cherokee County Banner*, 2 February 1916. In this regard, Brown adhered to the classic description of a Victorian gentleman—one steeped in discipline, strict personal ethics, social responsibility, and moral rectitude, struggling to create order in a newly industrializing world. Howe, "Victorian Culture in America," 12.

5. Jacksonville Centennial Corporation, *Jacksonville: The Story of a Dynamic Community* (Jacksonville, Texas: Jacksonville Centennial Corporation, 1972), 100; Hattie Joplin Roach, *The Hills of Cherokee: Historical Sketches of Life in Cherokee County* (Rusk, Texas: N.p., 1952), 170–71.

6. *Cherokee County Banner*, 11 February 1916.

7. Jacksonville Centennial, *Jacksonville*, 13.

8. *Cherokee County Banner*, 2 February 1916.

9. For more on the period's "striving mentality," see Burton J. Bledstein, *The Culture of Professionalism: The Middle Class and the Development of Higher Education in America* (New York: W. W. Norton, 1976).

10. Jacksonville Centennial, *Jacksonville*, 100; O. C. Payne, "Lem Brown and His 'New Way' Store," *Holland's Magazine* (September 1913), in *Saga of Cherokee County*, 24.

11. Jacksonville Centennial, *Jacksonville*, 100.

12. Customer Ledger 1876–77; Ledger 1874–75, 39, 56; Ledger F—1883, 348; Ledger J—1887, 525; all in Brown & Dixon, ETRC.

13. *Cherokee County Banner*, May 2, 1913.

14. In the opening pages of Daybook 1872, the following note appeared: "We Wm. Clark and Wm. Hyde have on October the 24th 1872 bought of Ingraham & Co. A mercantile firm composed of G. F. Ingraham and S. L. Anthom doing business in the town of Nacogdoches, Nacogdoches County the entire stock of goods, wares and merchandise of said firm have and do hereby agree to associate as equal partners under the firm name of Clark and Hyde in the conduct of a mercantile business at said place sharing profits and losses equally the stock resources and liabilities on said date appears as follows: Nacogdoches, Thursday, Oct. 24, 1872." Daybook 1 (October 1872–June 1873), Clark & Hyde Mercantile, ETRC. For information on their occupational status, see Ericson, *People of Nacogdoches County in 1870*, 13. For George F. Ingraham, see Carolyn Reeves Ericson, ed., *The People of Nacogdoches County in 1880: An Edited Census* (Nacogdoches: ETRC, 1988), 4.

15. *Nacogdoches* (Nacogdoches Altrusa Club, 1960), Dale Collection, Western History Collections, University of Oklahoma, Norman, Oklahoma (hereinafter WHC), 1–4. According to the census, the town's population was 3,188. U.S. Bureau of the Census, *Ninth Census 1870, Population*.

16. George F. Ingraham, one of the partners from whom Clark and Hyde purchased the store, served under William Clark during the Civil War in Company G of the Eighth Texas Infantry, demonstrating the meaningful ties of this merchant elite. Although originally a New Yorker, Ingraham resolved that since he had "cast his lot" with the South, he needed to fight on the side of the Confederacy. After returning from the Civil War, Ingraham affiliated with the Democratic Party, practiced law, and ultimately served as a judge for Nacogdoches County and the Second Judicial District. Among these many professional ventures, Ingraham found time to operate a dry goods store, aptly named Ingraham & Company, which later became the Clark & Hyde mercantile firm. Evidently, all three of these store owners distinguished themselves professionally in careers outside of retailing. NCGS, *Nacogdoches County Families*, 215, 371–72.

17. Daybook 1, Clark & Hyde, ETRC, 8, 28. According to the census, Mrs. William Clark was Amelia Clark, formerly Amelia Taylor. In 1870 the Clarks had two young children, two-year-old William and eight-month-old Mary. Apparently, William F. Hyde lived alone. Ericson, *People of Nacogdoches County in 1870*, 13.

18. Daybook 1, Clark & Hyde, ETRC, 103. Federhen et al. provide a detailed assessment of the proliferation and cultural meaning of a multitude of consumer items purchased for Victorian households; included in this discussion was the popularity of wall paper in creating a "background for domestic harmony." *Accumulation and Display*, 15.

19. Daybook 1, Clark & Hyde, ETRC, 151.

20. Ericson, *People of Nacogdoches Count in 1870*, 107.

21. Ledger 1870–73, Hardeman & Barret, ETRC, 283, 382.

22. A detailed compilation of documents and letters outlining Barret's role of quartermaster for the Nacogdoches District during the Civil War can be found in the L. T. Barret Collection (A-274), ETRC.

23. Devereaux, "History of Oil Springs," 150. For background on the Barret family, also see Chamberlain, "Lyne Toliaferro Barret," 8.

24. Ralph A. Wooster, "Wealthy Texans, 1870," *Southwestern Historical Quarterly* 74.1 (July 1970): 32.

25. Chamberlain, "Lyne Toliaferro Barret," 5–18.

26. Ericson, *People of Nacogdoches in 1870*, 105; NCGS, *Nacogdoches County Families*, 340.

27. Gladys Hardeman, "The History of Melrose," Gladys Hardeman Research Collection (A-69), ETRC, 19.

28. Ledger 1870–73, Hardeman & Barret, ETRC, 284, 21, 382, 384.

29. Alwyn Barr, *Black Texans: A History of African Americans in Texas, 1528–1995*, 2nd ed. (Norman: University of Oklahoma Press, 1996), 64; Smallwood, *Time of Hope*, 68–95.

30. Howe, "Victorian Culture in America," 19; Ledger 1870–73, Hardeman & Barret, ETRC, 22.

31. Schlereth, "Country Stores, County Fairs," 347; Ames, "Trade Catalogues," 8–14.

32. Ledger 1, Lewis Store (AR 1999-017), Austin History Center, Austin, Texas (AHC), 500. The store owner's name appears as A. B. Lewis in the ledgers, although in the census he is listed as Alfred D. Lewis. The discrepancy is due to either this researcher's inability to decipher his handwriting or a mistake occurring with the census taker—either is plausible.

33. See Ledger 2, ibid., 125–31, 137; U.S. Bureau of the Census, *Federal Census 1880: Population Schedules*, Travis County, Precinct No. 2, Enumeration District 138 (Oklahoma Historical Society, Oklahoma City, Oklahoma), 10.

34. Haywood, *Victorian West*, 38; Clark, *Pills, Petticoats, and Plows*, ix; Ownby, *American Dreams*, 9.

35. *Cherokee County Banner*, 2 February 1916.

36. The *Texas Intelligencer*, 9 January 1875, cited in *Cherokee County Banner*, 1 June 1917.

37. Don H. Biggers, *Shackelford County Sketches*, edited and annotated by Joan Farmer (Albany and Fort Griffin: Clear Fork Press, 1974), 6–7. "C.C. Cooper and John C. Lynch established ranches in Shackelford County, and in 1861, with employees and their families established a fortified settlement that they called Fort Hubbard." "Shackelford County," in Ron Tyler et al., ed., *The New Handbook of Texas* (Austin: Texas State Historical Association, 1996), 5:984.

38. Ledger 1876 [J. C. Lynch Store], John W. H. Davis Papers, 1876–1912 (2J136), Comfort, Kendall County, Grimes County, Center for American History, University of Texas, Austin (CAH), 13, 22, 115, 151, 161, 167; J. C. Lynch Account Book (2B178), CAH, 63.

39. Biggers, *Shackelford County Sketches*, 54. See also "Hubbard Creek," in Tyler et al., *New Handbook of Texas*, vol. 3, available at http://www.tshaonline.org/handbook/online/articles/rbhbq.

40. Lynch Account Book, CAH, 25, 33, 36, 54, 58.

41. Two sources discuss the ledger book from Schreiner's first year of business. The first is Charles's Schreiner's biographer, in Haley, *Charles Schreiner*, 12–13; the second is Gene Hollon, "Captain Charles Schreiner: The Father of the Hill Country," *Southwestern Historical Quarterly* 48.2 (October 1944): 145–68. Hollon explains that the account ledger was in the possession of Charles Schreiner's grandson Scott Schreiner, who allowed him access to its contents, 154. See also Neal Barrett, Jr., *Long Days and Short Nights: A Century of Texas Ranching on the YO, 1880–1980* (Mountain Home, Texas: Y-O Press, 1980); Don Hedgpeth, *Proud Promise: The Story of Schreiner Institute/College, 1923–1998* (Kerrville: Texas Press of the Guadalupe of Schreiner College, 1998).

42. This estate was valued at $6 million, when it was divided between the store owner's eight children in 1917. Hollon, "Captain Charles Schreiner," 159, 160.

43. Haley, *Charles Schreiner*, 68. See also Hollon, "Captain Charles Schreiner," 159, 160; Schreiner University website, at www.schreiner.edu/about/history.html.

44. E. McCurdy Bostic, "Elizabeth Fulton Hester," *Chronicles of Oklahoma* 6 (December 1928): 449–52.

45. Buster Springs and J. T. Inge (Mrs.), interview 6761, vol. 86, Indian Pioneer Collection (Indian Pioneer Papers), WHC.

46. Mrs. Frances Reeder, interview 7003, vol. 75, Indian Pioneer Collection (Indian Pioneer Papers), WHC; Bostic, "Elizabeth Fulton Hester."

47. Henderson County Historical Commission, *Family Histories of Henderson County, Texas, 1846–1981* (Dallas: Taylor, 1981), 205; J. J. Faulk, *History of Henderson County, Texas* (Athens, Texas: Athens Review, 1929), 269–72. Robert Lee [General] Gauntt was born during the Civil War in 1862, and his name is no doubt in homage to the famous southern general. At the time of Gauntt's birth, his father, John W. Gauntt, was serving a four-year stint in the Confederate army.

48. Gauntt Bros. Ledger 1887–88, Baylor University, Waco, Texas, 258, 285, 305; Faulk, *Henderson County*, 272.

49. Frederick Jackson Turner, *The Frontier in American History* (New York: Henry Holt, 1920), 154; Haywood, *Victorian West*, 3.

50. Dearan, *Halff of Texas*, 62. Admittedly, this assessment is from a popular history. I have tried to be mindful of relying on such sources for critical analysis. As David Jaffee has observed, local histories often present idealized, distorted, or uncritical depictions of historical characters. In his study of greater New England communities, Jaffee found that local histories of early communities presented distorted or idealized views of early settlers and attempted to create a particular, in this case hyper-patriotic, depiction of the past. David Jaffee, *People of the Wachusett: Greater New England in History and Memory, 1630–1860* (Ithaca: Cornell University Press, 1999), 239–49. With this in mind, I have tried to limit my use of such sources to factual data, rather than meaningful, uncritical interpretation.

51. Haywood, *Victorian West*, 6.

52. Angie Debo, *The Rise and Fall of the Choctaw Republic*, Civilization of the American Indian Series, vol. 6 (Norman: University of Oklahoma Press, 1961), 226.

53. *Oklahoma Star*, 23 November 1875.

54. For classic works on corporate growth and industrialism during the Gilded Age, see Charles A. Beard and Mary R. Beard, *The Rise of American Civilization* (New York: Macmillan, 1927); Vernon L. Parrington, *The Beginnings of Critical Realism in America, 1860–1920*, vol. 3, *Main Currents in American Thought* (Norman: University of Oklahoma Press, 1987); Richard Hofstadter, *The Age of Reform: From Bryan to F.D.R.* (New York: Vintage Books, 1960). For more recent works, see Glen Porter, *The Rise of Big Business, 1860–1910* (Arlington Heights, IL: Harlan Davidson, 1973); Alfred D. Chandler, *The Visible Hand: The Managerial Revolution in American Business* (Cambridge, Mass.: Belknap Press, 1977); Robert F. Himmelberg, ed., *The Rise of Big Business and the Beginnings of Antitrust and Railroad Regulation, 1870–1900* (New York: Garland, 1994); Charles W. Calhoun, ed., *The Gilded Age: Essays on the Origins of Modern America* (Wilmington, Del.: Scholarly Resources, 1996); David M. Tucker, *Mugwumps: Public Moralists of the Gilded Age* (Columbia: University of Missouri Press, 1998).

55. Much of this section is derived from Linda C. English, "Inside the Store, Inside the Past: A Cultural Analysis of McAlester's General Store," *Chronicles of Oklahoma* 81 (Spring 2003): 34–53.

56. For a good example, see Gerald L. Sparks, "James Jesse McAlester: The Choctaw Nation's Omnipresent Entrepreneur, 1871–1894" (master's thesis, University of Oklahoma, 1997).

57. For an interesting discussion of reactions to robber barons and "new money" entrepreneurs, see Hofstader's discussion of the "mugwump elite." In the absence of national sources of power and prestige, Hofstadter contended, the pillars of the local community were men of great importance in their own right. They often

came from elite families and old money. It is these same traditional elite who felt a sense of insecurity with the massive industrial, urban, and immigration changes of the late nineteenth century. Hofstadter, *Age of Reform*, 135–36. See also John G. Sproat, *"The Best Men": Liberal Reformers in the Gilded Age* (New York: Oxford University Press, 1968).

58. Oliver Knight, "An Oklahoma Indian Trader as a Frontiersman of Commerce," *Journal of Southern History* 23 (May 1957): 219.

59. While there are a number of histories that detail McAlester's early career, a particularly insightful article was written by Paul Nesbitt, based on an interview he conducted with McAlester. See Paul Nesbitt, "J. J. McAlester," *Chronicles of Oklahoma* 11 (June 1933): 758–64.

60. Ibid. More recent accounts include Sparks, "James Jesse McAlester," and Michael J. Hightower, "Cattle, Coal, and Indian Land: A Tradition of Mining in Southeastern Oklahoma," *Chronicles of Oklahoma* 62 (Spring 1984): 4–25.

61. Sparks, "James Jesse McAlester," 8. Despite gaining citizenship in the tribe, there was never any doubt among the Choctaws that McAlester was white or, conversely, that Mrs. Rebecca McAlester was Indian. According to the Choctaw census of 1885, Rebecca McAlester's racial heritage was listed as Indian, specifically Chickasaw. That McAlester profited from this racially mixed marriage there can be no doubt. He gained access to the Choctaw coalfields the only way one legitimately could—through marriage. Choctaw Nation Census, *Choctaw Census 1885*, Tubucksy [Tobucksy] County (Archive 121), 906–907, Oklahoma Historical Society (OHS), Oklahoma City. Of note, McAlester is listed in the 1885 census as having two thousand head of cattle and fifteen thousand bales of cotton, confirming that by the mid-1880s he had already acquired significant wealth.

62. H. Craig Miner, *The Corporation and the Indian: Tribal Sovereignty and Industrial Civilization in Indian Territory, 1865–1907* (Norman: University of Oklahoma Press, 1989), 59. The need to develop necessary business relationships in Indian Territory was also seen in the retailing activities of John and William Shirley, two brothers who were initially traders in the Chickasaw Nation but later opened a mercantile business, a hotel, a ranch, and a toll bridge in a community known as Cherokee Town. John Shirley entered into a contract with James Bond, an intermarried Chickasaw, to run several head of cattle: "'Permitted' citizens such as Shirley were limited by Chickasaw law in the amount of livestock they could hold, but Bond, being a full citizen, could use as much land as he wanted and could hold an unlimited number of livestock." Michael Tower, "Traders along the Washita: A Short History of the Shirley Trading Company," *Chronicles of Oklahoma* 65 (Spring 1987): 10.

63. Sparks, "James Jesse McAlester," 23; English, "Inside the Store," 37–38.

64. Nesbitt, "J. J. McAlester," 762.

65. Sales Ledger 1887–88, #161 (M2046), J. J. McAlester Collection, WHC, 62.

66. *McAlester Messenger*, 8 September 1905.

67. Knight, "Oklahoma Indian Trader," 215. For a picture of McAlester's home, see English, "Inside the Store," 47.

68. Sales Ledger 1879–80, #154, McAlester Collection, WHC, 150, 190, 244, 268; Mrs. Cook, interview cited in Knight, "Oklahoma Indian Trader," 215; *Endorsements and Recommendations of James J. McAlester, Candidate for U.S. Marshall of the Indian Territory Courts* (Atoka, Indian Territory, 1893), in Susan McAlester Barnes Collection (B-1, Part II, F-5), WHC.

69. Haywood, *Victorian West*, 16.

70. W. David Baird and Danney Goble, *The Story of Oklahoma* (Norman: University of Oklahoma Press, 1994), 282.

71. Miss Ella Robinson, "History of the Patterson Mercantile Company," *Chronicles of Oklahoma* 36 (Spring 1958): 55n5; Mary Jane Ward, *George Washington Grayson and the Creek Nation, 1843–1920* (Norman: University of Oklahoma Press, 1999), 102.

72. Daybook 1869–71, F. B. Severs Collection, OHS, 5, 67.

73. Ward, *George Washington Grayson*, 184, 196.

74. "Historical Notes," *Chronicles of Oklahoma* 17 (June 1939): 232.

75. Robinson, "Patterson Mercantile Company," 55n5.

76. Miss Sarah B. Trent, interview 8238, vol. 92, Indian Pioneer Collection (Indian Pioneer Papers), WHC.

77. *The New Encyclopedia of Texas*, ed. Ellis A. Davis and Edwin H. Grobe (Dallas: Texas Development Bureau, 1929), 3:2035.

78. Anna Martin to M. Chapman, 1904, Homer Martin Papers (microfilm M381), Southwest Collection, Texas Tech University, Lubbock, Texas (SWC); Stella Gipson Polk, *Mason and Mason County: A History*, rev. ed. (Burnet, Texas: Eakin Press, 1980), 48–52.

79. According to Wayne Austerman, although the El Paso mail probably never paid the contractors who established permanent mailing stations, the affiliation still reaped economic benefits for local service providers. For merchants, mail service attracted customers from the surrounding environs who might have otherwise stayed away or frequented a competitor's store. Wayne R. Austerman, *Sharp Rifles and Spanish Mules: The San Antonio–El Paso Mail, 1851–1881* (College Station: Texas A&M University Press, 1985). Other store merchants who served as postmasters were G. B. Hester, J. J. McAlester, and F. B. Severs.

80. Anna Martin to M. Chapman, 1904, Homer Martin Papers (Microfilm M381), SWC; Pat Ellebracht, "A True Texas Legend: Anna Mebus Martin and the Commercial Bank," *Financial History* 61 (Winter 1998): 24.

81. Daybook 1, 1885–87, Hedwig's Hill Store Records, SWC, 202, 215, 273.

82. Account Book 1, 1884–91, Hedwig's Hill Store, SWC, 1; Ellebracht, "True Texas Legend," 27; Margaret Bierschwale, *A History of Mason County, Texas, through 1964*, ed. Julius E. Devos, rev. ed. (Mason, Texas: Mason County Historical Commission, 1998), 106.

83. Clark, *Pills, Petticoats, and Plows*, 50.

84. *Oklahoma Star*, 23 November 1875.

85. Daniel J. Boorstin, *The Americans: The National Experience* (New York: Random House, 1965).

86. Carl Abbot, *Boosters and Businessmen: Popular Economic Thought and Urban Growth in the Antebellum Middle West* (Westport, Conn.: Greenwood Press, 1981).

87. Ward, *George Washington Grayson*, 196; Robinson, "Patterson Mercantile Company," 55n5.

88. Nesbitt, "J. J. McAlester," 764. See also Sparks, "James Jesse McAlester," 15–17.

89. Anderson, *Deep Creek Merchant*, 99–102.

90. H. Wayne Morgan, "An Age in Need of Reassessment: A View Beforehand," in H. Wayne Morgan, ed., *The Gilded Age: A Reappraisal* (Syracuse: Syracuse University Press, 1963), 13.

91. White, *"It's Your Misfortune,"* 307. See his discussion of western society, 307–16. The notion of white middle-class gentility in the West is problematized by Praetzellis and Praetzellis, who argue that in western regions symbols of gentility had power outside of the white middle class. To support their case, they cite examples such as a high-ranking Mexican Californio, a Chinese American merchant, African American porters, and an expensive brothel. Praetzellis and Praetzellis, "Mangling Symbols of Gentility."

92. Sales Ledger 1874–75, #152, Sales Ledger 1886–87, #160, Sales Ledger 1894–96, #173, McAlester Collection, WHC; Daybook 1, Clark & Hyde, ETRC, 56; Daybook 1, 1885–87, Hedwig's Hill Store, SWC, 215.

Chapter 2

1. Quoted from "Ten-Cent Cotton: Not Very Much of a Novelty—The Reasons for This Year's Boom," *New York Times*, March 8, 1903, 29.

2. October 29, 1885, Cotton Book 1885–86, Hermann Fischer Store Records, 1879–1904 (2D144), Barker Texas History Center, CAH.

3. Clark, *Pills, Petticoats, and Plows*, 293–98.

4. Hides and Skins 1888–91, Fischer Store Records, CAH.

5. Calvert, "Agrarian Texas," 197.

6. Walter L. Buenger, "Texas and the South," *Southwestern Historical Quarterly* 103 (January 2000): 324. Ty Cashion revisits this debate and argues for a "Texan West," prototypical of the American West, unlike its counterpart, East Texas, with its ties to the Old South. Ty Cashion, "What's the Matter with Texas? The Great Enigma of the Lone Star State in the American West," *Montana* 55 (Winter 2005): 2–15.

7. Foley, *White Scourge*, 28.

8. Foley offers a good description of these distinctions, ibid., 10.

9. Robert A. Calvert, "Nineteenth-Century Farmers, Cotton, and Prosperity," *Southwestern Historical Quarterly* 73 (April 1970): 510–11; John S. Spratt, *The Road to Spindletop: Economic Change in Texas, 1871–1901* (Dallas: Southern Methodist University Press, 1955), 61–83; Rupert N. Richardson et al., *Texas: The Lone Star State*, 8th ed. (Upper Saddle River, N.J.: Prentice-Hall, 2001), 277. For a discussion of labor relations, plantation owners, and African Americans, see Robert A. Calvert, ed., "The Freedmen and Agricultural Prosperity," *Southwestern Historical Quarterly* 76.4 (1973): 461–71. For more general discussions of farm life in late-nineteenth-century America, see Gilbert C. Fite, *The Farmers' Frontier, 1865–1900* (Albuquerque: University of New Mexico Press, 1974); Mary Ellen Jones, *Daily Life on the Nineteenth-Century American Frontier* (Westport, Conn.: Greenwood Press, 1998). Gilbert Fite discusses the poverty, economic swings, and general backwardness of southern agriculture in the nineteenth century and the modernizing effects of mechanization and diversification in the late 1930s. Gilbert C. Fite, *Cotton Fields No More: Southern Agriculture, 1865–1980* (Lexington: University of Kentucky Press, 1984). For a comprehensive look at Texas cotton culture in the twentieth century, see Thad Sitton and Dan K. Utley, *From Can See to Can't: Texas Cotton Farmers on the Southern Prairies* (Austin: University of Texas Press, 1997).

10. Foley, *White Scourge*, 11, 30. According to Foley, the area that he defines as "central Texas" encompasses the diamond-shaped region of Dallas in the north to Corpus Christi in the south, bounded by San Antonio in the west and Houston in the east. Ibid., 15.

11. Ibid., 1–2.

12. For the demographics of Central Texas, Foley cites a census agricultural report from 1880, which noted the composition of the workforce in the Blackland Prairie region as predominantly white, except in a handful of counties that maintained roughly an equal proportion of blacks to whites in 1880. However, Foley asserts that after 1880, whites began to outnumber blacks in these counties as well. Ibid., 225–26. See U.S. Bureau of the Census, *Report on Cotton Production in the United States; Also Embracing Agricultural and Physico-Geographical Descriptions of the Several Cotton States and of California, Part 1, Mississippi Valley and the Southwestern States, Volume 5, Cotton Production of the State of Texas* (Washington, D.C.: GPO, 1884), 819. For Melrose records, see Ericson, *People of Nacogdoches County in 1870*.

13. Ledger 1870–73, Hardeman & Barret, ETRC, 98.

14. Ericson, *People of Nacogdoches County in 1870*, 106.

15. Ibid., 106, 118, 121, 139; Ledger 1870–73, Hardeman & Barret, ETRC, 27, 80, 168, 170.

16. U.S. Bureau of the Census, *Ninth Census 1870*, 486, 495, 487, 506, 494, 489.

17. Ledger D, 1880–81, Brown & Dixon, ETRC, 178, 289, 303.

18. Ibid., 147, 228.

19. Ibid., 48.

20. Clark, *Pills, Petticoats, and Plows*, 277. There are a number of important studies that examine cotton farmers, the crop-lien system, and merchants' role in the economy of the New South. See, for example, Lawrence Goodwyn, *Democratic Promise: The Populist Moment in America* (New York: Oxford University Press, 1976); Michael Schwartz, *Radical Protest and Social Structure: The Southern Farmers' Alliance and Cotton Tenancy, 1880–1890* (New York: Academic Press, 1976); Jonathan M. Weiner, *Social Origins of the New South: Alabama, 1860–1885* (Baton Rouge: Louisiana State University Press, 1978); Steven Hahn, *The Roots of Southern Populism: Yeoman Farmers and the Transformation of the Georgia Upcountry, 1850–1890* (New York: Oxford University Press, 1983); Gavin Wright, *Old South, New South: Revolutions in the Southern Economy since the Civil War* (New York: Basic Books, 1986); Charles S. Aiken, *The Cotton Plantation South since the Civil War* (Baltimore: Johns Hopkins University Press, 1998); Scott Marler, "Merchants in the Transition to a New South: Central Louisiana, 1840–1880," *Louisiana History* 42 (Spring 2001): 165–92; Louis M. Kyriakoudes, "Lower-Order Urbanization and Territorial Monopoly in the Southern Furnishing Trade: Alabama, 1871–1890," *Social Science History* 26 (Spring 2002): 179–98.

21. Brown & Dixon Fond, ETRC, 1.

22. Ayers, *Promise of the New South*, 93.

23. Clark, *Pills, Petticoats, and Plows*, 274.

24. Marler, "Transition to a New South," 190–92; C. Vann Woodward, *Origins of the New South, 1877–1913* (1951; repr. Baton Rouge: Louisiana State University Press, 1971), 184.

25. Ayers, *Promise of the New South*, 418. Illiteracy rates remained high for southern blacks, ranging in 1880 from 70 percent in Kentucky to 82 percent in Mississippi.

26. The most likely candidate for store owner in the ledger book is J. N. Wilson. His name appears under the heading "Chireno Alliance" although he was probably in a partnership arrangement with others in the community. J. N. Wilson is listed in the 1880 census as a tax assessor. Chireno Ledger, 1887, "Chireno Alliance" (2C446), CAH, 346; Ericson, *People of Nacogdoches County in 1880*, 72.

27. Ericson, *People of Nacogdoches County in 1880*, 106–31.

28. Chireno Ledger, 1887, CAH, 131, 132, 143, 144.

29. *Cherokee County Banner*, 3 March 1916 (special edition featuring excerpts from *The Cherokee Advertiser*, 5 March 1872).

30. J. D. Sherrill Diary, 1884 (A1980.0244c), DeGolyer Library, Southern Methodist University (SMU), Dallas, Texas.

31. Ibid., also see entries for January 11, 19, 1884.

32. Ibid., November 28, 1882, SMU.

33. Walker, *Frontier Texas Mercantile*, 52.

34. Ledger D, 1880–81, 35; Ledger F, 1883, 286; Ledger H, 1885, 56; all in Brown & Dixon, ETRC.

35. Ericson, *People of Nacogdoches County in 1870*, 106, 118, 121, 139. According to Terry Jordan, the percentage of blacks born in southern states reached its apex before the Civil War and steadily dwindled after that, with the virtual cessation of black immigration to Texas after 1865. Terry Jordan, "A Century and a Half of Ethnic Change in Texas, 1836–1986," *Southwestern Historical Quarterly* 89 (April 1986): 385–422 (402).

36. *Federal Census of Cherokee County 1880*, transcribed by Sue Vaughn Taylor, ETRC, 366, 330, 317.

37. Ericson, *People of Nacogdoches County in 1870*, 105, 107.

38. Jordan, "Ethnic Change in Texas," 388. Also see Terry G. Jordan, "The Imprint of the Upper and Lower South on Mid-Nineteenth-Century Texas," *Annals of the Association of American Geographers* 57 (December 1967): 667–90.

39. Neer & James Account Ledger 1871–73, 1879, John & Marie Dutt Collection, Sam Houston Regional Library & Research Center (SHRL), Liberty, Texas, 60 (Easterling), 102 (McKinnon), 117 (Dawes).

40. Walter L. Buenger, *The Path to a Modern South: Northeast Texas between Reconstruction and the Great Depression* (Austin: University of Texas Press, 2001).

41. Cotton Book 1885–86, Fischer Store Records, CAH, November 1885; Terry Jordan, *German Seed in Texas Soil: Immigrant Farmers in Nineteenth-Century Texas* (Austin: University of Texas Press, 1966), 132–33.

42. Foley, *White Scourge*, 2; Terry D. Jordan et al., *Texas: A Geography*, Geographies of the United States Series (Boulder: Westview Press, 1984), 5. Also see Jordan, "Ethnic Change in Texas," 385.

43. J. L. McInnis Ledger 1874–75 (AR 1994-57), AHC, 89, 103; U.S. Bureau of the Census, *Federal Census 1880*, Travis County, 25 (40A).

44. McInnis Ledger 1874–75, 117 (Romine), 373 (O'Conner), 63 (Meeks). Also see U.S. Bureau of the Census, *Federal Census 1880*, Travis County, 38 (47C). For information on the community of Webberville, see Tyler et al., *New Handbook of Texas*, 6:867.

45. Debo, *Choctaw Republic*, 60, 114.

46. G. B. Hester Ledger 1874, Benjamin R. Cook Collection (C13), WHC, 10, 11, 29, 53, 189.

47. W. N. Jones Store Ledger 1871–74 (J-2 1137), Dovie Jones Collection, WHC, entry for December 27, 1872; Daybook 1869–71, Severs Collection, OHS, 32, 46, 97.

48. William P. Morton, interview 6099, vol. 65, Indian Pioneer Collection (Indian Pioneer Papers), WHC.

49. A. J. Kennedy, interview 6988, vol. 50, Indian Pioneer Collection (Indian Pioneer Papers), WHC, pages 3–13.

50. Robert M. Hamilton, interview 5998, vol. 37, Indian Pioneer Collection (Indian Pioneer Papers), WHC, pages 2–3.

51. Jimmy M. Skaggs, *The Cattle-Trailing Industry: Between Supply and Demand, 1866–1890* (Lawrence: University Press of Kansas, 1973); "Spring Cattle Driving," *New York Times*, April 14, 1876, 2.

52. Bierschwale, *Mason County, Texas*, 196; Skaggs, *Cattle-Trailing Industry*, 2; Foley, *White Scourge*, 26.

53. Foley, *White Scourge*, 26; "Spring Cattle Driving," *New York Times*, April 14, 1876, 2.

54. Hobart Huson, *Refugio: A Comprehensive History of Refugio County: From Aboriginal Times to 1955*, vol. 2, *Secession to 1955* (Woodsboro, Texas: Rooke Foundation, 1955), 264.

55. Account Ledger 1877, W. E. McCampbell & Bros. Records, col. 7597, Daughters of the Republic of Texas Library (DRTL), San Antonio, Texas, 84 (Dunman), 85 (West); Account Ledger 1876–77, ibid., 21 (O'Donald).

56. Account Ledger 1877, ibid., 31, 75, 100, 133, 140; Daybook 1877, 32. Costing anywhere from twenty to forty-five dollars, guns were an expensive purchase, and not all store customers could afford such an investment. All of the firearm purchases made through the McCampbell & Bros. store were recorded in Account Ledger 1877, the ledger reserved for successful town residents. In Account Ledger 1876–77, the ledger designated for common laborers (who tended to be either black or Mexican), there are purchases of firearm supplies such as powder, shot, and caps, but no expensive pistols.

57. Account Ledger, 1876–77, McCampbell & Bros., DRTL, 17, 30, 33, 90.

58. Daybook 1, 1885–87, 93 (Weidemann), Daybook 2, 1887–88, 101 (Tatsch), Hedwig's Hill Store, SWC.

59. Ellebracht, "True Texas Legend," 26.

60. Daybook 1, 1885–87, Hedwig's Hill Store, SWC, 374, 375, 429.

61. Daybook 2, 1887–88, ibid., 149, 331.

62. Jordan, *German Seed in Texas Soil*, 147.

63. Polk, *Mason and Mason County*, 48. On the issue of barbed wire and disputes between farmers and ranchers, see Robert Dykstra, *The Cattle Towns*, 6th ed. (New York: Atheneum, 1979).

64. Foley, *White Scourge*, 27.

65. Ibid.; Barr, *Reconstruction to Reform*, 81–83; White, *"It's Your Misfortune,"* 345.

66. Daybook 1, 1885–87, Hedwig's Hill Store, SWC, 369, 380, 430, 438.

67. "Overstocked Ranges: The Outlook for the Winter Not Good for the Cattle," *New York Times*, January 11, 1887, 5.

68. White, *"It's Your Misfortune,"* 344–45.

69. Fischer and Martin arrived after the Adelsverein migration (see Chapter 5).

70. Fischer Store Records, CAH; "Fischer, Texas," in Tyler et al., *New Handbook of Texas*, vol. 2, at http://www.tshaonline.org/handbook/online/articles/hnf48.

71. Jordan, *German Seed in Texas Soil*, 132–33 (132).

72. Ibid., 132–33.

73. Oscar Haas, *History of New Braunfels and Comal County, Texas, 1844–1946* (Austin: Steck, 1968), 150, 268.

74. Miner, *The Corporation and the Indian*, 58. For an in-depth discussion of the connection and controversy surrounding the MK&T and the Osage Coal and Mining Company, see Miner's chapter titled "Coal and Ties: The Confrontation," 58–76; also Sparks, "James Jesse McAlester," 7–8.

75. Hightower, "Cattle, Coal, and Indian Land," 7.

76. U.S. Department of the Interior, U.S. Geological Survey, *Mineral Resources of the United States for the Calendar Year 1887* (Washington, D.C.: GPO, 1888), 244–45.

77. Joseph B. Thorburn and Muriel H. Wright, *Oklahoma: A History of the State and Its People* (New York: Lewis Historical Publishing, 1929), 1:469–70.

78. Sales Ledger 1874–75, #152, January 1874; Sales Ledger 1875–78, #153, August 1876, McAlester Collection, WHC.

79. Robert Hamby, interview 7853, vol. 37, Indian Pioneer Collection (Indian Pioneer Papers), WHC.

80. Sales Ledger 1874–75, #152, McAlester Collection, WHC, 27, 3, 48. Excerpts from this discussion also appear in English, "Inside the Store," 41–43. The article also addresses the issue of whether miners paid more for items from the store than non-employees of the Osage Coal Company. After conducting a comparison of the costs of a number of different items including flour, syrup, and tobacco, the author concluded that coal miners were not singled out as targets of exploitation by the store owner. Those in other occupations, specifically sheep herding and retailing, paid similarly high prices on the same items. English, "Inside the Store," 44–46.

81. Sales Ledger 1874–75, #152, McAlester Collection, WHC, 75.

82. Ibid., 31, 54.

83. *Oklahoma Star*, 16 December 1876.

84. Pittsburg County Genealogical and Historical Society, *Pittsburg County, Oklahoma: People and Places* (Wolfe City, Texas: Henington Industries, 1997), 520.

Chapter 3

1. Clark, *Pills, Petticoats, and Plows*, 36.
2. Daybook 1, Clark & Hyde, ETRC, 18, 58, 61.
3. Ibid., 25, 29.
4. *Nacogdoches News*, July 20, 1877, 2.
5. Ericson, *People of Nacogdoches County in 1880*, 4. Interestingly, there is no occupation listed for Anna Hyde in the 1870, suggesting that hotel keeping was a relatively new role for Hyde in 1880. Ericson, *People of Nacogdoches County in 1870*, 13.
6. Ownby, *American Dreams*, 11. In a recent article, Lu Ann Jones has also argued that women (as well as African Americans) were less inclined to shop at country stores, which tended to be operated by white men, and instead chose to purchase items from itinerant peddlers. To be fair, Jones is making the case for the importance of itinerant merchants to the southern economy; she is not providing

an in-depth evaluation of the relationship between women and general stores in the postbellum period. Lu Ann Jones, "Gender, Race, and Itinerant Commerce in the New South," *Journal of Southern History* 66 (May 2000): 297–320. See also Ayers, *Promise of the New South*, 81–103; Grace Elizabeth Hale, *Making Whiteness: The Culture of Segregation in the South, 1890–1940* (New York: Pantheon Books, 1998), 168–79. The latter two books cast general stores as areas of white male social and economic control, emphasizing, for example, the appeal of store ownership to young white males in the South. In contrast, Mary Ryan argues that urban (New York, New Orleans, and San Francisco) women engaged in both consumer activities and public life throughout much of the nineteenth century. Mary P. Ryan, *Women in Public: Between Banners and Ballots, 1825–1880* (Baltimore: Johns Hopkins University Press, 1990), 77, 87.

7. Ownby, *American Dreams*, 11.

8. McInnis Ledger 1874–75, AHC, 79.

9. Jones, "Gender, Race, and Itinerant Commerce," 300, 302.

10. Ownby, *American Dreams*, 11.

11. Gloria Main asserts that informal borrowing and lending as well as oral agreements constituted the bulk of local exchanges in rural communities in colonial New England. Gloria L. Main, "Gender, Work, and Wages in Colonial New England," *William and Mary Quarterly* 51 (January 1994): 46. Marla Miller provides the examples of Lydia Duncan Champion and Tryphena Newton Cooke, whose needlework business is recorded in ledgers, yet under their husbands' names. Marla R. Miller, "Gender, Artisanry, and Craft Tradition in Early New England: The View through the Eye of a Needle," *William and Mary Quarterly* 60 (October 2003): 743–76. Finally, Wendy Gamber's work on the dressmaking and millinery trades in the nineteenth century suggests that, while men generally held the purse strings in the family and settled accounts with dressmakers and milliners, it was their wives who established relationships with artisans and frequented such shops. See her segment on the "Sexual Politics of Fashion," in Gamber, *The Female Economy*, 119–24.

12. According to the 1870 census, the sex ratio in Nacogdoches County was very balanced, with 4,806 men and 4,808 women. In Cherokee County (where Jacksonville is located), there was also a significant balance in the sex ratio, with 5,556 men to 5,523 women. *Census 1870, Selected Statistics by Age and Sex by Counties*, 636.

13. Daybook 1, Clark & Hyde, ETRC, 88, 91, 94, 96, 102, 103.

14. Customer Ledger 8/24/74–2/8/75, Brown & Dixon, ETRC, 14, 16, 17, 19, 20.

15. Daybook 1, Clark & Hyde, ETRC, 11. For other "per order" examples, see ibid., 14, 28, 126.

16. Ibid., 9, 14, 31.

17. Customer Ledger 8/24/74–2/8/75, Brown & Dixon, ETRC, 73.

18. Ibid., 22, 26, 29, 40, 42.

19. Howe, "Victorian Culture in America," 25. Contrary to Howe's thinking, however, Victorians were not the first to put forward idealized notions of domesticity, or the now defunct trope of separate spheres. A number of historians have argued that such rhetoric accompanied the rise of the middle class in America during the early decades of the nineteenth century. See Cott, *Bonds of Womanhood*; Mary P. Ryan, *Cradle of the Middle Class: The Family in Oneida County, New York, 1790–1865* (New York: Cambridge University Press, 1981); Karen Haltunnen, *Confidence Men and Painted Women: A Study of Middle-Class Culture in America, 1830–1870* (New Haven: Yale University Press, 1982); Stuart Blumin, *The Emergence of the Middle Class: Social Experience in the American City, 1790–1900* (Cambridge: Cambridge University Press, 1989).

20. As Barbara Welter argued in her influential essay "The Cult of True Womanhood," women, civilizing agents in their own right, created safe havens from the outside world for their families, protecting them from unsafe and immoral influences. Welter, "The Cult of True Womanhood," 152.

21. White, *"It's Your Misfortune,"* 307–309. For a discussion of the "white woman as civilizer," see Glenda Riley, *Women and Indians on the Frontier 1825–1915* (Albuquerque: University of New Mexico Press, 1984); newest edition, Glenda Riley, *Confronting Race: Women and Indians on the Frontier, 1815–1915* (Albuquerque: University of New Mexico Press, 2004). This perception has long been challenged by western women historians. See Joan M. Jensen and Darlis A. Miller, "The Gentle Tamers Revisited: New Approaches to the History of Women in the American West," *Pacific Historical Review* 49 (May 1980): 173–213; Elizabeth Jameson, "Women as Workers, Women as Civilizers: True Womanhood in the American West," in *The Women's West*, ed. Susan H. Armitage and Elizabeth Jameson (Norman: University of Oklahoma Press, 1987): 145–64. A more recent scholarly assessment of the preponderance and limitations of "true womanhood" in Texas is Adrienne Caughfield, *True Women and Westward Expansion* (College Station: Texas A&M University Press, 2005). For challenges to "true womanhood" arguments in Texas, see Elizabeth York Enstam, *Women and the Creation of Urban Life: Dallas, Texas, 1843–1920* (College Station: Texas A&M University Press, 1998); Angela Boswell, "The Meaning of Participation: White Protestant Women in Antebellum Houston Churches," *Southwestern Historical Quarterly* 99 (July 1995): 26–47; Angela Boswell, *Her Act and Deed: Women's Lives in a Rural Southern County, 1837–1873* (College Station: Texas A&M University Press, 2001).

22. Robert L. Griswold, "Anglo Women and Domestic Ideology in the American West in the Nineteenth and Early Twentieth Centuries," in *Western Women: Their Land, Their Lives*, ed. Lillian Schlissel, Vicki L. Ruiz, and Janice Monk (Albuquerque: University of New Mexico Press, 1988), 15.

23. *Cherokee County Banner*, 11 February 1916.

24. Linda Williams Reese, *Women of Oklahoma, 1890–1920* (Norman: University of Oklahoma Press, 1997), 33–34.

25. Customer Ledger 1874–75, November 13, 1876, Brown & Dixon, ETRC; *Federal Census of Cherokee County 1880*, ETRC, 181. There is no mention of Mrs. Smith's husband in the census; possibly she was a widow.

26. For a discussion of pianos and their role in Victorian society, see Federhen et al., *Accumulation and Display*, 79. Karen Haltunnen discusses Victorian parlors and their adornments from an urban perspective in "From Parlor to Living Room: Domestic Space, Interior Decoration, and the Culture of Personality," in Bronner, *Consuming Visions*, 157–89. Also see Grier, *Culture and Comfort*.

27. Anderson, *Deep Creek Merchant*, 129.

28. Wendy Gamber, "Tarnished Labor: The Home, the Market, and the Boardinghouse in Antebellum America," *Journal of the Early Republic* 22 (Summer 2002): 189.

29. Boydston, *Home and Work*, 159.

30. Karen Anderson, "Work, Gender and Power in the American West," *Pacific Historical Review* 61 (November 1992): 481.

31. Gamber, "Tarnished Labor," 180.

32. For a detailed discussion of female entrepreneurship at this time, see Wendy Gamber, "A Gendered Enterprise: Placing Nineteenth-Century Businesswomen in History," *Business History Review* 72 (Summer 1998): 188–217.

33. Gamber asserts that most women operated "boardinghouses," which were most often converted dwellings of simple "homes" with extra rooms to let—as opposed to "hotels," which were usually run by men and tended to be more luxurious, expensive, and architecturally elaborate than boardinghouses (although Gamber concedes that there was considerable overlap). Ibid., 181.

34. Ericson, *People of Nacogdoches County in 1870*, 8.

35. Enstam, *Women and the Creation of Urban Life*, 42. Enstam's study of the frontier period in Dallas history (1843–80) provides ample evidence of working women engaging in public life, which counters notions that women were protected from work during the Victorian era. Also see Gamber, "Tarnished Labor," 181–83.

36. Daybook 1, Clark & Hyde, ETRC, 27.

37. Laurie Mercier, "'We Are Women Irish': Gender, Class, Religious, and Ethnic Identity in Anaconda, Montana," in *Writing the Range: Race, Class, and Culture in the Women's West*, ed. Elizabeth Jameson and Susan Armitage (Norman: University of Oklahoma Press, 1997), 316.

38. Ericson, *People of Nacogdoches County in 1880*, 7–8.

39. Wolf Ledger, 1872–75 (AR 1991-72), AHC, 203, 234, 252. Also see the *1872 Austin City Directory*, where Schaffer is listed as a store clerk for Charles Wolf, AHC, 24.

40. Wolf Ledger, 1872–75, AHC, 154, 162; Ledger: Cash Received/Out, Charles Wolf Ledger, AHC, 20.

41. Fritz Sittel, interview 5827, vol. 84, Indian Pioneer Collection (Indian Pioneer Papers), WHC; Pittsburg County Genealogical and Historical Society, *Pittsburg County, Oklahoma*, 370, 517; Sales Ledger 1897–1900, #177, McAlester Collection, WHC, 265, 626.

42. *Star-Vindicator*, 3 November 1877, 3; Laborer Account Book 1877–79, box 36, McAlester Collection, WHC.

43. Haywood, *Victorian West*, 265.

44. Sandra L. Myres, *Westering Women and the Frontier Experience, 1800–1915* (Albuquerque: University of New Mexico Press, 1982), 243.

45. Evidence of these large purchase orders appears in Sales Ledger 1897–1900, #177, 265, 626, Sales Ledger 1877–80, #154, 426, 514, and Sales Ledger 1894–97, #174, 412–13, all in McAlester Collection, WHC.

46. In Nacogdoches County, "housekeeper" denoted an occupation performed outside the household in 1870, but by the 1880 census the title was given to married women who kept house—no longer a distinct occupation. See Ericson, *People of Nacogdoches County in 1870*; and Ericson, *People of Nacogdoches County in 1880*.

47. Boydston, *Home and Work*, 142–63. Again, such divisions were largely based on gender: men's labor outside home was considered "work" and women's labor inside the home was not.

48. Ledger B 1877–78, Brown & Dixon, ETRC, 124.

49. Customer Ledger 6/1876–3/29/1877, Brown & Dixon Company Records, ETRC (no page numbers).

50. Customer Ledger 10/29/77–8/31/78, Brown & Dixon Company Records, ETRC, 55.

51. Julie Roy Jeffrey, *Frontier Women: "Civilizing" the West? 1840–1880* (New York: Hill and Wang, 1979; rev. ed., 1998), 78; Joan Jensen, *Loosening the Bonds: Mid-Atlantic Farm Women, 1750–1850* (New Haven: Yale University Press, 1986).

52. Boydston, *Home and Work*, 120–41; Enstam, *Women and the Creation of Urban Life*, 42.

53. Boydston, *Home and Work*, 120–41; Catherine E. Kelly, *In the New England Fashion: Reshaping Women's Lives in the Nineteenth Century* (Ithaca: Cornell University Press, 1999), 35. A good example provided in Kelly's study of New England is her discussion of Persis Hastings Russell, a woman who assumed responsibility of her husband's store while he was away on buying trips. Kelly also observes that changing market dynamics, including the general intensification of market activity and more sophisticated credit practices in the midcentury, led to a diminished role for women in the family business. For discussion of women participating in the female exchange economy in the late eighteenth and early nineteenth centuries, also see Jensen, *Loosening the Bonds*; Laurel Thatcher Ulrich's, "Martha Ballard and Her Girls," in Stephen Innes, ed., *Work and Labor in Early America* (Chapel Hill: University of North Carolina Press, 1988), 70–105; and Ulrich, *A Midwife's*

224 NOTES TO PAGES 94–99

Tale. Ulrich finds evidence in Martha Ballard's diary of the existence of a separate female economy existing beneath the level of traditional documentation.

54. Sales Ledger 1874–75, #152, McAlester collection, WHC, 54, 56, 58, 61, 102. It is quite possible that these miners initially moved to the Choctaw lands, obtained employment, and thereafter sent for their wives. Alternatively, the men might have traveled with their wives in the initial migration. In any case, despite the scarcity of women's names, purchases documented in the ledgers imply the presence of women in the McAlester region in the early stages of settlement.

55. Jeffrey, *Frontier Women*, 136.

56. Myres, *Westering Women*, 242.

57. Sales Ledger 1875–78, #153, McAlester Collection, WHC, 124.

58. Ibid., 260.

59. Ibid., 217.

60. Sales Ledger 1874–75, #152, McAlester Collection, WHC, 24.

61. Sales Ledger 1875–78, #153, ibid., 124.

62. In her examination of the dressmaking and millinery trades in the nineteenth century, Wendy Gamber argues that dressmaking was not simply an extension of women's traditional domestic skills but a trade acquired only after much training in a workshop, not in the home. Gamber locates her study in an urban setting—specifically Boston, where apprenticeship opportunities were available to young working-class women. However, Gamber concedes that many women knew how to sew and often made their own clothing to save money. Gamber, *The Female Economy*, 135.

63. Gauntt Bros. Ledger, Baylor University, 187.

64. Wolf Ledger, 1872–75, AHC, 7.

65. *General Directory of the City of Austin, Texas, for 1877–1878* (Houston: Mooney & Morrison), 78.

66. Daybook 1, Clark & Hyde, ETRC, 36, 45, 180.

67. Ericson, *People of Nacogdoches County in 1880*, 4.

68. Account Ledger 1877, McCampbell & Bros., DRTL, 108.

69. Huson, *Refugio*, 176, 177, 266 (177).

70. Account Ledger 1877, McCampbell & Bros., DRTL, 307.

71. Account Ledger 1876–77, McCampbell & Bros., DRTL, 16.

72. This issue is discussed in detail in the next chapter.

73. Account Ledger 1876–77, McCampbell & Bros., DRTL, 54.

74. Ibid., 72.

75. Sales Ledger 1874–75, #152, 335, Sales Ledger 1875–78, #153, 214, 279, and Sales Ledger 1881, #155, 22, 45, 131, 166, all in McAlester Collection, WHC.

76. Compare the entries for Ann Shaw and Elvira Peters/Edwards from the Account Ledger 1876–77 (54, 108, 143) with, particularly, the entries for Mrs. Kate Duncan, Mrs. Susan Dugat, Mrs. Eliza Buck in Account Ledger 1877 (31, 70, 479), McCampbell & Bros., DRTL.

77. Daybook 1, Clark & Hyde, 46. See entire ledger for examples. Specific female account holders include Mrs. A. J. Hyde, Mrs. Sleet, Mrs. S. A. Durst, Mrs. Edwards, Mrs. Gough, Mrs. Love, Mrs. Ingraham, Miss Ingraham, and Mrs. Roberts.

78. Ibid., 15, 16, 25, 34, 88, 91, 95, 97, 106. For Ellen Rolligan, see ibid., 152, 156, 158. She also appears in the ledger as Ellen Walker (by her name it says Rolligan or Walker), 145, 167, 185. There is no Ellen Walker in the census for the period—if this is a separate person, then she is somehow associated with Ellen Rolligan. In Daybook 2, June 1873–January 1874, the same situation occurs on Eliza White's account, 101. She is listed in the census as a mulatto housekeeper. Ericson, *People of Nacogdoches County in 1870*, 13.

79. Ericson, *People of Nacogdoches County in 1870*, 30, 51; Ericson, *People of Nacogdoches County in 1880*, 14, 9. In the census, Ellen's last name is spelled Roligan.

80. Gauntt Bros. Ledger, Baylor University, 6.

81. Ibid., 107.

82. Nancy Woloch, *Women and the American Experience*, 2nd ed. (New York: McGraw-Hill, 1994), 130; Sklar, *Catherine Beecher*; Catharine Beecher, *The Evils Suffered by American Women and American Children, the Causes and the Remedy* (New York: Harper and Brothers, 1846), 12.

83. Sarah Ann Harlan, interview 8248, vol.106, Indian Pioneer Collection (Indian Pioneer Papers), WHC; Muriel H. Wright, "Sarah Ann Harlan: From Her Memoirs of Life in the Indian Territory," *Chronicles of Oklahoma* 39.3 (Fall 1961): 310; Bostic, "Elizabeth Fulton Hester."

84. Daybook 1872–73, Severs Collection, OHS, 75.

85. Mollie is mentioned in an earlier entry in the ledger. The entry for November 19, 1872, reads, "Miss Mollie Willison (Teacher), Cash paid for merchandise per bill rendered $48.40." Significant in the entry is the distinction of Miss, clarifying Mollie's marital status and the inclusion of her occupation as a teacher. Ibid., 52.

86. Ibid., 85, 198.

87. Jeffrey, *Frontier Women*, 112–13.

88. Muriel H. Wright, "Old Boggy Depot," *Chronicles of Oklahoma* 5 (March 1927): 7. For ledger entries, see G. B. Hester, Ledger 1874, Benjamin Cook Collection, WHC, 106.

89. Pittsburg County Genealogical and Historical Society, *Pittsburg County, Oklahoma*, 443–44; Sales Ledger 1891–92, #169, McAlester Collection, WHC, 30.

90. Sales Ledger 1899–1900, #177, McAlester Collection, WHC, 806.

Chapter 4

1. West, "Reconstructing Race," 20; U.S. Congress, Senate, 39th Congress, 1st Session, 1865, 43.

2. Ronald Takaki discusses the implications of the coming of the railroad and the 1871 Indian Appropriation Act for both Indian tribal power and property.

See Ronald T. Takaki, *Iron Cages: Race and Culture in Nineteenth-Century America* (New York: Alfred A, Knopf, 1979), 171–75.

3. West, "Reconstructing Race," 23. It should be noted that just a few "radicals" in Congress shared in the dream of forty acres and a mule. By and large, neither the majority of government officials nor Americans in general supported the redistribution of southern property into the hands of the freedmen.

4. More information on the background of this discussion can be found in Calvert, "Nineteenth-Century Farmers," 510–11; Spratt, *Road to Spindletop*, 61–83; Richardson et al., *Texas*, 277; Calvert, "Freedmen and Agricultural Prosperity"; Fite, *Cotton Fields No More*; and Sitton and Utley, *From Can See to Can't*.

5. Buenger, *Path to a Modern South*, 51.

6. Customer Ledger 8/24/74–2/8/75, 40, Ledger B, 1877–78, 140, and Ledger E, 1882, 103, all in Brown & Dixon, ETRC. According to Sitton and Conrad, "Nelson Sneed" achieved some financial independence before the end of the Civil War. He was permitted by his owner to work for others, which enabled him to accumulate money and buy his freedom. He later joined with Andy Bragg in the founding of a freedmen's settlement in Cherokee County named Andy. See Thad Sitton and James H. Conrad, *Freedom Colonies: Independent Black Texans in the Time of Jim Crow* (Austin: University of Texas Press, 2005), 39.

7. Barr, *Black Texans*, 64–65. See also Ruthe Winegarten, *Black Texas Women: 150 Years of Trial and Triumph* (Austin: University of Texas Press, 1995); Smallwood, *Time of Hope*, 68–95.

8. Ayers, *The Promise of the New South*, 93.

9. Quote from Harold D. Woodman, *King Cotton and His Retainers: Financing and Marketing the Cotton Crop of the South, 1800–1925* (Lexington: University of Kentucky Press, 1968), 308–309. For a discussion of bookkeeping practices, also see Clark, *Pills, Petticoats, and Plows*, 272–74; Ownby, *American Dreams*, 71–72.

10. Ledger F, 1883, Brown & Dixon, ETRC, 177.

11. Ledger D, 1880–81, Brown & Dixon, ETRC, 228. According to the 1880 census, Sandy Chandler was a Mississippi-born farmer, thirty-five years of age, African American, his wife's name was Martha, and he had five children ranging in age from eight to sixteen. *Federal Census of Cherokee County 1880*, ETRC, 366.

12. *Federal Census of Cherokee County 1880*, 368, 229.

13. Ledger D, 1880–81, Brown & Dixon, ETRC, 229.

14. Unfortunately, there is little continuity of the spelling of Mr. Kessentiner's name in either the ledgers or the census. He appears in the 1880 census as "March Kisentiner." See *Federal Census of Cherokee County 1880*, ETRC, 317.

15. Ibid., 170.

16. Ledger F, 1883, Brown & Dixon, 167.

17. *Federal Census of Cherokee County 1880*, ETRC, 317.

18. Ledger H, 1885, Brown & Dixon, ETRC, 29.

19. Perry Bolden appears in the census as Perry Boland, the head of a large household, including his wife and eight children. His occupation is listed as farmer. At the time of the census, his eldest son, also named Perry, resided in his household, and both of them appear in the McKinney & Brown records. See *Federal Census of Cherokee County 1880*, ETRC, 330. According to ledger entries, Bolden secured the account of Denis Cristial in 1877. Ledger B, 1877–78, Brown & Dixon, ETRC, 125.

20. Customer Ledger 1876–77, August 16, 1876, Brown & Dixon, ETRC.

21. Ledger D, 1880–81, Brown & Dixon, ETRC, 147.

22. Crouch, "Spirit of Lawlessness"; Crouch, *Freedmen's Bureau*; Barr, *Reconstruction to Reform*; Smallwood, *Time of Hope*; Campbell, *Grass-Roots Reconstruction*; Smallwood, Crouch, and Peacock, *Murder and Mayhem*, 71.

23. *Cherokee County Banner*, August 4, 1916; "Newspaper Obituaries," Cherokee County, Texas, 1910–1922, book 2 (Copyright 1989: Compiled, printed, bound by Helen Wooddell Crawford), 140, ETRC.

24. Hardeman, "History of Melrose," 31–32. Committee members included E. H. Hobbs (chairman), L. T. Barret (secretary), B. R. Brown, D. Atkins, R. Leak, B. M. Walker, H. W. Riddle, John Hobbs, Henry Hobbs, Eli Hobbs, James Jacobs, O. H. Hamil, M. L. Patton, C. Chireno, D. Thomason, I. Goen, and E. A. Day. According to the 1870 census, the value of property for some of the members listed (those listed in census) are as follows: E. H. Hobbs ($3,000), L. T. Barret ($3,000), E. Brown ($1,800), B. R. Brown ($250), R. Leak (Leek) ($5,500), B. M. Walker ($1,080), H. W. Riddle ($1,080–wife), James Jacobs ($3,000), M. L. Patton ($9,430), D. Thomason ($600), E. A. Day ($1,000). U.S. Bureau of the Census, *Ninth Census 1870*.

25. Item 5, folder 15 (A-274), L. T. Barret Collection, ETRC, 1.

26. Ibid., 5.

27. Ledger F, 1883, Brown & Dixon, ETRC, 487.

28. Ledger D, 1880–81, ibid., 289.

29. Ledger B, 1877–78, ibid., 336.

30. Eric Foner, *Reconstruction: America's Unfinished Revolution, 1863–1877* (New York: Harper and Row, 1988), 96.

31. Barr, *Black Texans*, 64–65; Crouch, *Freedmen's Bureau*, 59–64; Winegarten, *Black Texas Women*, 90–92; Smallwood, *Time of Hope*, 68–95.

32. Ledger 1870–73, Hardeman & Barret, ETRC, 27, 80, 122, 144; Ericson, *People of Nacogdoches County in 1870*, 121, 139, 105. Beside George Garret's name in the ledger is in brackets "(alias Hamil)," as it turns out, he appears in the census as George Hamil.

33. While the freedom to educate their children was new for African Americans, the fact that many white farmers in Hardeman & Barret ledgers also purchased educational materials suggests that both whites and blacks in the Nacogdoches area privileged the education of their children. For examples, see Ledger 1870–73, Hardeman & Barret, ETRC, 21, 34, 59, 61, 67, 139, 145, 160, 163, 346.

34. List of Goods 1879–82, McCampbell & Bros., DRTL, 7.

35. Charles Carpenter, *History of American Schoolbooks* (Philadelphia: University of Pennsylvania Press, 1963), 85; Elizabeth Kolmer, "The McGuffey Readers: Exponents of American Classical Liberalism," *Journal of General Education* 27 (Winter 1976): 314.

36. Carol Billman, "McGuffey's Readers and Alger's Fiction: The Gospel of Virtue according to Popular Children's Literature," *Journal of Popular Culture* 11 (Winter 1977): 614–15. In accordance with the prevailing attitudes of the day, McGuffey in his stories lauded the value of both healthy competition and individualism in achieving one's goals; indeed, such attributes were necessary components of the progress mentality so endemic to Gilded Age belief systems. However, McGuffey warned his young readers against the excessive materialism, ruthless acquisition, and big-scale capitalism of the period. Instead, he promoted the idea that "money isn't everything" and, rather, that joy should come from hard work, frugality, and generosity. Thus, McGuffey's message aligned more closely with Hofstadter's traditional Mugwumps and their aversion to the cutthroat capitalism associated with the period's robber barons. In this sense, McGuffey's readers mirrored the conservatism and anti-industrialism of persons living in rural settings, who developed a distaste for cities, large factories, and corporate greed. Billman, "McGuffey's Readers," 617–18; Hofstadter, *Age of Reform*, 135–36.

37. In fact, it has been estimated that from seventy-five to eighty million copies of the speller were printed. According to its publisher, thirty-five million copies were produced from 1855 to 1890. In describing the popularity of Webster's speller, historian Charles Carpenter asserted, "Printing presses were worn out printing the book and it was at this time that the term *Blue-Black Speller* became a household word all over the country." Carpenter, *American Schoolbooks*, 151.

38. Ledger 1870–73, Hardeman & Barret, ETRC, 80; Ledger F, 1883, Brown & Dixon Company Records, ETRC, 487.

39. William Hampton Adams and Steven D. Smith, "Historical Perspectives on Black Tenant Farmer Material Culture: The Henry C. Long General Store Ledger at Waverly Plantation, Mississippi," in Theresa A. Singleton, ed., *The Archaeology of Slavery and Plantation Life* (Orlando: Academic Press, 1985), 309–34 (330); Ownby, *American Dreams*, 74.

40. Cited in Leon F. Litwack, *Been in the Storm So Long: The Aftermath of Slavery* (New York: Vintage Books, 1979), 309, 411. Not to take away from this account, but five dollars a month seems a little low for the period. Litwack notes that the average wage hand in Reconstruction Texas (and Arkansas) could expect to make anywhere from fifteen to twenty-five dollars a month. Smallwood puts the wage scale from two to fifteen dollars a month for male field hands and from two to ten dollars for female. Smallwood, *Time of Hope*, 43. According to the Texas Agricultural Bureau, even as late as 1887–88, the average monthly income for a farm laborer in Nacogdoches County was only twelve dollars. L. L. Foster, *Forgotten*

Texas Census: First Annual Report of the Agricultural Bureau of the Department of Agriculture, Insurance, Statistics, and History, 1887–1888 (reissue; Austin: Texas State Historical Association, 2001), 167.

41. Ledger 1870–73, Hardeman & Barret, ETRC, 225. Again, store owner L. T. Barret denoted former slaves in his ledger by the distinction "F.M.C." or "F.W.C" for free man or woman of color, reinforcing that, while African Americans were certainly integrated into the larger economic system, racial boundaries persisted (even in private ledgers). Menefee's account was secured by M. (Monroe) Pleasant, a white farmer. His debts, which were accrued over a number of months in summer and fall of 1870, were paid in full by Pleasant on February 14, 1871. "Securing" in this example suggests a clear economic tie between the parties involved. Perhaps, Menefee was a tenant or cropper on Pleasant's land, and the landowner covered his debts after he received his crop payment. "Securing" could also mean providing permission for store purchases—Edward Ayers notes that, even to obtain the smallest of items from the local store, tenants often had to receive permission from their landlord, who might hold a lien on their crop and thus the final say over how they spent their money. *Promise of the New South*, 90.

42. Of course, comparable purchases to Menefee's—harmonicas, tumblers, and shoe cologne—were also made by the store's white customers, including those of the store owner himself, L. T. Barret. See Ledger 1870–73, Hardeman & Barret, ETRC, 22, 34.

43. Ledger D, 1880–81, Brown & Dixon, ETRC, 228.

44. The 10 percent interest charge seems to have been an additional charge assessed by the store owners on particularly large purchases made by some of their clientele, particularly African Americans. In the same ledger, the purchases totaling $4.00 by Perry Bolden on April 30, 1881, received a similar 10 percent added interest charge. Ibid., 147. In other examples, the store owners charged accounts a 12 percent interest charge on balances that carried over to the next year (and a new ledger book). For example, see Alex Alexander's account record on January 13, 1882. Ledger E, 1882, Brown & Dixon, 49. This 12 percent interest charge is considerably lower than the 25 percent store interest rates on credit accounts discussed by other historians. As Thomas Clark described in his classic study of southern country stores, there is the possibility that the merchants buried additional "interest" charges in inflated prices and markups. For a discussion of high interest rates and markups, see Ayers, *Promise of the New South*, 92; Clark, *Pills, Petticoats, and Plows*, 273–74; Woodman, *King Cotton*, 303.

45. Ledger D, 1880–81, Brown & Dixon, ETRC, 178.

46. Bushman, *Refinement of America*, 438. For a study of propertied blacks in the South, see Loren Schweninger, *Black Property Owners in the South, 1790–1915* (Urbana: University of Illinois Press, 1990).

47. Shane White and Graham White, *Stylin': African American Expressive Culture from Its Beginnings to the Zoot Suit* (Ithaca: Cornell University Press, 1998),

128. Also see Robin D. G. Kelley, *Race Rebels: Culture, Politics, and the Black Working Class* (New York: Free Press, 1994), 50–51. For an archeological perspective, see Paul Mullins, "Race and the Genteel Consumer: Class and African American Consumption," *Historical Archaeology* 33 (1999): 22–38; Praetzellis and Praetzellis, "Mangling Symbols of Gentility," 651.

48. Ledger 1870–73, Hardeman & Barret, ETRC, 45, 83, 147.

49. Bobby M. Wilson, "Race in Commodity Exchange and Consumption: Separate but Equal," *Annals of the Association of American Geographers* 95.3 (2005): 595.

50. Affirming this point in the ledgers is the fact that Perry Bolden Jr.'s account received a credit of $44.80 from the net proceeds of one bale of cotton in December 1881. Ledger D, 1880–81, Brown & Dixon, ETRC, 289. Hardeman & Barret's ledgers featured a separate "cotton account" entry, listing customer's credits received from cotton. Ledger 1870–73, Hardeman & Barret, ETRC, 357.

51. Crouch, *Freedmen's Bureau*, 46; Smallwood, *Time of Hope*; Lawrence D. Rice, *The Negro in Texas, 1874–1900* (Baton Rouge: Louisiana State University Press, 1971); Alwyn Barr, "African Americans in Texas: From Stereotypes to Diverse Roles," in Buenger and Calvert, *Texas through Time*, 57–67.

52. Barr, *Black Texans*, 92. For an informative discussion of the experiences of urban blacks in post–Civil War San Antonio, see Kenneth Mason, *African Americans and Race Relations in San Antonio, Texas, 1867–1937* (New York: Garland, 1998).

53. *General Directory of the City of Austin*, 87.

54. Wolf Ledger, 1872–75, AHC, 52. Chambers appears in the ledger as Lem. Chambers.

55. U.S. Bureau of the Census, *Federal Census 1880*, Travis County, 287.

56. Foley, *White Scourge*, 28–29. Identifying the regions of Mexican settlement in the mid-nineteenth century, Kenneth Stewart and Arnoldo De Leon note that most Mexicans lived in the sparsely populated regions of southern Texas and two counties in south central Texas, Bexar and Goliad. Kenneth L. Stewart and Arnold De Leon, *Not Room Enough: Mexicans, Anglos, and Socioeconomic Change in Texas, 1850–1900* (Albuquerque: University of New Mexico Press, 1993), 13. According to the 1887 agricultural census, there were only 37 Mexicans among a total county population of 1,245. Foster, *Forgotten Texas Census*, 187.

57. Account Ledger 1876–77, McCampbell & Bros., DRTL, 8, 9, 12.

58. Ibid., 17, 28, 30, 47, 48, 61, 98; Account Ledger 1877, ibid., 25, 39, 53, 59, 67.

59. Account Ledger 1877, ibid., 31, 70, 479.

60. Account Ledger 1876–77, ibid., 16, 47, 61, 72, 81, 108, 143.

61. Ibid., 72, 81, 108, 120.

62. Ibid., 49, 90, 115, 121.

63. Account Ledger 1877, ibid., 84; Huson, *Refugio*, 262.

64. Huson, *Refugio*, 256; Account Ledger 1876–77, McCampbell & Bros., DRTL, 50, 83.

65. Account Ledger 1876–77, McCampbell & Bros., DRTL, 77, 141; Account Ledger 1877, ibid., 327, 409.

66. For "making whiteness," see for example David R. Roediger, *The Wages of Whiteness: Race and the Making of the American Working Class* (London: Verso, 1991); Noel Ignatiev, *How the Irish Became White* (New York: Routledge, 1995); Matthew Frye Jacobson, *Whiteness of a Different Color: European Immigrants and the Alchemy of Race* (Cambridge: Harvard University Press, 1998); Hale, *Making Whiteness*; Brander Rasmussen, ed., *The Making and Unmaking of Whiteness* (Durham: Duke University Press, 2001).

67. Account Ledger 1877, 31, 79, 109, 458, Account Ledger 1876–77, 22, 23, 26, 95, W. E. McCampbell & Bros., DRTL.

68. Ledger 1870–73, Hardeman & Barret, ETRC, 12, 34, 59, 139, 144, 224, 393, 443, 493.

69. Ownby, *American Dreams*, 72.

70. Huson, *Refugio*, 136.

71. Marler, "Transition to a New South," 165–92. A similar argument against territorial monopolies in Alabama is found in Kyriakoudes, "Lower-Order Urbanization."

72. R. Halliburton, Jr., *Red over Black: Black Slavery among the Cherokee Indians* (Westport: Greenwood Press, 1977). Also see the numerous books by Daniel F. Littlefield, *The Cherokee Freedmen: From Emancipation to American Citizenship* (Westport: Greenwood Press, 1978), *Africans and Creeks: From the Colonial Period to the Civil War* (Westport: Greenwood Press, 1979), *The Chickasaw Freedmen: A People without a Country* (Westport: Greenwood Press, 1980), and *Africans and Seminoles: From Removal to Emancipation* (Jackson: Banner Books, University Press of Mississippi, 2001).

73. West, "Reconstructing Race," 23.

74. James P. Ronda, "'We Have a Country': Race, Geography, and the Invention of Indian Territory," *Journal of the Early Republic* 19 (Winter 1999): 739–55. For a discussion of racial classification among the Choctaws, see Jeffrey Burton, *Indian Territory and the United States, 1866–1906: Courts, Government, and the Movement for Oklahoma Statehood* (Norman: University of Oklahoma Press, 1995), 119–20.

75. Murray R. Wickett, *Contested Territory: Whites, Native Americans, and African Americans in Oklahoma, 1865–1907* (Baton Rouge: Louisiana State University Press, 2000), 35.

76. Claudio Saunt, "The Paradox of Freedom: Tribal Sovereignty and Emancipation during the Reconstruction of Indian Territory," *Journal of Southern History* 70 (January 2004): 63–94; Wickett, *Contested Territory*, 7–13.

77. Ronda, "We Have A Country," 753–54.

78. Brian W. Dippie, *The Vanishing American: White Attitudes and U.S. Indian Policy* (Middletown, Conn.: Wesleyan University Press, 1982), 245. Burton discusses

the role of white labor in undermining tribal governments in his *Indian Territory*, 117. Also see Miner, *The Corporation and the Indian*.

79. *Oklahoma Star*, 23 November 1875. Significantly the masthead for the paper was "Progress and a Higher Civilization."

80. Dippie, *Vanishing American*, 247.

81. See Madison Grant, *The Passing of the Great Race* (New York: C. Scribner's Sons, 1916).

82. Wickett, *Contested Territory*, 37, 39.

83. Dippie, *Vanishing American*, 253.

84. Ronda, "We Have a Country," 753–54.

85. Ibid., 755.

86. Daybook 1871–72, box 29, McAlester, WHC, 5.

87. Debo, *Choctaw Republic*, 117–18.

88. Through his relationship with the Pusleys and marriage into the tribe, McAlester certainly gained legal rights to the Choctaw Nation's resources. Yet the dimensions and legalities of his exploitation of coal reserves proved a contentious issue among the Choctaws. McAlester was embroiled in a number of legal battles and personal conflicts with a number of Choctaw leaders in the decades that followed. See Sparks, "James Jesse McAlester."

89. Daybook 1874–75, #152, McAlester Collection, WHC, 107.

90. Daybook 1875–78, #153, McAlester Collection, WHC, 210, 243.

91. Ibid., 214, 279.

92. Daybook 1874–75, #152, McAlester Collection, WHC, 133, 183.

93. Daybook 1875–78, #153, McAlester Collection, WHC, 38, 75, 77, 115, 116, 121, 124.

94. Ibid., 74, 115.

95. With no census for the 1870s and the fact that these are both rather common Choctaw names, it is difficult to establish tribal affiliation. Many of the citizens listed above, including McAlester himself, appeared in Hastain's *Index* from 1908, a compilation of Choctaw-Chickasaw deeds and allotments. Isam Jefferson does not appear in the index, and unfortunately there are multiple William Moores listed. The index is almost thirty years after the fact, which is also problematic. E. Hastain, ed., *Index to the Choctaw-Chickasaw Deeds and Allotments* (Muskogee, Okla., 1908), WHC.

96. Debo, *Choctaw Republic*, 144, 163–66. Also see Sparks, "James Jackson McAlester," 21–22; Miner, *The Corporation and the Indian*, 64. Duncan Aldrich finds similar rifts among the Cherokees during the same period, noting the connection of whiteness with the merchant class. Duncan M. Aldrich, "General Stores, Retail Merchants, and Assimilation: Retail Trade in the Cherokee Nation, 1838–1890," *Chronicles of Oklahoma* 57 (Summer 1979): 130–32.

97. Wickett, *Contested Territory*, 39.

98. Daybook 1875–78, #153, McAlester Collection, WHC, 75, 116, 124.

99. Ibid., 115.

100. Charles Middleton, interview 7181, vol. 63, Indian Pioneer Collection (Indian Pioneer Papers), WHC.

101. W. N. Jones Store Ledger 1871–74 (J-2, 1137), Dovie Jones Collection, WHC, 22.

102. Ibid., 12. For translations, see Will T. Nelson, ed., *English Choctaw Dictionary*, 5th ed. (Oklahoma City: Oklahoma City Council of Choctaws, 1975).

103. Daybook 1869–71, Severs Collection, OHS, 10, 14, 24.

104. Miss Sarah B. Trent, interview 8238, vol. 92, Indian Pioneer Collection (Indian Pioneer Papers), WHC.

105. Daybook 1869–71, Severs Collection, OHS, 55, 58.

106. Ibid., 128, 215.

107. Ownby, *American Dreams*, 72–73.

Chapter 5

1. Anna Martin to M. Chapman, 1904, Homer Martin Papers (microfilm M381), SWC.

2. Jordan, "Ethnic Change in Texas," 411.

3. Terry G. Jordan, "The German Settlement of Texas after 1865," *Southwest Historical Quarterly* 73 (October 1969): 193.

4. Frederick Law Olmstead, *A Journey through Texas: or, A Saddle-Trip on the Southwestern Frontier* (New York: Dix, Edwards, 1857; reprint, Austin: University of Texas Press, 1978), 160, 424, 428.

5. Ibid., 431.

6. Roger Daniels, "The Immigrant Experience in the Gilded Age," in Calhoun, *Gilded Age*, 76 (quote), 65; Roger Daniels, *Coming to America: A History of Immigration and Ethnicity in American Life* (Princeton: Visual Education, 1990), 151.

7. Miner, *The Corporation and the Indian*, 58, and the chapter "Coal and Ties: The Confrontation," 58–76; Sparks, "James Jesse McAlester," 7–8.

8. Hightower, "Cattle, Coal, and Indian Land," 7.

9. Knight, "Oklahoma Indian Trader," 210.

10. Daybook 1874–75, #152, McAlester Collection, WHC, 126, 56, 54, 31.

11. Hightower, "Cattle, Coal, and Indian Land," 10.

12. Ibid. This trend can be substantiated by later census data. In the 1910 census records, the number of immigrants from England was listed at 227, from Scotland 133, and from Wales 105. In comparison, there were 1,398 from Italy, 395 from Austria, 178 from Germany, and 379 from Russia. Similarly in the 1920 census, the largest immigrant groups listed were Italians at 912, followed by Mexicans at 343, and Russians at 272. There were only 149 from England and 40 from Ireland in the later census. U.S. Bureau of the Census, *Thirteenth Census of the United States 1910, Vol. III, Population,* 476, and *Fourteenth Census of the United States 1920, State Compendium, Oklahoma,* 43.

13. U.S. Bureau of the Census, *Twelfth Census of the United States 1900, Schedule No.1, Population*, Enumeration District 81 (manuscript), 285A and 286A. Some of this discussion appears in English, "Inside the General Store."

14. Baird and Goble, *Story of Oklahoma*, 278–79.

15. Barbara J. Rozek, *Come to Texas: Attracting Immigrants, 1865–1915* (College Station: Texas A&M University Press, 2003).

16. Jordan, "German Settlement of Texas," 197–98.

17. Jordan, *German Seed in Texas Soil*, 55.

18. Walter Struve, *Germans and Texas: Commerce, Migration, and Culture in the Days of the Lone Star Republic* (Austin: University of Texas Press, 1996), 46–48; Jordan, *German Seed in Texas Soil*, 41–43.

19. Ellebracht, "True Texas Legend," 24.

20. Jordan, *German Seed in Texas Soil*, 53–54.

21. Jordan, "Ethnic Change in Texas," 409–10.

22. Jordan, "German Settlement of Texas," 211.

23. U.S. Bureau of the Census, *Ninth Census 1870*, The Statistics of the Population of the United States, Population of Civil Divisions Less than Counties, Table III, 274.

24. *Austin-Daily Statesman*, May 13, 1913.

25. Wolf and East Family Sketches, 1867–1971, Creator Sketch, Wolf Family Papers (AR.U.006), AHC.

26. *Austin-Daily Statesman*, May 13, 1913.

27. Ibid., May 24, 1913, Wolf Family Papers (AR.U.006), AHC.

28. Wolf Ledger, 1872–75, AHC, 52, 7; *General Directory of the City of Austin*, 78.

29. Wolf Ledger, 1872–75, AHC, 284, 291, 293, 79, 299, 371, 100, 255, 227, 407, 427, 281, 271, 245, 240, 289.

30. Ibid., 5, 12, 21, 50, 55, 100, 118, 127.

31. Most of the early Texas settlers, especially those in the 1840s migrations, came from the same regions in Germany—the Middle and High German provinces of Nassau, Electoral Hesse, Upper Hesse–Darmstadt, Alsace, Thuringia, the Heilbronn area of Württemburg, as well from the Low German areas of Oldenburg, southern Hannover, Brunswick (Braunschweig), the Münsterland, and Mecklenburg. The Wetterau, a region in Upper Hesse–Darmstadt north of Frankfurt-am-Main, was a particularly important source of Texas settlers. Lesser numbers came from Holstein, Waldeck, Anhalt, and portions of the Prussian Rhine Province. Jordan, *German Seed in Texas Soil*, 33.

32. Anna Martin to M. Chapman, 1904, Homer Martin Papers (microfilm M381), SWC.

33. There is a discrepancy in the historical records concerning this date; the family arrived either on December 10, 1845, or January 10, 1846, depending on the source. See "Henry Julius Behrens," in *Mason County Historical Book* (Mason

County Historical Commission, 1986), 8. There is an earlier version, similarly titled the *Mason County Historical Book* (Mason County Historical Commission and Mason County Historical Society, 1976), 13, Texas Tech University, Lubbock, TX. I have gone with the later date since it is derived from an early interview with Behrens. Regardless of the arrival date in Texas, both sources have the family leaving for New Braunfels on February 2, 1846.

34. "Henry Julius Behrens," *Mason County Historical Book* (1986), 9.

35. Ibid.; *Mason County Historical Book* (1976), 13, 14.

36. Daybook 2, 1887–88, Hedwig's Hill Store, SWC, 266.

37. "Henry Julius Behrens," *Mason County Historical Book* (1986), 10; *Mason County Historical Book* (1976), 15.

38. Anna Martin to M. Chapman, 1904, Homer Martin Papers (microfilm M381), SWC.

39. Ibid.

40. Mack Walker, "The Old Homeland and the New," in Glen E. Lich and Dona B. Reeves, eds., *German Culture in Texas, A Free Earth: Essays from the 1978 Southwest Symposium* (Boston: Twayne, 1980), 76–77.

41. Ibid., 74–75.

42. See Customer Account Book 1, 1884–91, 4, 13, 39, 46, 50, 129, and Daybook 1, 1885–87, 10, 351, 383, 398, 506, Hedwig's Hill Store, SWC. For family histories, see *Mason County Historical Book* (1976), 10, 60, 98, 131, 151, 165, 205, 241, 277, 278.

43. R. L. Biesele, "The First German Settlement in Texas," *Southwestern Historical Quarterly* 34 (April 1931): 335. A league of land was the Spanish measurement: 4,428.4 acres.

44. Ibid., 338; "Johann Freidrich Ernst," in Tyler et al., *New Handbook of Texas*, 2:884.

45. Jordan, *German Seed in Texas Soil*, 41; Tyler et al., *New Handbook of Texas*, 3:850, 2:884.

46. Miriam Korff York, *Friedrich Ernst of Industry: Research on Life, Family, Acquaintances, and Conditions of the Times* (Giddings, Texas: Nixon, 1989), 61.

47. Ibid., 148.

48. Hermann Ernst Account Book 1876–95 (3C61), CAH, 111. See also C. Klim's account, ibid., 107, 108, 112, 113.

49. Ibid., 86. See also entry for Wm. Hander, April 13, 1875, ibid., 77, 78, 80; also ibid., 87.

50. York, *Friedrich Ernst of Industry*, 153; Ernst Account Book, 1876–95, CAH, 110, 118.

51. Tyler et al., *New Handbook of Texas*, 3:850.

52. Ernst Account Book, 1876–95, CAH, 113.

53. Ernst Account Book, 1860–75, CAH, 49.

54. Ibid., 1876–95, 82.

55. Ibid., 1860–75, 55. Cash and interest payments also appear in ibid., 1876–95, 95.

56. Ibid., 1860–75, 62.

57. Ibid., 1876–95, 94.

58. Biesele, "First German Settlement in Texas," 339.

59. Anna Martin to M. Chapman, 1904, Homer Martin Papers (microfilm M381), SWC. Louis Martin was hanged in Eagle Pass, Texas, near the end of the war. Ellebracht, "True Texas Legend," 25.

60. Hollon, "Captain Charles Schreiner," 149. Also see Haley, *Charles Schreiner*, 4.

61. Walter D. Kamphoefner, "New Perspectives on Texas Germans and the Confederacy," *Southwestern Historical Quarterly* 102.4 (1999): 441–55.

62. "Started with a Country Store—Martin's Family Bank at Mason Traces Growth to Humble Start by Mother of Late President," Homer Martin Papers (microfilm M381), SWC. It would be interesting to know more about the relationship between Martin and Schreiner, but unfortunately, this is all that was mentioned and there are no other sources that discuss this.

63. Jordan, *German Seed in Texas Soil*, 135.

64. Ibid., 141, 143.

65. Ernst Account Book, 1860–75, CAH, 75.

66. Prince von Solms-Braunfels cited in Bierschwale, *Mason County, Texas*, 192.

67. Ibid. Jordan, *German Seed in Texas Soil*, 144, 147.

68. Gilbert J. Jordan, "German Cultural Heritage in the Hill Country of Texas," in Lich and Reeves, *German Culture in Texas*, 176–88.

69. For examples, see Daybook 3, 1888–90, Hedwig's Hill Store, SWC, 1, 3. Also see Hermann Ernst Account Book, Fischer Store Records, May 30, July 27, 1886.

70. Gauntt Bros. Ledger, Baylor University, 45, 49, 259.

71. Penne L. Restad, *Christmas in America: A History* (New York: Oxford University Press, 1995); Stephen Nissenbaum, *The Battle for Christmas* (New York: Alfred A. Knopf, 1996); Leigh Eric Schmidt, *Consumer Rites: The Buying and Selling of American Holidays* (Princeton, N.J.: Princeton University Press, 1995); Elizabeth H. Pleck, *Celebrating the Family: Ethnicity, Consumer Culture, and Family Rituals* (Cambridge, Mass.: Harvard University Press, 2000).

72. Pleck, *Celebrating the Family*, 43.

73. Restad, *Christmas in America*, 54.

74. Clark, *Pills, Petticoats, and Plows*, 100.

75. Schmidt, *Consumer Rites*, 35.

76. Clark, *Pills, Petticoats, and Plows*, 100.

77. Ibid., 104–105.

78. Daybook 1, 1885–86, Wadsworth (William B.) Ledgers (2H127), CAH, 226, 231, 248, 249.

79. Ledger F, 1883, Brown & Dixon, ETRC, 522.

80. Ibid., 545; Ledger H, 1885, ibid., 516.

81. *Texas Intelligencer*, January 9, 1875, reprinted in the *Cherokee County Banner*, June 1, 1917.

82. *Oklahoma Star*, December 16, 1876.

83. Restad, *Christmas in America*, 71.

84. Jordan, "German Cultural Heritage,"178.

85. Hermann Seele, *The Cypress and Other Writings of a German Pioneer in Texas*, Translated by Edward C. Breitenkamp (Austin: University of Texas Press, 1979), 96–97.

86. Haley, *Charles Schreiner*, 14–15.

87. Daybook 1, 1885–87, Hedwig's Hill Store, SWC, 183, 185, 189, 188, 190, 194.

88. Jordan, "German Cultural Heritage," 176.

89. Elizabeth Silverthorne, *Christmas in Texas* (College Station: Texas A&M University Press, 1990), 65.

90. While such cohesion distinguishes the rural German immigrant experience in Texas, there is still much scholarly work to be done on the German urban experience in Texas during the nineteenth century.

Chapter 6

1. Richard W. Leeman, *"Do Everything" Reform: The Oratory of Frances E. Willard*, Great American Orators Series 15 (New York: Greenwood Press, 1992), 112–13.

2. Catherine Gilbert Murdock, *Domesticating Drink: Women, Men, and Alcohol in America, 1870–1940* (Baltimore: Johns Hopkins University Press, 1998), 11.

3. Nancy G. Garner, "'A Prayerful Public Protest': The Significance of Gender in the Kansas Woman's Crusade of 1874," *Kansas History* 20 (Winter 1997–98): 218. According to Garner, the national woman's crusade was so popular among women reformers that, during the winter and spring of 1873–74, more than fifty-six thousand Anglo-Protestant women participated in the campaign to close down saloons with prayer and hymns. Ibid., 215–16.

4. McInnis Ledger 1874–75, AHC, 10.

5. Wolf Ledger, 1872–75, AHC, 19, 147.

6. Clark, *Pills, Petticoats, and Plows*, 15.

7. According to H. A. Ivy, a Texas prohibitionist, while a number of counties vacillated between wet and dry in the 1870s and 1880s, there were only three dry counties in Texas by 1887—Jasper, Rockwall, and Jones Counties. H. A. Ivy, *Rum on the Run in Texas: A Brief History of Prohibition in the Lone Star State* (Dallas: Temperance Publishing, 1910), 27.

8. Ibid., 14, 15, 37, 99; Allan M. Winkler, "Drinking on the American Frontier," *Quarterly Journal of Studies on Alcohol* 29 (June 1968): 431, 434, 435; Murdock, *Domesticating Drink*, 16, 51; Ownby, *American Dreams*, 11.

9. Ivy, *Rum on the Run*, 20.

10. Gregg Cantrell, "'Dark Tactics': Black Politics in the 1887 Texas Prohibition Campaign," *Journal of American Studies* 25.1 (April 1991): 86.

11. James D. Ivy, *No Saloon in the Valley: The Southern Strategy of Texas Prohibitionists in the 1880s* (Waco, Baylor University Press, 2003), 7.

12. Ibid., 7–23.

13. Debo, *Choctaw Republic*, 48.

14. Ibid., 177, 189. Federal law restricting the sale of liquor in Indian Territory prompted particularly entrepreneurial saloon keepers to set up shop just outside of the borders of Indian Territory; see Blake Gumprecht, "A Saloon on Every Corner: Whiskey Towns of Oklahoma Territory, 1889–1907," *Chronicles of Oklahoma* 74 (Summer 1996): 146–73.

15. Sales Ledger 1874–75, #152, McAlester Collection, WHC, 153, 179, 229, 289, 293.

16. For examples, see the following collections: Wolf Ledger 1872–75, AHC, 12, 52; Ledger 1870–73, Hardeman & Barret, ETRC, 4, 44, 172, 173; McInnis Ledger 1874–75, AHC, 53, 55; Account Book 1848–50, Lockranzy, Texas Ledger (A1982.339c), SMU; R. C. Doom & Company Account Ledger, Day Journal (file 1, box 1), SHRL, 5, 171, 178; L. B. Wood Daybook 1859–62, Polk County Records, SHRL, 321, 326, 330, 343.

17. Account Ledger 1869–73, Rowlett Store (B-39), ETRC, September 4, 10, 12, 1869.

18. Wolf Ledger 1872–75, AHC, 92.

19. Clark & Hyde Mercantile Collection, 2 vols., ETRC; Gauntt Bros. Ledger, Baylor University.

20. Ledger F, 1883, Brown & Dixon, ETRC, 167.

21. Account Ledger 1877, McCampbell & Bros., DRTL, 70.

22. Ledger H, 1885, Brown & Dixon, ETRC, 39.

23. *Texas Intelligencer*, January 9, 1875. There was also an active UFT chapter in Nacogdoches in the mid-1880s. A minute book from the year 1885–86 includes a list of the organization's members, reports on council meetings, officer elections, and treasury records. *United Friends of Temperance*, Fairview Council, Nacogdoches, Texas Minute Book 1885–86 (B-37), ETRC.

24. Ivy, *No Saloon in the Valley*, 63.

25. Ernst Account Book, 1876–95, CAH, 98; Account Book 1884–86, see July 6, 7, 9, 11, 20, 21 [1886?], Fischer Store Records, CAH.

26. Daybook 1, 1885–87, 145, 269, and Daybook 2, 1887–88, Hedwig's Hill Store, SWC, 103.

27. Murdoch, *Domesticating Drink*, 66–67.

28. Ibid., 52–62.

29. H. Wayne Morgan, *Drugs in America: A Social History, 1800–1980* (Syracuse: Syracuse University Press, 1981), 40. See also Patricia M. Tice, *Altered States: Alcohol and Other Drugs in America* (Rochester: Strong Museum, 1992), 41–71.

30. Wolf Ledger 1872–75, AHC, 52.

31. Ledger 1870–73, Hardeman & Barret, ETRC, 83.

32. Cantrell, "Dark Tactics," 91–92.

33. Morgan, *Drugs in America*, 32.

34. Clark, *Pills, Petticoats, and Plows*, 204.

35. Morgan, *Drugs in America*, 38.

36. Ledger 1870–73, Hardeman & Barret, ETRC, 604; Ledger F, 1883, Brown & Dixon, ETRC, 11; Sales Ledger 1877–80, #154, McAlester Collection, WHC, 190.

37. Morgan, *Drugs in America*, 2.

38. Daybook 1, Clark & Hyde, ETRC, 107, 112, 144; morphine purchases appear in ibid., 55, 58. Daybook 1870–72, box 29, McAlester Collection, WHC, 162. For cocaine examples, see Daybook 1, Clark & Hyde, ETRC, 4.

39. Ledger 1870–73, Hardeman & Barret, ETRC, 1.

40. Sales Ledger 1875–78, #153, McAlester Collection, WHC, 7.

41. Daybook 1869–71, Severs Collection, OHS, 149, 153.

42. Daybook 1, 1885–86, Wadsworth Ledgers, CAH, 4, 6, 20, 35, 40, 133, 140, 155. Quinine was also used for the treatment of malaria, which was common in lowland regions.

43. Daybook 1871–72, box 29, McAlester Collection, WHC, 91.

44. Clark, *Pills, Petticoats, and Plows*, 204.

45. For examples, see Daybook 2, 1886, Wadsworth Ledgers, CAH, 27; Account Book, Fischer Store Records, CAH, May 28, 1886; Daybook 1869–71, Severs Collection, OHS, 46.

46. Daybook 1869–71, Severs Collection, OHS, 44, 147.

47. Clark, *Pills, Petticoats, and Plows*, 205.

48. Account Ledger 1876–77, 14, 57, and Account Ledger 1877, 109, 193, McCampbell & Bros., DRTL; Daybook 1, 1885–86, Wadsworth Ledgers, CAH, 38, 40, 60; Daybook 1869–71, Severs Collection, OHS, 4, 19, 34, 48; Sales Ledger 1875–78, #153, McAlester Collection, WHC, 10, 18, 29, 38; Daybook 1, 1885–87, Hedwig's Hill Store, SWC, 29, 56, 450.

49. Ericson, *People of Nacogdoches County in 1870*, 104–40.

50. Brown & Dixon, ETRC; *Federal Census of Cherokee County 1880*, ETRC; Clark & Hyde, ETRC; Ericson, *People of Nacogdoches County in 1870*.

51. Census records indicate that the population of Austin in 1870 was 4,428. *Tenth Census 1880*, 455.

52. McAlester's ledgers indicate that credit played an important role in mining communities also, as local miners cashed their company's check at McAlester's store to cover their debts.

53. Ledger D, 1880–81, Brown & Dixon, ETRC, 178, 289, 303.

54. Daybook 1, 1885–87, Hedwig's Hill Store, SWC, 362, 364.

55. Robert G. Barrows, "Urbanizing America," in Calhoun, *Gilded Age*, 92.

56. Ownby, *American Dreams*, 17, 80.

57. Adams and Smith, "Black Tenant Farmer Material Culture." Historical archeologists and anthropologists have produced important works utilizing account records from general stores, including William Hampton Adams, Steven Smith, Margaret Purser, and James Wettstaed. See Adams and Smith, "Black Tenant Farmer Material Culture"; Margaret Purser, "Consumption as Communication in Nineteenth-Century Paradise Valley, Nevada," *Historical Archaeology* 26 (1992): 106–16; James R. Wettstaed, "A Look at Early Nineteenth-Century Life in an Ozarks Mining Town: The View from the Company Store," *Plains Anthropologist* 45 (2000): 85–97.

58. Wesson, "Southern Country Store,"164–65.

59. Wettstaed, "Ozarks Mining Town," 89.

60. Gauntt Bros. Ledger, Baylor University, 73, 77. For a discussion of tobacco in American culture and the shift to packaged cigarettes, see Iain Gately, *Tobacco: The Story of How Tobacco Seduced the World* (New York: Grove Press, 2001); Jordan Goodman, *Tobacco in History: The Cultures of Dependence* (London: Routledge, 1993).

61. Daybook 1874–75, #152, McAlester Collection, WHC, 54.

62. Ibid., 31.

63. *Oklahoma Star*, December 16, 1875.

64. Doris D. Fanelli, "William Polk's General Store in Saint George's Delaware," *Delaware History* 19 (1981): 212–28.

65. While Perkins notes the availability of luxury items on the Kentucky frontier (and this is largely her point), the fact remains that common necessities appeared most frequently on customer accounts, particularly among customers in the lowest tax levels. Perkins, "The Consumer Frontier," 498.

66. Schlereth, "Country Stores, County Fairs," 347.

67. Ledger 1, Lewis Store, AHC, 500.

68. Daybook 1, Clark & Hyde, ETRC, 8, 28, 103.

69. Ledger 1870–73, Hardeman & Barret, ETRC, 225.

70. Ledger D, 1880–81, Brown & Dixon, ETRC, 228, 178.

71. Ledger 1870–73, Hardeman & Barret, ETRC, 27, 80, 122, 144; Ericson, *People of Nacogdoches County in 1870*, 121, 139, 105. For luxury items, see Ledger 1870–73, Hardeman & Barret, ETRC, 21, 34, 59, 61, 67, 139, 145, 160, 163, 346.

72. Daybook 1, 1885–87, Hedwig's Hill Store, SWC, 183, 185, 189, 188, 190, 194.

Bibliography

Primary Sources

Ledger and Manuscript Collections

Austin History Center (AHC), Austin, Texas
    Lewis Store Records. AR 1999-017
    J. L. McInnis Ledger. AR 1994-57
    Wolf General Merchandise Store. AR 1991-72
Baylor University, Waco, Texas
    Gauntt Bros. Ledger 1887–1888
Center for American History (CAH), University of Texas, Austin, Texas
    Chireno Ledger, 1887, "Chireno Alliance." 2C446
    John W. H. Davis Papers, 1876–1912. 2J136
    Hermann Ernst Account Book. 3C61
    Hermann Fischer Store Papers, 1879–1904. 2D144
    J. C. Lynch Account Book. 2B178
    William B. Wadsworth Ledgers. 2H127
Daughters of the Republic of Texas Library (DRTL), San Antonio, Texas
    W. E. McCampbell & Bros. Records. Col. 7597
DeGolyer Library, Southern Methodist University (SMU), Dallas, Texas
    Lockranzy, Texas Ledger. 1 vol. A1982.339c
    J. D. Sherrill Diaries, 1882, 1884. A1980.0244c
East Texas Research Center (ETRC), Nacogdoches
    L. T. Barret Collection. A-274
    Bondies, Rohte & Co. Daybook. 1 vol. B-96
    Brown & Dixon Company Records. B-70
    Clark & Hyde Mercantile Company Records. 2 vols. B-97
    Gladys Hardeman Collection. A-69
    Hardeman & Barret General Merchandise Records. 1 vol. 1. B-38
    Rowlett Store, 1 vol. B-39
    United Friends of Temperance, Fairview Council, Minute Book, 1885–1886. B-37

Oklahoma Historical Society (OHS), Oklahoma City, Oklahoma
  Lottie Durham Collection. #713, Box 1, Box 1
  Industrial Development & Parks Commission Collection. #11298, Box 1, Box 1
  Oklahoma Historical Society Photograph Collection, 1860s–2006. #2406, Box 6c Towns (Box 4)
  F. B. Severs Collection. M1996.45
Sam Houston Regional Library & Research Center (SHRL & RC), Liberty, Texas
  R. C. Doom & Company Account Ledger. Day Journal, Box 1, File 1
  Neer & James Account Ledger. John & Marie Dutt Collection. 1 vol.
  L. B. Wood Day Book, 1859–1862. 1 vol. Polk County Records
Southwest Collection (SWC), Texas Tech University, Lubbock, Texas
  Hedwig's Hill Store Records. A111.7
  Homer Martin Papers
Western History Collections (WHC), University of Oklahoma, Norman, Oklahoma
  Benjamin R. Cook Collection. C13
  Dale Collection. Nacogdoches Altrusa Club. *Nacogdoches*. Booklet, Call No. F 394.N32 B5 1960
  Indian Pioneer Collection (Indian Pioneer Papers)
  Dovie Jones Collection. J-2 1137
  J. J. McAlester Collection. M2046
  Sudie (Susan) McAlester Barnes Collection. PB 36.G74

Published Directories

General Directory of the City of Austin, Texas, for 1877–1878. Houston: Mooney & Morrison, 1878. Austin History Center, Austin, Texas.

Hastain, E., ed. *Hastain's Index: Index to the Choctaw-Chickasaw Deeds and Allotments*. Muskogee, Okla.: 1908. Western History Collection, Norman, Oklahoma.

Newspapers and Magazines

Austin-Daily Statesman
Cherokee Advertiser
Cherokee County Banner
Holland's Magazine
McAlester Messenger
Nacogdoches News
New York Times
Oklahoma Star, McAlester, Choctaw Nation
Star-Vindicator, McAlester, Choctaw Nation
Texas Intelligencer

Government Publications

Choctaw Nation Census. *Choctaw Census, 1885*. Tubucksy [Tobucksy] County, Archive 121, Oklahoma Historical Society, Oklahoma City.

———. *Census for the Choctaw Nation, 1896.* Archives Division, Oklahoma Historical Society, Oklahoma City.

Foster, L. L. (commissioner). *Forgotten Texas Census: First Annual of the Agricultural Bureau of the Department of Agriculture, Insurance, Statistics, and History, 1887–1888.* Austin: Texas State Historical Association, 2001.

U.S. Bureau of the Census. *Federal Census 1880: Population Schedules.* Travis County, Precinct No. 2, Enumeration District 138. Oklahoma Historical Society, Oklahoma City, Oklahoma.

———. *Fourteenth Census of the United States 1920, State Compendium, Oklahoma.* Washington D.C.: Government Printing Office.

———. *Ninth Census of the United States 1870, Population.* Vol. 1. Washington, D.C.: Government Printing Office, 1872. Series M593, Roll #1599. *Population of Civil Divisions less than Counties*, Table III–State of Texas.

———. *Report on Cotton Production in the United States: Also Embracing Agricultural and Physico-Geographical Descriptions of the Several Cotton States and of California. Part 1: Mississippi Valley and the Southwestern States, Volume 5: Cotton Production of the State of Texas.* Washington, D.C.: Government Printing Office, 1884.

———. *Tenth Census of the United States 1880, Population.* Washington, D.C.: Government Printing Office, 1883.

———. *Thirteenth Census of the United States 1910, Volume III, Population.* Washington, D.C.: Government Printing Office.

———. *Twelfth Census of the United States 1900, Schedule No.1, Population.* Enumeration District 81. Manuscript. Government Documents, University of Oklahoma Library.

U.S. Department of the Interior. U.S. Geological Survey. *Mineral Resources of the United States for the Calendar Year 1887.* Washington, D.C.: Government Printing Office, 1888.

Unpublished Documents

Ericson, Carolyn Reeves, ed. *The People of Nacogdoches County in 1870: An Edited Census.* East Texas Research Center, Nacogdoches, 1977.

———. *The People of Nacogdoches County in 1880: An Edited Census.* East Texas Research Center, Nacogdoches, 1988.

Federal Census of Cherokee County 1880. Transcribed by Sue Vaughn Taylor. East Texas Research Center, Nacogdoches, Texas.

Hardeman, Gladys. "The History of Melrose." Gladys Hardeman Research Collection (A-69), East Texas Research Center, Nacogdoches, 1964–65.

The Saga of Cherokee County, Texas. Papers compiled by Helen Crawford. East Texas Research Center (ETRC), Nacogdoches, Texas.

Secondary Sources
Books and Journal Articles

Abbot, Carl. *Boosters and Businessmen: Popular Economic Thought and Urban Growth in the Antebellum Middle West.* Westport, Conn.: Greenwood Press, 1981.

Abelson, Elaine. *When Ladies Go A-Thieving: Middle-Class Shoppers in the Victorian Department Store.* New York: Oxford University Press, 1989.

Adams, William Hampton, and Steven D. Smith. "Historical Perspectives on Black Tenant Farmer Material Culture: The Henry C. Long General Store Ledger at Waverly Plantation, Mississippi." In *The Archeology of Slavery and Plantation Life,* ed. Theresa A. Singleton, 309–34. Orlando: Academic Press, 1985.

Agnew, Aileen B. "The Retail Trade of Elizabeth Sanders and the 'Other' Consumers of Colonial Albany." *Hudson Valley Regional Review* 14 (1997): 35–55.

Aiken, Charles S. *The Cotton Plantation South since the Civil War.* Baltimore: Johns Hopkins University Press, 1998.

Aldrich, Duncan M. "General Stores, Retail Merchants, and Assimilation: Retail Trade in the Cherokee Nation, 1838–1890." *Chronicles of Oklahoma* 57 (Summer 1979): 119–36.

Allen, Irving Lewis. *The Language of Ethnic Conflict: Social Organization and Lexical Culture.* New York: Columbia University Press, 1983.

Ames, Kenneth L. *Death in the Dining Room and Other Tales of Victorian Culture.* Philadelphia: Temple University Press, 1992.

———. "Meaning in Artifacts: Hall Furnishing in Victorian America." *Journal of Interdisciplinary History* 9 (Summer 1978): 19–46.

———. "Trade Catalogues and the Study of Culture." In Federhen et al., *Accumulation and Display,* 8–14.

Anderson, Charles G. *Deep Creek Merchant: The Story of William Henry "Pete" Snyder.* Snyder, Texas: Snyder Publishing, 1984.

Anderson, Karen. "Work, Gender, and Power in the American West." *Pacific Historical Review* 61 (November 1992): 481–99.

Atherton, Lewis E. *The Pioneer Merchant in Mid-America.* Columbia: University of Missouri Press, 1939.

———. *The Southern Country Store, 1800–1860.* Baton Rouge: Louisiana State University Press, 1949.

Austerman, Wayne R. *Sharp Rifles and Spanish Mules: The San Antonio–El Paso Mail, 1851–1881.* College Station: Texas A&M University Press, 1985.

Ayers, Edward L. *The Promise of the New South: Life after Reconstruction.* New York: Oxford University Press, 1992.

Baird, W. David, and Danney Goble. *The Story of Oklahoma.* Norman: University of Oklahoma Press, 1994.

Barr, Alwyn. *Black Texans: A History of African Americans in Texas, 1528–1995.* 1973. 2nd edition. Norman: University of Oklahoma Press, 1996.

———. *Reconstruction to Reform: Texas Politics, 1876–1906*. University of Texas Press, 1971. Reprint, Dallas: Southern Methodist University Press, 2000.

Barrett, Neal, Jr. *Long Days and Short Nights: A Century of Texas Ranching on the YO, 1880–1980*. Mountain Home, Texas: Y-O Press, 1980.

Barrows, Robert G. "Urbanizing America." In Calhoun, *Gilded Age*, 91–110.

Beecher, Catherine. *The Evils Suffered by American Women and American Children, the Causes and the Remedy*. New York: Harper and Brothers, 1846.

Benson, Susan Porter. *Counter Cultures: Saleswomen, Managers, and Customers In American Department Stores, 1890–1940*. Urbana: University of Illinois Press, 1986.

Biderman, Rose G. *They Came to Stay: The Story of the Jews of Dallas, 1870–1997*. Austin: Eakin Press, 2002.

Bierschwale, Margaret. *A History of Mason County, Texas, through 1964*. Edited by Julius E. Devos. Revised ed. Mason, Texas: Mason County Historical Commission, 1998.

Biesele, R. L. "The First German Settlement in Texas." *Southwestern Historical Quarterly* 34 (April 1931): 334–39.

Biggers, Don H. *Shackelford County Sketches*. Edited and annotated by Joan Farmer. Albany and Fort Griffin: Clear Fork Press, 1974.

Billman, Carol. "McGuffey's Readers and Alger's Fiction: The Gospel of Virtue according to Popular Children's Literature." *Journal of Popular Culture* 11 (Winter 1977): 614–18.

Bledstein, Burton J. *The Culture of Professionalism: The Middle Class and the Development of Higher Education in America*. New York: W. W. Norton, 1976.

Blumin, Stuart. *The Emergence of the Middle Class: Social Experience in the American City, 1790–1900*. Cambridge: Cambridge University Press, 1989.

Boorstin, Daniel J. *The Americans: The National Experience*. New York: Random House, 1965.

Bostic, E. McCurdy. "Elizabeth Fulton Hester." *Chronicles of Oklahoma* 6 (December 1928): 449–52.

Boswell, Angela. *Her Act and Deed: Women's Lives in a Rural Southern County, 1837–1873*. College Station: Texas A&M University Press, 2001.

———. "The Meaning of Participation: White Protestant Women in Antebellum Houston Churches." *Southwestern Historical Quarterly* 99 (July 1995): 26–47.

Boydston, Jeanne. *Home and Work: Housework, Wages, and the Ideology of Labor in the Early Republic*. New York: Oxford University Press, 1990.

Breen, T. H. "'Baubles of Britain': The American and Consumer Revolution of the Eighteenth Century." *Past and Present* 119 (1988): 73–104.

Brewer, John, and Roy Porter, eds. *Consumption and the World of Goods*. London: Routledge, 1993.

Bronner, Simon, ed. *Consuming Visions: Accumulation and Display of Goods in America, 1880–1920*. Winterthur: Henry Francis du Pont Winterthur Museum, 1989.

Buenger, Walter L. *The Path to a Modern South: Northeast Texas between Reconstruction and the Great Depression.* Austin: University of Texas Press, 2001.

———. "Texas and the South." *Southwestern Historical Quarterly* 103 (January 2000): 309–24.

Buenger, Walter L., and Robert A. Calvert, eds. *Texas through Time: Evolving Interpretations.* College Station: Texas A&M University Press, 1991.

Burton, Jeffrey. *Indian Territory and the United States, 1866–1906: Courts, Government, and the Movement for Oklahoma Statehood.* Norman: University of Oklahoma Press, 1995.

Bushman, Richard L. *The Refinement of America: Persons, Houses, Cities.* New York: Alfred A. Knopf, 1992.

Butler, Anne M. *Daughters of Joy, Sisters of Misery: Prostitutes in the American West, 1865–1890.* Urbana: University of Illinois Press, 1985.

Calhoun, Charles W., ed. *The Gilded Age: Essays on the Origins of Modern America.* Wilmington, Del.: Scholarly Resources, 1996.

Calvert, Robert A. "Agrarian Texas." In Buenger and Calvert, *Texas through Time*, 197–228.

———. "The Freedmen and Agricultural Prosperity." *Southwestern Historical Quarterly* 76.4 (1973): 461–71.

———. "Nineteenth-Century Farmers, Cotton, and Prosperity." *Southwestern Historical Quarterly* 73 (April 1970): 509–21.

Calvert, Robert A., Arnoldo De Leon, and Gregg Cantrell. *The History of Texas*, 4th ed. Wheeling, Ill.: Harlan Davidson, 2007.

Campbell, Randolph B. *Grass-Roots Reconstruction in Texas, 1865–1880.* Baton Rouge: Louisiana State University Press, 1998.

Cantrell, Gregg. "'Dark Tactics': Black Politics in the 1887 Texas Prohibition Campaign." *Journal of American Studies* 25.1 (April 1991): 85–93.

Carpenter, Charles. *History of American Schoolbooks.* Philadelphia: University of Pennsylvania Press, 1963.

Carson, Cary, Ronald Hoffman, and Peter J. Albert, eds. *Of Consuming Interests: The Style of Life in the Eighteenth Century.* Charlottesville: University Press of Virginia, 1994.

Cashion, Ty. "What's the Matter with Texas? The Great Enigma of the Lone Star State in the American West." *Montana: The Magazine of Western History* 55 (Winter 2005): 2–15.

Caughfield, Adrienne. *True Women and Westward Expansion.* College Station: Texas A&M University Press, 2005.

Chamberlain, C. K. "Lyne Toliaferro Barret: A Pioneer Texas Wildcatter." *East Texas Historical Journal* 6 (March 1968): 5–18.

Clark, Thomas D. *Pills, Petticoats, and Plows: The Southern Country Store.* Bobbs-Merrill Company, 1944. Reprint, Norman: University of Oklahoma Press, 1964.

Coleman, Jon T. "The Men in McArthur's Bar: The Cultural Significance of the Margins." *Western Historical Quarterly* 31 (2000): 47–68.
Cott, Nancy F. *The Bonds of Womanhood: "Woman's Sphere" in New England, 1780–1835.* New Haven: Yale University Press, 1977.
Crawford, Henry B. "George W. Singer and Dry Goods Retailing on the West Texas–South Plains Frontier, 1880–1890." *West Texas Historical Association Year Book* 69 (1993): 18–33.
Crouch, Barry A. *The Freedmen's Bureau and Black Texans.* Austin: University of Texas Press, 1992.
———. "A Spirit of Lawlessness: White Violence, Texas Blacks, 1865–1868." *Journal of Social History* 18 (Winter 1984): 217–32.
Daniels, Christine. "'Getting His [or Her] Livelihood': Free Workers in Slave Anglo-America, 1675–1810." *Agricultural History* 71 (Spring 1997): 125–61.
Daniels, Roger. *Coming to America: A History of Immigration and Ethnicity in American Life.* Princeton: Visual Education, 1990.
Davis, Ellis A., and Edwin H. Grobe, eds. *The New Encyclopedia of Texas*, vol. 3. Dallas: Texas Development Bureau, 1929.
Day, Gary, ed. *Varieties of Victorianism: The Uses of a Past.* New York: St. Martin's Press, 1998.
Dearan, Patrick. *Halff of Texas: A Merchant Rancher of the Old West.* Austin: Eakin Press, 2000.
Debo, Angie. *The Rise and Fall of the Choctaw Republic.* Civilization of the American Indian Series, vol. 6. Norman: University of Oklahoma Press, 1961.
Deetz, James. *In Small Things Forgotten: An Archeology of Early American Life.* New York: Anchor Books, 1977, rev. 1996.
Degler, Carl N. *At Odds: Women and the Family from the Revolution to the Present.* New York: Oxford University Press, 1981.
Devereaux, Linda Ericson. "A History of Oil Springs." In *The Bicentennial Commemorative History of Nacogdoches*, 149–55. Nacogdoches Jaycees, 1976.
Dippie, Brian W. *The Vanishing American: White Attitudes and U.S. Indian Policy.* Middleton, Conn.: Wesleyan University Press, 1982.
Dykstra, Robert. *The Cattle Towns.* 6th ed. New York: Atheneum, 1979.
Ellebracht, Pat. "A True Texas Legend: Anna Mebus Martin and the Commercial Bank." *Financial History* 61 (Winter 1998): 24–37.
Emmons, David M. "Constructed Province: History and the Making of the Last American West." *Western Historical Quarterly* 25 (1994): 437–59.
English, Linda C. "Inside the General Store, Inside the Past: A Cultural Analysis of McAlester's General Store." *Chronicles of Oklahoma* 81 (Spring 2003): 34–53.
———. "Recording Race: General Stores and Race in the Late Nineteenth-Century Southwest," *Southwestern Historical Quarterly* 110 (October 2006): 190–217.
———. "Revealing Accounts: Women's Lives and General Stores." *The Historian* 64 (Spring/Summer 2002): 567–85.

Enman, John A. "Coal Company Store Prices Questioned: A Case Study of The Union Supply Company Store, 1905–1906." *Pennsylvania History* 41 (1971): 53–62.

Enstam, Elizabeth York. *Women and the Creation of Urban Life: Dallas, Texas 1843–1920*. College Station: Texas A&M University Press, 1998.

Fanelli, Doris D. "William Polk's General Store in Saint George's, Delaware." *Delaware History* 19 (1981): 212–28.

Faulk, J. J. *History of Henderson County, Texas*. Athens, Texas: Athens Review, 1929.

Federhen, Deborah Anne, et al., ed. *Accumulation and Display: Mass Marketing Household Goods in America, 1880–1920*. Winterthur: Henry du Pont Winterthur Museum, 1986.

Fishback, Price V. Did Coal Miners "Owe Their Souls to the Company Store'? Theory and Evidence from the Early 1900s." *Journal of Economic History* 46 (December 1986): 1011–29.

Fite, Gilbert C. *Cotton Fields No More: Southern Agriculture, 1865–1980*. Lexington: University of Kentucky Press, 1984.

———. *The Farmers' Frontier, 1865–1900*. Albuquerque: University of New Mexico Press, 1974.

Flesher, Dale L., and Michael G. Schumacher. "A Natchez Doctor's Ledgers as a Source of History, 1804–1809." *Journal of Mississippi History* 58 (1996): 177–92.

Foley, Neil. *The White Scourge: Mexicans, Blacks, and Poor Whites in Texas Cotton Culture*. Berkeley and Los Angeles: University of California Press, 1997.

Foner, Eric. *Reconstruction: America's Unfinished Revolution, 1863–1877*. New York: Harper and Row, 1988.

Fox, Richard Wightman, and T. Jackson Lears, eds. *The Culture of Consumption: Critical Essays in American History, 1880–1980*. New York: Pantheon Books, 1983.

Foy, Jessica H., and Thomas J. Schlereth, eds. *American Home Life, 1880–1930: A Social History of Spaces and Services*. Knoxville: University of Tennessee Press, 1992.

Furlough, Ellen. "Gender and Consumption in Historical Perspective: A Selected Bibliography." In *The Sex of Things: Gender and Consumption in Historical Perspective*, ed. Victoria de Grazia and Ellen Furlough, 389–409. Berkeley and Los Angeles: University of California Press, 1996.

Gamber, Wendy. *The Female Economy: The Millinery and Dressmaking Trades, 1860–1930*. Urbana: University of Illinois Press, 1997.

———. "A Gendered Enterprise: Placing Nineteenth-Century Businesswomen in History." *Business History Review* 72 (Summer 1998): 188–217.

———. "Tarnished Labor: The Home, the Market, and the Boardinghouse in Antebellum America." *Journal of the Early Republic* 22 (Summer 2002): 177–204.

Garner, Nancy G. "'A Prayerful Public Protest': The Significance of Gender in the Kansas Woman's Crusade of 1874." *Kansas History* 20 (Winter 1997–98): 214–29.

Gately, Iain. *Tobacco: The Story of How Tobacco Seduced the World*. New York: Grove Press, 2001.

Gay, Peter. *The Bourgeois Experience: Victoria to Freud*. Vol.1. New York: W. W. Norton, 1984.

———. *Education of the Senses*. Vol. 2, of Gay, *Bourgeois Experience*. New York: W. W. Norton, 1986.

———. *The Cultivation of Hatred*. Vol. 3, of Gay, *Bourgeois Experience*. New York: W. W. Norton, 1993.

———. *The Naked Heart*. Vol. 4, of Gay, *Bourgeois Experience*. New York: W. W. Norton, 1995.

———. *Pleasure Wars*. Vol. 5, of Gay, *Bourgeois Experience*. New York: W. W. Norton, 1998.

Glennie, Paul. "Consumption within Historical Studies." In *Acknowledging Consumption: A Review of New Studies*, ed. Daniel Miller, 164–203. London: Routledge, 1995.

Glickman, Lawrence B. "Bibliographic Essay." In *Consumer Society in American History: A Reader*, ed. Lawrence B. Glickman, 399–414. Ithaca: Cornell University Press, 1999.

Goodman, Jordan. *Tobacco in History: The Cultures of Dependence*. London: Routledge, 1993.

Goodwyn, Lawrence. *Democratic Promise: The Populist Moment in America*. New York: Oxford University Press, 1976.

Grant, Madison. *The Passing of the Great Race*. New York: C. Scribner's Sons, 1916.

Grier, Katherine. *Culture and Comfort: People, Parlors, and Upholstery*. Rochester, N.Y.: Strong Museum, Distributed by the University of Massachusetts Press, 1988.

Gumprecht, Blake. "A Saloon on Every Corner: Whiskey Towns of Oklahoma Territory, 1889–1907." *Chronicles of Oklahoma* 74 (Summer 1996): 146–73.

Haas, Oscar. *History of New Braunfels and Comal County, Texas, 1844–1946*. Austin: Steck, 1968.

Hahn, Steven. *The Roots of Southern Populism: Yeoman Farmers and the Transformation of the Georgia Upcountry, 1850–1890*. New York: Oxford University Press, 1983.

Hale, Grace Elizabeth. *Making Whiteness: The Culture of Segregation in the South, 1890–1940*. New York: Pantheon Books, 1998.

Haley, J. Evetts. *Charles Schreiner, General Merchandise: The Story of a Country Store*. Austin: Texas State Historical Association, 1944.

Halliburton, R., Jr. *Red over Black: Black Slavery among the Cherokee Indians*. Westport: Greenwood Press, 1977.

Haltunnen, Karen. *Confidence Men and Painted Women: A Study of Middle-Class Culture in America, 1830–1870*. New Haven: Yale University Press, 1982.

Haywood, C. Robert. *Victorian West: Class and Culture in Kansas Cattle Towns*. Lawrence: University Press of Kansas, 1991.

Hedgpeth, Don. *Proud Promise: The Story of Schreiner Institute/College, 1923–1998.* Kerrville: Texas Press of the Guadalupe of Schreiner College, 1998.

Henderson County Historical Commission. *Family Histories of Henderson County, Texas, 1846–1981.* Dallas: Taylor, 1981.

Hightower, Michael J. "Cattle, Coal, and Indian Land: A Tradition of Mining in Southeastern Oklahoma." *Chronicles of Oklahoma* 62 (Spring 1984): 4–25.

"Historical Notes." *Chronicles of Oklahoma* 17 (June 1939): 232.

Hofstadter, Richard. *The Age of Reform: From Bryan to F.D.R.* New York: Vintage Books, 1960.

Hollon, Gene. "Captain Charles Schreiner: The Father of the Hill Country." *Southwestern Historical Quarterly* 48.2 (October 1944): 145–68.

Horowitz, Daniel. *The Morality of Spending: Attitudes toward the Consumer Society, 1875–1940.* Baltimore: Johns Hopkins University Press, 1985.

Howe, Daniel Walker, ed. *Victorian America.* Pennsylvania: University of Pennsylvania Press, 1976.

———. "Victorian Culture in America." In Howe, *Victorian America*, 3–28.

Hunt, Lynn. "Introduction: History, Culture, and Text." In *The New Cultural History*, ed. Lynn Hunt, 1–22. Berkeley and Los Angeles: University of California Press, 1989.

Huson, Hobart. *Refugio: A Comprehensive History of Refugio County: From Aboriginal Times to 1955.* Volume 2, *Secession to 1955.* Woodsboro, Texas: Rooke Foundation, 1955).

Ivy, H. A. *Rum on the Run in Texas: A Brief History of Prohibition in the Lone Star State.* Dallas: Temperance Publishing, 1910.

Ivy, James D. *No Saloon in the Valley: The Southern Strategy of Texas Prohibitionists in the 1880s.* Waco: Baylor University Press, 2003.

Jacksonville Centennial Corporation. *Jacksonville: The Story of a Dynamic Community.* Jacksonville: Jacksonville Centennial Corporation, 1972.

Jaffee, David. "Peddlers of Progress and the Transformation of the Rural North, 1760–1860." *Journal of American History* 78 (September 1991): 511–35.

———. *People of the Wachusett: Greater New England in History and Memory, 1630–1860.* Ithaca: Cornell University Press, 1999.

———. "The Village Enlightenment in New England, 1760–1820." *William and Mary Quarterly* 47 (July 1990): 327–46.

Jameson, Elizabeth. "Women as Workers, Women as Civilizers: True Womanhood in the American West." In *The Women's West*, ed. Susan H. Armitage and Elizabeth Jameson, 145–64. Norman: University of Oklahoma Press, 1987.

Jameson, Elizabeth, and Susan Armitage, eds. *Writing the Range: Race, Class, and Culture in the Women's West.* Norman: University of Oklahoma Press, 1997.

Jeffrey, Julie Roy. *Frontier Women: "Civilizing" the West? 1840–1880.* 1979. Revised edition, New York: Hill and Wang, 1998.

Jensen, Joan. *Loosening the Bonds: Mid-Atlantic Farm Women, 1750–1850.* New Haven: Yale University Press, 1986.
Jensen, Joan M., and Darlis A. Miller. "The Gentle Tamers Revisited: New Approaches to the History of Women in the American West." *Pacific Historical Review* 49 (May 1980): 173–213.
Jones, Lu Ann. "Gender, Race, and Itinerant Commerce in the New South." *Journal of Southern History* 66 (May 2000): 297–320.
Jones, Mary Ellen. *Daily Life on the Nineteenth-Century American Frontier.* Westport, Conn.: Greenwood Press, 1998.
Jordan, Gilbert J. "German Cultural Heritage in the Hill Country of Texas." In Lich and Reeves, *German Culture in Texas,* 176–88.
Jordan, Terry G. "A Century and a Half of Ethnic Change in Texas, 1836–1986." *Southwestern Historical Quarterly* 89 (April 1986): 385–422.
———. *German Seed in Texas Soil: Immigrant Farmers in Nineteenth-Century Texas.* Austin: University of Texas Press, 1966.
———. "The German Settlement of Texas after 1865." *Southwest Historical Quarterly* 73 (October 1969): 193–212.
———. "The Imprint of the Upper and Lower South on Mid-Nineteenth-Century Texas." *Annals of the Association of American Geographers* 57 (December 1976): 667–90.
Jordan, Terry G., et al. *Texas: A Geography.* Geographies of the United States Series. Boulder: Westview Press, 1984.
Kamphoefner, Walter D. "New Perspectives on Texas Germans and the Confederacy." *Southwestern Historical Quarterly* 102.4 (1999): 441–55.
Kelley, Robin D. G. *Race Rebels: Culture, Politics, and the Black Working Class.* New York: Free Press, 1994.
Kelly, Catherine E. *In the New England Fashion: Reshaping Women's Lives in the Nineteenth Century.* Ithaca: Cornell University Press, 1999.
Kennedy, Michael V. "'Cash for His Turnips': Agricultural Production for Local Markets in Colonial Pennsylvania, 1725–1783." *Agricultural History* 74 (2000): 587–608.
Kerber, Linda K. "Separate Sphere, Female Worlds, Woman's Places: The Rhetoric of Women's History." *Journal of American History* 75 (June 1988): 9–39.
Knight, Oliver. "An Oklahoma Indian Trader as a Frontiersman of Commerce." *Journal of Southern History* 23 (May 1957): 203–19.
Kolmer, Elizabeth. "The McGuffey Readers: Exponents of American Classical Liberalism." *Journal of General Education* 27 (Winter 1976): 309–16.
Kucich, John, and Dianne F. Sadoff, eds. *Victorian Afterlife: Postmodern Culture Rewrites the Nineteenth Century.* Minneapolis: University of Minnesota Press, 2000.
Kyriakoudes, Louis M. "Lower-Order Urbanization and Territorial Monopoly in the Southern Furnishing Trade: Alabama, 1871–1890." *Social Science History* 26 (Spring 2002): 179–98.

Leach, William. *Land of Desire: Merchants, Power, and the Rise of a New American Culture.* New York: Pantheon Books, 1993.
Lears, T. Jackson. *Fables of Abundance: A Cultural History of Advertising in America.* New York: Basic Books, 1994.
Lebsock, Suzanne. *The Free Women of Petersburg: Status and Culture in a Southern Town, 1784–1860.* New York: Norton, 1984.
Leeman, Richard W. *"Do Everything" Reform: The Oratory of Frances E. Willard.* Great American Orators Series 15. New York: Greenwood Press, 1992.
Lerner, Gerda. "The Lady and the Mill Girl: Changes in the Status of Women in the Age of Jackson." *Mid-Continental American Studies Journal* 10 (Spring 1969): 5–15.
Lich, Glen E., and Dona B. Reeves, eds. *German Culture in Texas, a Free Earth: Essays from the 1978 Southwest Symposium.* Boston: Twayne, 1980.
Littlefield, Daniel F. *Africans and Creeks: From the Colonial Period to the Civil War.* Westport: Greenwood Press, 1979.
———. *Africans and Seminoles: From Removal to Emancipation.* Jackson: Banner Books, University Press of Mississippi, 2001.
———. *The Cherokee Freedmen: From Emancipation to American Citizenship.* Westport: Greenwood Press, 1978.
———. *The Chickasaw Freedmen: A People without a Country.* Westport: Greenwood Press, 1980.
Litwack, Leon F. *Been in the Storm So Long: The Aftermath of Slavery.* New York: Vintage Books, 1979.
Lucas, John. "Republican versus Victorian: Radical Writing in the Later Years of the Nineteenth Century." In *Rethinking Victorian Culture,* ed. Juliet John and Alice Jenkins, 29–45. New York: St. Martin's Press, 2000.
Main, Gloria L. "Gender, Work, and Wages in Colonial New England." *William and Mary Quarterly* 51 (January 1994): 39–66.
Marler, Scott. "Merchants in the Transition to a New South: Central Louisiana, 1840–1880." *Louisiana History* 42 (Spring 2001): 165–92.
Martin, Ann Smart. "Makers, Buyers, and Users: Consumerism as a Material Culture Framework." *Winterthur Portfolio* 28.2–3 (1993): 141–57.
Mason, Kenneth. *African Americans and Race Relations in San Antonio, Texas, 1867–1937.* New York: Garland, 1998.
Mason County Historical Commission. *Mason County Historical Book.* Mason: Mason County Historical Commission and Mason County Historical Society, 1976.
———. *Mason County Historical Book.* Mason: Mason County Historical Commission, 1986.
McKendrick, Neil, John Brewer, and J. H. Plumb. *The Birth of Consumer Society: The Commercialization of Eighteenth-Century England.* Bloomington: Indiana University Press, 1982.
McReynolds, Edwin C. *Oklahoma: A History of the Sooner State.* Norman: University of Oklahoma Press, 1954.

McWilliams, James E. "Work, Family, and Economic Improvement in Late-Seventeenth-Century Massachusetts Bay: The Case of Joshua Buffum." *New England Quarterly* 74 (2001): 355–84.
Meyer, Deborah J. C., and Laurel E. Wilson. "Bringing Civilization to the Frontier: The Role of Men's Coats in 1865 Virginia City, Montana Territory." *Clothing and Textiles Research Journal* 16 (1998): 19–26.
Miller, Marla R. "Gender, Artisanry, and Craft Tradition in Early New England: The View through the Eye of a Needle." *William and Mary Quarterly* 60 (October 2003): 743–76.
Milner, Clyde A., II, Carol A. O'Connor, and Martha A. Sandweiss, eds. *The Oxford History of the American West.* New York: Oxford University Press, 1994.
Miner, Craig H. *The Corporation and the Indian: Tribal Sovereignty and Industrial Civilization in Indian Territory, 1865–1907.* 1976. New ed. Norman: University of Oklahoma Press, 1989.
Moore, Alexander. "Daniel Axtell's Account Book and the Economy of Early South Carolina." *South Carolina Historical Magazine* 95 (October 1994): 280–301.
Morgan, H. Wayne. *Drugs in America: A Social History, 1800–1980.* Syracuse: Syracuse University Press, 1981.
———, ed. *The Gilded Age: A Reappraisal.* Syracuse: Syracuse University Press, 1963.
Mullins, Paul. "Race and the Genteel Consumer: Class and African American Consumption." *Historical Archaeology* 33 (1999): 22–38.
Murdock, Catherine Gilbert. *Domesticating Drink: Women, Men, and Alcohol in America, 1870–1940.* Baltimore: Johns Hopkins University Press, 1998.
Myres, Sandra L. *Westering Women and the Frontier Experience, 1800–1915.* Albuquerque: University of New Mexico Press, 1982.
Nacogdoches County Genealogical Society. *Nacogdoches County Families.* Dallas: Curtis Media, 1985.
Nacogdoches Jaycees. *The Bicentennial Commemorative History of Nacogdoches.* Nacogdoches: Nacogdoches Jaycees, 1976.
Nelson, Will T., ed. *English Choctaw Dictionary.* Fifth edition. Oklahoma City: Oklahoma City Council of Choctaws, 1975.
Nesbitt, Paul. "J. J. McAlester." *Chronicles of Oklahoma* 11 (June 1933): 758–64.
Nissenbaum, Stephen. *The Battle for Christmas.* New York: Alfred A. Knopf, 1996.
Noel, Thomas J. *The City and the Saloon: Denver, 1858–1916.* Lincoln: University of Nebraska Press, 1982.
Nugent, Walter. "Where Is the American West? Report on a Survey." *Montana: The Magazine of Western History* 42 (Spring 1992): 2–23.
Olmstead, Frederick Law. *A Journey through Texas; or, A Saddle-Trip on the Southwestern Frontier.* New York: Dix, Edwards, 1857. Reprint, Austin: University of Texas Press, 1978.
Ownby, Ted. *American Dreams in Mississippi: Consumers, Poverty, and Culture, 1830–1998.* Chapel Hill: University of North Carolina Press, 1999.

Parsons, Elaine Frantz. "Risky Business: The Uncertain Boundaries of Manhood in the Midwestern Saloon." *Journal of Social History* 34 (2000): 283–307.

Perkins, Elizabeth A. "The Consumer Frontier: Household Consumption in Early Kentucky." *Journal of American History* 78 (September 1991): 486–510.

Pleck, Elizabeth H. *Celebrating the Family: Ethnicity, Consumer Culture, and Family Rituals*. Cambridge, Mass.: Harvard University Press, 2000.

Pittsburg County Genealogical and Historical Society. *Pittsburg County, Oklahoma: People and Places*. Wolfe City, Texas: Henington Industries, 1997.

Polk, Stella Gipson. *Mason and Mason County: A History*. Revised ed. Burnet, Texas: Eakin Press, 1980.

Praetzellis, Adrian, and Mary Praetzellis. "Mangling Symbols of Gentility in the Wild West: Case Studies in Interpretative Archeology." *American Anthropologist* 103 (September 2001): 645–54.

Purser, Margaret. "Consumption as Communication in Nineteenth-Century Paradise Valley, Nevada." *Historical Archeology* 26 (1992): 106–16.

Reese, Linda Williams. *Women of Oklahoma, 1890–1920*. Norman: University of Oklahoma Press, 1997.

Restad, Penne L. *Christmas in America: A History*. New York: Oxford University Press, 1995.

Richardson, Rupert N., et al. *Texas: The Lone Star State*. 8th ed. Upper Saddle River, N.J.: Prentice-Hall, 2001.

Ridge, Martin. "The American West: From Frontier to Region." *New Mexico Historical Quarterly* 64 (April 1989): 125–41.

Riley, Glenda. *Confronting Race: Women and Indians on the Frontier, 1815–1915*. Albuquerque: University of New Mexican Press, 2004.

———. *Women and Indians on the Frontier, 1825–1915*. Albuquerque: University of New Mexico Press, 1984.

Roach, Hattie Joplin. *The Hills of Cherokee: Historical Sketches of Life in Cherokee County*. Rusk, Texas: N.p., 1952.

Robinson, Miss Ella. "History of the Patterson Mercantile Company." *Chronicles of Oklahoma* 36 (Spring 1958): 53–64.

Ronda, James P. "'We Have a Country': Race, Geography, and the Invention of Indian Territory." *Journal of the Early Republic* 19 (Winter 1999): 739–55.

Rozek, Barbara J. *Come to Texas: Attracting Immigrants, 1865–1915*. College Station: Texas A&M University Press, 2003.

Ryan, Mary P. *Cradle of the Middle Class: The Family in Oneida County, New York, 1790–1865*. New York: Cambridge University Press, 1981.

———. *Women in Public: Between Banners and Ballots, 1825–1880*. Baltimore: Johns Hopkins University Press, 1990.

Saunt, Claudio. "The Paradox of Freedom: Tribal Sovereignty and Emancipation during the Reconstruction of Indian Territory." *Journal of Southern History* 70 (January 2004): 63–94.

Schlereth, Thomas J. "Country Stores, County Fairs and Mail Order Catalogues: Consumption in Rural America." In Bronner, *Consuming Visions*, 339–75.

———. *Victorian America: Transformations in Everyday Life, 1876–1915*. New York: HarperCollins, 1991.

Schlissel, Lillian, Vicki L. Ruiz, and Janice Monk, eds. *Western Women: Their Land, Their Lives*. Albuquerque: University of New Mexico Press, 1988.

Schmidt, Leigh Eric. *Consumer Rites: The Buying and Selling of American Holidays*. Princeton, N.J.: Princeton University Press, 1995.

Schwartz, Michael. *Radical Protest and Social Structure: The Southern Farmers' Alliance and Cotton Tenancy, 1880–1890*. New York: Academic Press, 1976.

Seele, Herman. *The Cypress and Other Writings of a German Pioneer in Texas*. Translated by Edward C. Breitenkamp. Austin: University of Texas Press, 1979.

Shi, David E. "Review of Stanley Coben's *Rebellion against Victorianism: The Impetus for Cultural Change in 1920s America*." *American Historical Review* 97 (October 1992): 1301–1302.

Silverthorne, Elizabeth. *Christmas in Texas*. College Station: Texas A&M University Press, 1990.

Sitton, Thad, and James H. Conrad. *Freedom Colonies: Independent Black Texans in the Time of Jim Crow*. Austin: University of Texas Press, 2005.

Sitton, Thad, and Dan K. Utley. *From Can See to Can't: Texas Cotton Farmers on the Southern Prairies*. Austin: University of Texas Press, 1997.

Skaggs, Jimmy M. *The Cattle-Trailing Industry: Between Supply and Demand, 1866–1890*. Lawrence: University Press of Kansas, 1973.

Sklar, Kathryn Kish. *Catherine Beecher: A Study in American Domesticity*. New Haven: Yale University Press, 1973.

Smallwood, James M. *Time of Hope, Time of Despair: Black Texans during Reconstruction*. Port Washington, N.Y.: Kennikat Press, 1981.

Smallwood, James M., Barry A. Crouch and Larry Peacock. *Murder and Mayhem: The War of Reconstruction in Texas*. College Station: Texas A&M University Press, 2003.

Sparks, Gerald L. "James Jesse McAlester: The Choctaw Nation's Omnipresent Entrepreneur, 1871–1894." Masters thesis, University of Oklahoma, 1997.

Spratt, John S. *The Road to Spindletop: Economic Change in Texas, 1871–1901*. Dallas: Southern Methodist University Press, 1955.

Stansell, Christine. *City of Women: Sex and Class in New York, 1789–1860*. New York: Alfred A. Knopf, 1986.

Stewart, Kenneth L., and Arnold De Leon. *Not Room Enough: Mexicans, Anglos, and Socioeconomic Change in Texas, 1850–1900*. Albuquerque: University of New Mexico Press, 1993.

Struve, Walter. *Germans and Texas: Commerce, Migration, and Culture in the Days of the Lone Star Republic*. Austin: University of Texas Press, 1996.

Takaki, Ronald T. *Iron Cages: Race and Culture in Nineteenth-Century America*. New York: Alfred A. Knopf, 1979.

Thorburn, Joseph B., and Muriel H. Wright. *Oklahoma: A History of the State and Its People*. Vol. 1. New York: Lewis Historical Publishing, 1929.

Tice, Patricia M. *Altered States: Alcohol and Other Drugs in America*. Rochester: Strong Museum, 1992.

Tower, Michael. "Traders along the Washita: A Short History of the Shirley Trading Company." Chronicles of Oklahoma 65 (Spring 1987): 4–15.

Turner, Frederick Jackson. *The Frontier in American History*. New York: Henry Holt, 1920.

Tyler, Ron, et al., ed. *The New Handbook of Texas*. Austin: Texas State Historical Association, 1996.

Ulrich, Laurel Thatcher. "Martha Ballard and Her Girls." In *Work and Labor in Early America*, ed. Stephen Innes, 70–105. Chapel Hill: University of North Carolina Press, 1988.

———. *A Midwife's Tale: The Life of Martha Ballard, Based on Her Diary, 1785–1812*. New York: Vintage Books, 1990.

Walker, Donald R. *A Frontier Texas Mercantile: The History of Gibbs Brothers and Company, Huntsville, 1841–1940*. Huntsville: Texas Review Press, 1997.

Ward, Mary Jane. *George Washington Grayson and the Creek Nation, 1843–1920*. Norman: University of Oklahoma, 1999.

Weiner, Jonathan M. *Social Origins of the New South: Alabama, 1860–1885*. Baton Rouge: Louisiana State University Press, 1978.

Welter, Barbara. "The Cult of True Womanhood, 1820–1860." *American Quarterly* 18 (Summer 1966): 151–75.

Wesson, Kenneth R. "The Southern Country Store Revisited: A Test Case." *Alabama Historical Quarterly* 42 (Fall/Winter 1980): 157–66.

West, Elliott. *The Contested Plains: Indians, Goldseekers, and the Rush to Colorado*. Lawrence: University Press of Kansas, 1998.

———. "Reconstructing Race." *Western Historical Quarterly* 34 (Spring 2003): 7–26.

———. *The Saloon on the Rocky Mountain Mining Frontier*. Lincoln: University of Nebraska Press, 1979.

———. "Scarlet West: The Oldest Profession in the Trans-Mississippi West." *Montana: The Magazine of Western History* 31 (1981): 16–27.

Wettstaed, James R. "A Look at Early Nineteenth Century Life in an Ozarks Mining Town: The View from the Company Store." *Plains Anthropologist* 45 (2000): 85–97.

White, Richard. *"It's Your Misfortune and None of My Own": A New History of the American West*. Norman: University of Oklahoma Press, 1991.

White, Shane, and Graham White. *Stylin': African American Expressive Culture from Its Beginnings to the Zoot Suit*. Ithaca: Cornell University Press, 1998.

Wickett, Murray R. *Contested Territory: Whites, Native Americans, and African Americans in Oklahoma, 1865–1907.* Baton Rouge: Louisiana State University Press, 2000.

Wilson, Bobby M. "Race in Commodity Exchange and Consumption: Separate but Equal." *Annals of the Association of American Geographers* 95.3 (September 2005): 587–606.

Winegarten, Ruthe. *Black Texas Women: 150 Years of Trial and Triumph.* Austin: University of Texas Press, 1995.

Winkler, Allan M. "Drinking on the American Frontier." *Quarterly Journal of Studies on Alcohol* 29 (June 1968): 413–45.

Woloch, Nancy. *Women and the American Experience.* 2nd ed. New York: McGraw-Hill, 1994.

Woodman, Harold D. *King Cotton and His Retainers: Financing and Marketing the Cotton Crop of the South, 1800–1925.* Lexington: University of Kentucky Press, 1968.

Woodward, C. Vann. *Origins of the New South, 1877–1913.* 1951. Reprint, Baton Rouge: Louisiana State University Press, 1971.

Wooster, Ralph A. "Wealthy Texans, 1870." *Southwestern Historical Quarterly* 74.1 (July 1970): 24–35.

Worster, Donald. *Under Western Skies: Nature and History in the American West.* New York: Oxford University Press, 1992.

Wright, Gavin. *Old South, New South: Revolutions in the Southern Economy since the Civil War.* New York: Basic Books, 1986.

Wright, Muriel H. "Old Boggy Depot." *Chronicles of Oklahoma* 5 (March 1927): 4–16.

———. "Sarah Ann Harlan: From Her Memoirs of Life in the Indian Territory." *Chronicles of Oklahoma* 39.3 (Fall 1961): 158–79.

Wrobel, David M., and Michael C. Steiner, eds. *Many Wests: Place, Culture, and Regional Identity.* Lawrence: University Press of Kansas, 1997.

Wunder, John R., ed. *At Home on the Range: Essays on the History of Western Social and Domestic Life.* Westport, Conn.: Greenwood Press, 1985.

York, Miriam Korff. *Friedrich Ernst of Industry: Research on Life, Family, Acquaintances, and Conditions of the Times.* Giddings, Texas: Nixon, 1989.

Index

Account book. *See* Ledger (definition)
Adelsverein, 152–53, 159, 172
African Americans: alcohol purchases and, 182; distinguished in ledgers, 6, 98–100, 107–108, 120–21, 128, 132, 197, 229n44; education and, 11, 112–15, 192, 199; experiences during Reconstruction, 6–7, 10, 58, 63, 105–23, 125, 133, 182, 196, 199, 228nn40–41; illiteracy rates among, 60, 108, 112–13; in Indian Territory, 11, 65, 99, 124–25, 127–28, 132; purchasing patterns of, 1, 58–59, 107–10, 112–23, 192; sharecropping and, 7, 54, 56–58, 63–65, 106, 108, 117–18, 189. *See also* Racial violence
Alcohol, 81, 173–82, 186, 193, 198; temperance campaigns against, 20, 173–81, 198, 237n3, 237n7
Alger, Horatio, 44, 195
American Indians: frontier threats of, 155–56; intermarriage and, 41, 44, 126–27, 129–31; and racial divisions, 10–11, 40–44, 106, 124–33, 197, 199; tribal power and, 105–106, 124, 126. *See also* Chickasaw Indians; Choctaw Nation; Creek Nation; Indian Territory
Anacher, James, 129
Anderson, Chief George, 42
Anderson, George (Freedman), 107
Anderson, Miss Annie. *See* Severs, Mrs. Annie (Anderson)

Archibald, Edward, 38
Arnwine, Cal, 62
Asbury Mission, 42
Athens, Texas, 18, 36, 96, 100, 165, 178, 187, 190
Atherton, Lewis, 14–16
Atkins, Lou, 102
"Aunt Violet," 99, 128
Austin, Texas, 18, 64, 89, 96–97, 118, 153, 156, 182, 187

Ballard, Zach, 122
Bankston, George, 184
Barbed wire, 42, 70–72
Barber, A. H., 122
Barber, R. R., 120
Barret, Lyne T., 6, 8–9, 28–30, 34, 50, 56, 63, 111, 183, 195; family purchases of, 28, 30–31, 50; oil exploits and, 29, 50
Barret, Mrs. Angelina (wife of Lyne T. Barret), 28
Barret, Peter, 117
Barrow, H. V., 120
Bauer, Jacob (and family), 159, 170
Bauer, John, 70
Baxter, William, 184
Bedford, George, 167
Beecher, Catherine, 100–101
Behrens, Henry Julius, 155–57; family of, 155–56
Behrens Community School, 156
Berryhill, Abbie, 101–102
Biedermeier movement, 158–59

259

260 INDEX

Blakely, Mrs. A., 6
Boarding houses. *See* Hotel keeping
Boldebuck, H., 175
Bolden, Perry, 58–59, 63, 110–12, 133, 187, 227n19
Bolden, Perry Jr. (son), 112, 227n19
Bowen, Larry, 75
Bowers, Mrs. Annie, 94–95
Brandenberger, Gottlieb, 181
Bremen, Germany, 152, 157
Brenham, Texas, 161
Brinkman, Alexander, 96
Brinkman, Mrs. Regina, 96–97, 154
Brown, Charles, 75
Brown, Dixon & Company (aka Brown & Dixon). *See* McKinney & Brown store
Brown, J. L. (Lem), 25–26
Brown, Mrs. Mary Elizabeth (wife), 84–85
Brown, William A. (W. A.), 23–26, 32–32, 49–50, 58, 84, 107, 168, 179
Brown County, Texas, 71
Bruce, C. D. and A. C., 167
Brueggerhoff & Heidenheimer, 118
Bryant, Mandy, 109–10
Buck, Mrs. Eliza, 120
Buenger, Andreas, 161–62
Buford, Cesar, 109
Buford, Jake, 113, 192
Buhring, Henry, 131
Bureau of Immigration, 152
Burgess, Toney, 66
Burleson, John, 81
Byington, Nancy, 99
Byrd, Charles Jr., 56–57

Caberro, Telesforo, 121
Cade, I.T., 18, 130, 177
Caffro, Antonio, 151
Campbell, Dr. W. H., 24–25
"Camp Mason," 156
Camp Verde, 34
Cartlidge, Enoch, 94, 151
Cartlidge, Sam, 184
Cass, Noel, 129
Castell, Texas, 156

Catalogues, 17, 19
Cattle ranching: in Indian Territory, 18, 38, 41–43, 66, 73, 77, 130–31, 186; in Texas, 18, 33–35, 37, 45, 48, 52–54, 65–73, 77, 119, 161, 164–65, 170, 186–88, 195, 197
Chambers, Caroline (wife of Lemuel), 119, 154, 182
Chambers, Lem (Lemuel), 118–19
Chandler, Sandy, 58–59, 63, 108–109, 112, 115–16, 133, 187, 192
Charles Schreiner General Merchandise, 8–9, 34
Cheadle, Judge James, 48
Checote, Capt. Samuel, 42, 131
Cherino, Texas, 18, 30, 60, 187
Cherino Alliance, 60, 216n26
Chessher, A. J., 83
Chickasaw Indians, 39–40, 101–102, 212n62
Chiffey, Miss Mary, 102
Choctaw, Oklahoma & Gulf Railroad, 48
Choctaw Nation: alcohol laws in, 177–78; cattle ranching, 66, 73; Choctaw Light Horse Company, 40; coal exploits in, 74–76, 94, 128, 150–51, 232n88; cotton production in, 65, 73, 76; female teachers in, 101–103; government of, 40, 48, 66; racial dynamics in, 125–31, 197, 212n61, 232n95; teaching in, 35, 101–103, territory of, 19, 37–43, 151. *See also* Indian Territory
Christmas rituals, 166–71, 199
Civil War, 10, 27–29, 34, 39, 42, 148, 155–56, 162–63
Clapp & Brown, 24
Clark, Mrs. William, 28, 192, 209n17
Clark, Thomas D., 14–16, 32, 60, 78–81, 185, 196, 229n44
Clark, William, Jr. (father), 27
Clark, William, III, 26–27, 50, 82, 184, 192, 195, 208n14
Clark & Hyde mercantile store, 26, 78, 82–83, 88, 96, 99–100, 103, 178, 184, 187

Clarkson, Robert P., 122
Clay County, Texas, 71
Cleary, J. J., 94
Coal mining, in Indian Territory, 39–40, 73–77, 94, 128, 148, 150–51, 187, 190, 219n80
Cole, Chief Coleman (Choctaw), 40
Coleman, Dick, 59, 62
Colorado City, Texas, 48, 86
Colorado County, 63–64
Comal County, Texas, 52–53, 64–65, 72, 154, 180
Comanche, Texas, 18
Comanche County, 61
Commercial Bank (Mason, Texas), 45
"Committee of Safety," 111–12, 197, 227n24
Concharty Town, I.T., 42
Confederacy, 10, 27–29, 34, 39, 42, 53, 112, 162–63, 208n16. *See also* Civil War
Conner, A., 65
Consumer culture, studies of, 15
Consumerism. *See* Consumer culture; Consumption
Consumption: definition, 11; studies of, 15
Cookenboo, H., 167
Cothran, Mr., 185
Cotton farming, 7, 10, 18, 24, 44, 52–57, 58, 61–66, 68, 71, 73, 76–77, 106, 117, 119, 161, 186–89, 215n9, 216n20; tenant farming, 54–55, 57, 196. *See also* Sharecropping
Coudrons, T. M., 61
Cowan, J. T., 75
Craft, John, 175
Crane, Dr. William Carey, 176
Credit, merchants and, 13, 17, 20, 50, 52–53, 58–64, 66–67, 69–70, 77, 106–109, 123, 133, 162, 187–88, 195, 199, 229n44
Creek Nation, 18, 42–44, 66–67, 101–102, 177, 185; racial dynamics in, 125–26, 131–32. *See also* Indian Territory

"Crossroads, the," 39, 73–74, 150
Curtis Act, 126

Dagan, John, 184
Dallas, Texas, 64, 92–93
Dargetz, William, 75
Davis, C. H., 102
Davis, Miss, 100
Davis, Miss Sally E., 6
Davis, Mrs., 100
Davis, William, 165
Dawes, Irwin, 64
Daybook (definition), 12
Deep Creek, Texas, 48–49
Delona, Jesse, 175
Derit, Mr. and Mrs. Lou, 92
Dickson & Green mercantile, 61
Dixon, Lon (Alonzo), 23–26, 179, 183
Donalson, James, 94
Dorsey, D. W., 184
Doughty, W. B., 121
Doyle, Archie, 102
Drugs. *See* Medicinal purchases
Dubois, Felix, 120
Duffy, A. A., 184
Dugat, Mrs. Susan, 120, 179
Duncan, Henry, 66
Duncan, Mrs. Kate, 120, 122
Dunman, A. M., 69
Dunman, R. L., 98, 121
Dunn, Mike, 76, 94, 151, 190
Durst, George and Bernhardt, 159
Durst, Mrs. Susan A., 88–89, 99

Easterling, A. E., 63
Eckert, Louis, 70
Education, 24–26, 30, 32–33, 35–36, 39, 49, 60, 101, 106, 112–14, 130, 156, 161, 192, 199, 227n33. *See also* African Americans; Teachers
Edwards, Ellen, 109
Element (ship), 159
Elementary Spelling Book, The (Webster), 114, 228n37
Elk House, 89–90
Elliot, Henry, 122

262 INDEX

Ellis, Ben C., 123
El Paso–San Antonio mail line, 45
Ernst, Friedrich, 159–60, 162
Ernst, Hermann, 154, 160–62, 180
Eufaula, I.T., 43, 47

Fairfield, Ala., 189
Faltin, August, 34
F. B. Severs's Cash Store, 8, 42–43, 101–102, 131–32, 177, 184–85
Fence cutting. *See* Barbed wire
Fendall, Mrs. Sarah, 90
Fields, Andy, 132
Fields, Henry, 121
Fife, Dorsey, 102
Fischer, Hermann, 52–53, 64–65, 72, 154, 180; ledger transactions, 52–53, 185
Fischer's Store, Texas (town), 18, 73, 180, 187, 194
Five Tribes (Indian Territory), 10, 65, 124
Fixoco, Cono, 66
Folsom, Judge Ellis, 129–30
Folsom family, 129
Fort Gibson, I.T., 42
Fort Hubbard, Texas, 18
Fort Mason, Texas, 156
Frebely, John, 52
Fredericksburg, Texas, 155–56, 159
Freedmen and freedwomen. *See* African Americans
Freedmen's Bureau, 106, 112–13
Frerichs, Freidrich, 64
Fristoe, Henry C., 32
Fuller, J. H., 61
Fulton, Rev. Defau Tallerand, 101

Galveston, Texas, 7, 148, 152, 154–55, 157, 159, 171
Gardner, Zach, 65
Garret, George, 113, 192
Gauntt, Gen. Robert Lee, 36, 210n47
Gauntt, J. R. (Bob), 36
Gauntt, William M. (Bill), 36, 165

Gauntt Bros. mercantile, 36, 96, 100, 165, 178, 190; female patrons of, 100
Gay, Charles, 83
Geistweidt, William, 71
General Allotment Act, 126
General Directory of the City of Austin, Texas for 1877–1878, 96, 118
Germans: cattle ranching and, 68–72, 161, 164–65; Christmas rituals, 166, 169–71, 192, 199; Civil War and, 155–56, 162–63; consumption patterns, 11, 157, 161–62, 165–66, 170–71, 180–81, 197–99; cotton production of, 64, 161; demographics of, 147–49; farming practices of, 163–64; frontier experiences of, 154–56; immigration patterns of, 22, 34, 52, 72, 147–49, 151–55, 157, 159–60, 172, 234n31; surnames of, 64, 154
Gilded Age, The (Twain and Warner), 49
Gilded Age acquisitiveness, 19–20, 24, 37–38, 44, 49–51, 194
Gonzales, Texas, 153
Goodlaw, Judge, 178
Goodson, John T., 83
Goodson, Mrs. S. A., 83
Goram, Richard, 128
Gover, Samuel, 83
Granger, Gen. Gordon, 7
Gray, Dick, 117, 182
Gray, Henry, 117
Greenwood, Hanibal, 121
Griffith, L. E., 82
Grote, Fritz, 71

Haden, Sandy, 65
Hailey, Dr. Daniel M., 74–76, 150
Halff, Mayer, 37
Hall, George, 122
Hall, Mrs. Harriet, 6
Hamilton, Robert, 67
Hampton, Wade, 129–30
Hancock, Samuel, 65

Hardeman, Bailey, 30
Hardeman, Blackstone, Jr., 6, 9, 29–30, 50, 63
Hardeman, Dr. Blackstone, Sr. (father), 6, 30
Hardeman, Gladys, 111
Hardeman & Barret General Merchandise (store), 3, 5–9, 28–29, 56–58, 63, 111, 113–15, 117, 122, 182, 184, 187
Hardeman family, 29–30
Harlan, Sarah Ann, 101
Harrell Institute, 44
Hasse, Henry, Jr., 159
Haynes, Miss Mary S., 6
Heard, Henry B., 120
Hedwig's Hill, Texas, 8, 18, 45–46, 50, 68–72, 77, 147, 153–55, 157, 159, 162, 165, 170–72, 180–81, 186–87, 192, 194, 197–98
Hester, Daisy, 36
Hester, George Benjamin (G. B.), 35, 65–66, 101–102, 177
Hester, Mrs. Elizabeth Fulton (wife), 35, 101–102
Hidetown, Texas, 18, 48
Hill Country (aka Texas Hill Country), 22, 34, 52, 64, 67–68, 70, 72, 149, 151, 154–55, 159, 163, 165, 170–72, 187, 192, 197
Holmes, Mrs. Mike, 91
Hood, Mrs. Hattie, 95
Hotel keeping, 79, 86–91, 222n33
Houston, Texas, 7, 64, 153, 159
Houston East & West Railroad Company, 27
Humphries, Sallie, 99
Hyde, Dr. George S., 78–79, 184
Hyde, Letty (married to Paul Hyde), 82, 100
Hyde, Mrs. Anna J., 78–79, 82, 86–88, 99
Hyde, William F., 26–27, 208n14, 209n17

Immigration patterns, 19–20, 22, 147–55, 157, 159–60, 197, 199, 233n12, 234n31. *See also* Germans; Indian Territory

Indianola, Texas, 152–53, 155, 157, 159
Indian Territory: alcohol sales in, 177–78, 238n14; cattle ranching in, 18, 38, 42, 66, 73, 77, 130–31, 186; Civil War, 10; coal mining in, 73–77, 94, 148, 151, 190; cotton production in, 65–66, 73, 76–77; migration to, 67, 95, 101, 148, 150–51, 172, 197, 233n12; population growth, 9–10, 18; racial divisions in, 10–11, 41–42, 44, 106, 124–33; and surrounding region, 17–18, 106, 186, 202n13; teachers in, 100–103. *See also* Choctaw Nation; Creek Nation
Industry, Texas, 18, 154, 160–62, 164, 180, 187
Ingraham, G. F., 26, 82–83, 208n14, 208n16
Ingraham, Miss Elsie, 99–100
International & Great Northern Railroad, 25
Irion, Robert and Helena, 89
Irwin, A. D., 66
Irwin, Joshua, 66

Jacksonville, Texas, 18–19, 23, 25–26, 32–33, 49, 58–59, 61–63, 82, 84–85, 92, 107, 115–16, 123, 132, 168–69, 178–79, 187, 192, 194
Jacksonville Education Association, 25, 32
Jacobs, Hannah (Margaret Jacobs's daughter), 5
Jacobs, Margaret, 3–9, 13, 22
Jacobs, May (Margaret's daughter), 5
Jefferson, Isam, 129
Jefferson, Thomas, 126
Johnson, Mrs. Amanda, 6
Johnson, Pres. Andrew, 105
Johnson, Tom, 28
Jones, John C., 189
Jones, W. N., 66, 130–31, 177
"Judge Rea," 97
Junction, Texas, 35
Juneteenth, 7

INDEX

Kansas merchants, 32; cattle towns in, 37, 68, 91; temperance campaigns, 174–75
Keith, U. A., 76, 151, 190
Keller, Adolf, 70
Keller, John, 159, 170
Kennedy, A. J., 67
Kensing, Henry, 187–88
Kentucky, frontier purchasing in, 12, 191, 240n65
Kerr County, Texas, 34
Kerrville, Texas, 9, 18, 34–35, 163, 170
Kessentiner, March, 58, 63, 109, 116, 187, 192
Keyser family, 70–71
Knights of the Rising Sun, 7
Knights of the White Camellia, 7, 58
Knolle, Emil, 180
Knolle, Ernst F. G. (and brother Frederick), 161–62
Kohler, Viggo, 121–22
Kothmann, D., 170
Kothmann, Fritz, 71, 159, 170
Krebs, I.T., 151
Ku Klux Klan, 7, 58
Kyle, Starling, 56–57, 113, 192

Lacy, Sam, 63, 108–109
Lavender, Mrs. E. K., 6
Layton, T. W., 61
Ledbetter Salt Works, 33
Ledger (definition), 12; separation by race and class, 119–21
Leifeste, Christian, 155
Leifeste, Christophe and Henry, 159
Lerue, Mrs., 100
Levi, Simeon, 131
Lewis, Alfred, 31–32, 191–92, 209n32
Lewis, Ashby W. (son), 31–32
Lewis Roy (African American customer), 119
Linartz, Herm, 64
Long, Henry, 189
Lorenz, Fritz, 188
Louisiana retailing, 60

Love, Thomas, 85
Lynch, Judge John C., 33–34

Maley, George, 120
Manhattan, Kans., 174–75
Manning, Mary (teacher), 33
Manor, Texas, 18, 31, 187, 191
Mariana ("Mexican" customer), 119
Marshall, John W., 109
Martin, Anna, 8, 44–46, 50, 68–72, 104, 147–48, 153–55, 157–58, 162–63, 165, 170–72, 180–81, 195, 197–98; store transactions, 46, 69–71, 159, 170, 181, 187–88, 192
Martin, Charles (husband), 45, 50, 156, 162–63
Martin, Charles (son), 45, 180
Martin, Louis (uncle), 152, 157
Martin, Max, 45
Martin, Mrs., 89
Mason County, Texas, 44, 70–71, 154, 157, 164–65
Matagorda, Texas (town), 18, 167, 184, 187
Matagorda Bay, 152, 157
Mayfield, Ed, 88
McAlester, I.T., 18, 48, 73–74, 89–91, 94–95, 99, 103–104, 168–69, 183, 187, 190, 194, 196; location of McAlester family home, 41; South McAlester, 48
McAlester, James Jackson (J. J.), 38–44, 47–51, 73–76, 89, 95, 103, 126, 127–29, 131, 133, 150–51, 169, 177, 190, 195, 212n61, 232n88; store transactions, 19, 73, 75–76, 89–91, 93–95, 98–99, 103, 127–29, 151, 184, 189, 190, 197; wholesale locations of, 50, 177
McAlester, Mrs. Rebecca (Burney), 39–42, 128, 212n61
McAlester & Hannaford, 39
McCain, Jonathon H., 167
McCampbell, Charlie, 122
McCampbell, Thomas P., 97, 119

McCampbell, William E., 97–99, 119, 121, 132–33, 179
McCampbell & Bros. store. *See* W. E. McCampbell & Bros. store
McElroy, Mrs. Fannie, 95–96
McGuffey's readers, 113–14, 195, 228n36
McInnis, J. L., 65, 81, 175
McKinney, Dixon, 129
McKinney, William, 24–25, 107
McKinney & Brown store, 19, 23, 25, 58–59, 62–63, 82–83, 85, 92, 107–10, 112–17, 123, 132–33, 168, 178, 187, 189, 192
McKinnon, Stephen, 64
McKnight, Jeff, 79
McLaughlin, Paddy, 151
McMullen, J., 75
McNabb, Jonathon, 184
Medicinal purchases, 182–86, 193
Meeks, John, 65
Meier, Frederick, 88
Melrose, Texas, 3–7, 9, 18, 28, 56–57, 61, 63, 111–13, 115, 122–23, 182, 187, 196
Melrose Petroleum Company, 29
Menefee, Charles, 115, 192
Merchants: community life and, 16; credit practices of, 13, 17, 50, 52–53, 55, 58–64, 66–67, 69–70, 77, 106–108, 123, 133, 162, 187–88, 195, 199, 229n44; elite status of, 17, 20, 23–24, 27–34, 41, 46, 49–51, 153, 195, 199, 211n57; land speculation and, 47–48, 51; moral development and education, 24–26, 32–33, 35–36, 44, 46, 51, 161, 194–95; shady practices of, 13, 59–60, 108; town boosters, 24, 47. *See also* Credit
Meshemahtubbie family, 129
Meusebech, Baron von, 152
Mexican Americans, 106, 107, 119–20, 230n56; surnames of (e.g., "Arcadia," "Telesferro," "Phillisana," "Pancho," "Germo," and "Trinidad"), 120–21, 123, 128
Mining. *See* Coal mining

Mission of Our Lady of Guadalupe of Nacogdoches, 26
Mississippi, consumer purchasing, 16, 81–82, 123, 133, 189. *See also* Ownby, Ted
Missouri-Kansas-Texas Railway (MK&T or the Katy), 74–75, 128, 150, 177
Mize, Mrs. H. M., 91
MK&T. *See* Missouri-Kansas-Texas Railway (MK&T or the Katy)
Moon, D. P., 184
Moore, Sam, 129–30
Moore, William, 129–30
Morton, Levi, 61
Morton, William P., 66–67
Muskogee, I.T., 35–36, 44, 47, 102
Muskogee Day Nursery, 36

Nacogdoches, Texas, 18, 26–27, 50, 61, 78, 83, 87–88, 96, 103, 111, 123, 178, 187; county of, 7, 57, 79, 113
Nacogdoches News, 79
Neel, Henry, 121
Neely, Tom, 83
Neer & James mercantile, 63
Netty, Miss (teacher), 33
New Braunfels, Texas, 52, 72, 153–54
"Nig" (African American customer), 120
Nunn, T. N. (Tommy), 48–49

Oakland, Texas, 18, 63
O'Conner, Michael, 65
Oklahoma (pre-statehood). *See* Indian Territory
Oklahoma Star, 37–38, 47, 76, 126, 169
Okmulgee, I.T., 18, 42, 44, 66–67, 102, 131–32, 184–85, 194
Old Boggy Depot, I.T., 18, 35, 65, 102, 177
Olmstead, Frederick Law, 148–49, 162
Opiates, 183–84
Orlando, Louis, 88
Osage Mining Company, 38, 40, 73–76, 128, 150, 219n80. *See also* Coal mining

Owen, Mrs., 100
Owen, Robert L., 36
Owens, Salone, 129
Ownby, Ted, 16, 81–82, 123, 133, 188–89

Parkinson-Trent (store), 67
Parks, Miss P., 6
Patton, Professor, 83
Perryman, George, 42
Peters, Eliza, 98–99
Peters, Elvira (Edwards), 97, 120–21
Pinkard, John, 109–10, 178–79
Pluenneke, Conrad, 155, 159, 170
Polk, William, 191
Porter, Pleasant, 131, 185
Postal services, 8, 45, 72–73, 160, 213n79
Powers, Jesse, 56–57, 113, 192
"Preacher Tremble" (name in J. C. Lynch's ledgers), 33
Pusley, Billy, 127
Pusley, Eastman, 129
Pusley, Joshua, 74, 127, 150
Pusley family, 40, 128–29

Racial violence, 7, 58, 105, 110–12, 133. *See also* Ku Klux Klan
Rafferty, J. S., 121–22
Ragland, Dr. John S., 120
Rainbolt, Robert, 88
Ratchford, James Wiley and George Robertson, 123
Rawson, Robert, 102
Reconstruction, 6–7, 12, 16, 19–20, 22, 29–30, 58, 63, 105–107, 110–13, 115, 125, 182, 197, 199, 228n40
Refugio, Texas, 18, 68–69, 97, 99, 113, 119, 121, 123, 128, 132–33, 179, 186, 197
Reichenau, A. A., 170
Reichenau, Max, 70
Renfrow, Wade, 190
Republicans (Radical), 30, 58, 112, 125, 152, 162
Republic of Texas, 6, 27, 30, 152, 159, 164

Reynolds, Mrs., 100
Reynolds & Hannaford, 39
Richardson, Annie, 96
Richardson, Rosie, 100
Riddle, G. W., 129
Robinson's Academy, 101
Rolligan, Ellen (married to Henry Rolligan), 100
Romine, Jasper, 65
Rowlett store, 178
Rugeley, F. L., 167
Rusk, Berry, 57

Sachtleben, C., 64
Saint George's, Del., 191
"Salina Red," 99
San Antonio, Texas, 7, 37, 52, 64, 70, 148, 164
Sanders, Ellen, 99
San Felipe, Texas, 159
Sargent, M., 61
Savage, Ed, 184
Schaffer, Charles, 89
Schlamens, Otto, 64
Schlereth, Thomas, 17
Schools. *See* Education; Teachers
Schreiner, Charles, 9, 34–35, 163, 210nn41–42; businesses owned by, 35; store description, 9. *See also* Charles Schreiner General Merchandise
Schreiner Institute, 35
Schulz, M., 164
Schurz, Carl, 105
Seele, Friedrich Hermann, 169–70
Seiper, John G., 160
Sellars, Beriah (character in *The Gilded Age*), 49
Seminole Indians, 125
Severs, Frederick Benjamin (F. B.), 42–44, 47, 50, 66–67, 101–102, 126, 131–32, 195; businesses owned by, 43–44, 47
Severs, Mrs. Annie (Anderson), 42–43, 131
Shackelford County, Texas, 33

Sharecropping, 7, 53–58, 61, 63–65, 77, 106, 108, 117–18, 189, 196. *See also* Cotton farming
Shaw, Ann, 98–99, 120–21
Sherrill, J. D., 61–62
Shreveport, La., 7
Simmons, T. R., 161
Simon, Conrad, 159
Simon, Mrs., 180
Simpson, A. J., 82
Simpson, Dr. J. T., 59, 168
Simpson, John, 57
Sirrell, Harry, 167
Sittel, Edward and Lena, 89–91
Sittel, Fritz, 90
Sleet, Mrs. Arkansas (widow of Philip Sleet), 83, 96, 99
Smith, Mrs. Susan Smith, 85, 92
Snead, Nelse, 107, 226n6
Snyder, Nellie, 86
Snyder, William Henry (Pete), 48–49, 86
Solms-Braunfels, Prince Carl von, 152, 164
Stark, Mrs. David, 91
Star Vindicator (McAlester, I.T., newspaper), 90
Stewart, J. G., 165
Stewart, W. S., 167
Stoehr, Madam L., 162, 164
Stoker, John, 75
Stone, Manning & Co. store, 191
Store owners. *See* Merchants
Stubbs, George, 64
Sullivan, Miss Mollie, 95
Sullivan, Will, 190

Tatsch, William, 69
Taylor, Dick and Darthula, 56–57
Taylor, E., 184
Taylor, Texas, 32
Teachers, 33, 35, 42, 100–103, 161, 225n85
Temperance. *See* Alcohol
Texas: Constitution of 1876, 176; Declaration of Independence of, 27, 30; population growth in, 10, 148; racial divisions in, 10, 22, 105–23, 132–33, 215n12; region and, 17–18, 186–88, 214n6; temperance campaigns in, 175–77, 179–80, 193, 198–99, 237n7. *See also* Cattle ranching; Confederacy; Cotton farming; Germans; Hill Country (aka Texas Hill Country); Immigration patterns
Texas Intelligencer (Jacksonville), 33, 168, 179
Texas Rangers, 163
Thompson, Giles, 66
Thompson, Judge James, 40
Ticknor, George, 169
Tiger, Moty, 131
Tilery, John, 107
Tilley, Mrs. Joe, 92
Toups, Joe, 120
Travis County, Texas, 65
Trent, Sarah, 44, 131
Tronier, Frederick (and son Otto), 151
Trumbo, George, 128
Turner, Frederick Jackson, 11, 36–37
Turtle Creek, Texas, 34

United Friends of Temperance, 176
Uzzell, Mrs., 184

Verein zum Schutze deutscher Einwander in Texas. See *Adelsverein*
Victoria, Texas, 153
Victorianism, 19–21, 30, 38, 49, 84, 86, 166, 181, 195, 204n29, 206nn37–38, 209n18, 221n19
Vicy (African American customer), 99, 128
Vineyard, George, 123

Wade, Washington, 129–30
Wadsworth, William, 167, 184; Christmas purchasing at store, 167
Walker, Tandy, 40, 74, 150
Waverly Plantation, Miss., 189
WCTU. *See* Woman's Christian Temperance Union (WCTU)

Webberville, Texas, 18, 65, 81, 175, 186
Webster (American Indian customer), 129
Weidemann, Theodor, 69
Weihnachtsmann, 169
"Weldon" (McAlester's geologist), 39
W. E. McCampbell & Bros. store, 69, 97–99, 113, 119–23, 128, 132–33, 195, 197
West, A. J., 120
West, A. M., 69
West, B. F., 120–21
West, Dick, 120
Wettstaed, James, 190–91
White, C. C., 151
Willard, Frances, 174, 176–77
Williams, James, 184
Williams, Mrs. C., 184
Williamson, Miss, 100
Willison, Miss Mollie, 102, 225n85
Wilson, William, 102
Withers, Miss Edna, 103
Withers, Mrs. Harriet (Hattie) Olivia Coleman, 103
Wolf, Charles, 18, 89, 96, 153, 175, 178
Wolf General Merchandise store, 89, 96, 118, 153–54, 175, 178, 182
Woman's Christian Temperance Union (WCTU), 174, 176
Women: consumption and work patterns of, 21, 78–104, 120–21, 196–97, 219n6, 220n11; domesticity and, 21, 44–45, 84, 88, 104, 199, 207n39, 221n21, 224n62; hotel keeping and, 78–79, 86–91; informal economy and, 92–93, 223n53; teaching profession and, 100–103; temperance activities, 173–77, 181, 237n3. *See also* Martin, Anna
Woolf, David, 75
Wooten, J. J., 94, 151

Yarger, David, 102
Yates, William, 128
Young, Simma, 79
Yount, Rosa, 99

Zano (African American customer), 120–21

www.ingramcontent.com/pod-product-compliance
Lightning Source LLC
Chambersburg PA
CBHW020833160426
43192CB00007B/634